Searching for Scientific Womanpower

SEARCHING
for SCIENTIFIC
WOMANPOWER

Technocratic Feminism and the Politics
of National Security, 1940–1980

LAURA MICHELETTI PUACA

THE UNIVERSITY OF NORTH CAROLINA PRESS   CHAPEL HILL

*This book was published with the assistance of the
Authors Fund of the University of North Carolina Press.*

© 2014 THE UNIVERSITY OF NORTH CAROLINA PRESS

The paper in this book meets the guidelines for permanence
and durability of the Committee on Production Guidelines for
Book Longevity of the Council on Library Resources.

The University of North Carolina Press has been
a member of the Green Press Initiative since 2003.

Complete cataloging information for this title is
available from the Library of Congress.

ISBN 978-1-4696-1081-8 (pbk.: alk. paper)

ISBN 978-1-4696-1082-5 (ebook)

18 17 16 15 14   5 4 3 2 1

Parts of this book have been reprinted in revised form from "Cold War Women:
Professional Guidance, National Defense, and the Society of Women Engineers,
1950–1960," in *The Educational Work of Women's Organizations, 1890–1960*,
edited by Anne Meis Knupfer and Christine Woyshner (New York: Palgrave
Macmillan, 2008), 57–77, with permission of Palgrave Macmillan.

To Brian, *with love and gratitude*

CONTENTS

ILLUSTRATIONS

ACKNOWLEDGMENTS

The origins of this book can be traced to my experience as an undergraduate at Douglass College, Rutgers University, where I was first introduced to women's history. It was in Dee Garrison's women's history survey class that I undertook the task of interviewing my grandmother for a project on women and World War II. Hearing her stories made me curious about the lives of other women of her generation, and to this end, I decided to conduct my senior honors thesis on the impact of the war on Douglass alumnae. As I scoured student newspapers, yearbooks, and various manuscript materials, I was amazed at the number of stories detailing the wartime recruitment of women into scientific fields. After enrolling in the Ph.D. program in women's history at the University of North Carolina at Chapel Hill, I embarked on what would eventually become a full-scale investigation of this topic.

While working on this project, I enjoyed the support and assistance of numerous individuals and organizations. First, I would like to acknowledge those institutions that generously funded my work. Its early stages were supported by a Woodrow Wilson Fellowship in Women's Studies, a Schlesinger Library Grant from the Radcliffe Institute for Advanced Study at Harvard University, a Mowry Research Award from the University of North Carolina's Department of History, an Off-Campus Research Fellowship from the University of North Carolina's Graduate School, and a Spencer Fellowship for Research Related to Education. My new institutional home, Christopher Newport University, provided additional support. I am especially indebted to history department chairs Phillip Hamilton and Eric Duskin, deans of the College of Arts and Humanities Steven Breese and Lori Underwood, and provost Mark Padilla and his office. Their assistance made possible not only extended research trips to new archives and publication funds but also a year-long academic leave that allowed me to accept an American Association of University Women Postdoctoral Research Fellowship. Without the support of these individuals, offices, and organizations, the completion of this book would not have been possible.

I am also grateful to the archivists, librarians, and other individuals who helped me make my way through countless documents and the research process. The staff at the American Association of University Women Archives, the Karnes Archives and Special Collections at Purdue, the Columbia University Rare Book and Manuscript Library, the Institute Archives and Special Collections at MIT, the National Archives at College Park, the National Federation of Business and Professional Women's Clubs Archives, and the Rockefeller Archive Center provided invaluable guidance. In particular, I would like to thank Donald Glassman and Martha Tenney at the Barnard College Archives; Eisha Neely at the Division of Rare and Manuscript Collections at Cornell; Diana Carey, Sarah Hutcheon, Jane Knowles, and Ellen Shea at the Radcliffe Institute's Schlesinger Library; Tom Frusciano at Rutgers University's Special Collections and University Archives; Troy Eller English and Deborah Rice at Wayne State University's Walter P. Reuther Library; and Tanya Zanish-Belcher at Iowa State University's Special Collections Department. Friends and family members who opened their homes to me during long research trips include Fran and George Anderson, Jan and Neal Butler, Melissa Skwira and Mark Morency, Sandra VanBurkleo, and Katya Varlamova. I am incredibly appreciative for their hospitality and generosity. Back at home, I benefited from the reference and technical assistance of Amy Boykin, Susan Barber, Beth Young, Johnnie Gray, and Jesse Spencer. Helen Haller of Sigma Delta Epsilon–Graduate Women in Science also furnished me with materials from her files. Jennifer Fitzpatrick in Christopher Newport University's Department of History provided invaluable clerical help at regular intervals and crucial moments.

This book has also benefited tremendously from the thoughtful feedback of friends and colleagues. Graduate school compatriots René Luis Alvarez, Anna Bailey, David L. Davis, Anne-Lise Halvorsen, Pam Lach, Hilary Marcus, Katie Otis, Nancy Schoonmaker, and Tomoko Yagyu read and commented on early drafts. So did a number of professors at UNC who advised me on various stages of the project, such as Peter Filene, Jerma Jackson, Michael Hunt, Sylvia Hoffert, Jim Leloudis, and Catherine Marshall. I am grateful for their wise counsel. Andrew Falk, Amanda Herbert, Gwen Kay, Sally Gregory Kohlstedt, Laura McEnaney, Chris Ogren, Kathy Peiss, and Leandra Zarnow also offered astute comments on later conference papers and chapter drafts. Margaret Rossiter's influence is especially felt, both through her written work and her personal encouragement. Unfailingly generous with her time and advice, she not only helped me clarify my ideas but also guided me to new sources that few other people would have known. I have similarly benefited from the scholarship and encouragement of Linda Eisenmann, whose careful reading and constructive comments have improved this work immensely. Jane DeHart likewise read several iterations of the manuscript materials and provided invaluable guidance, especially in the final throes of the project. I am also grateful to the University of North Carolina Press for its support and guidance in producing this work, and especially for the editorial assistance of Chuck Grench, Paula Wald, and Nancy Raynor. Kurt Piehler, who initially oversaw my undergraduate honors thesis, has watched this project develop over many years and has been a continual source of support long after he first encouraged me to enter the field. My greatest intellectual debt is to Jacquelyn Hall, a model advisor, mentor, scholar, and friend. Her close attention to countless drafts as well as her broader theoretical and conceptual suggestions have enriched this project immeasurably. She challenged me at every step and taught me much about the craft of historical writing. Moreover, she has been unswerving in her support, guidance, and encouragement and has always believed in me, even when my own confidence faltered.

Less tangible, but no less important, has been the support of family and friends throughout this long process. Christopher Newport University's Department of History has provided a friendly and welcoming place to work. Lexy Bucklew, Carley Everett, Lacy Bramblett, and Lora Cooper all provided excellent and often last-minute child care, especially as deadlines loomed. Andrew, Kristen, Noah, and Lauren Falk have not only helped me celebrate this project's milestones but also taught me how to make time for needed breaks. Audrey Statelman made numerous trips from New Jersey to Virginia to provide both moral support and extended child care, when they were desperately needed. Other members of my family, including my brother, Dave Micheletti; my aunt and uncle, Fran and George Anderson; my aunt Rose Grammer; and my in-laws, Michael and Sally Puaca, have provided continual encouragement. So have my parents, Ann and Richard Micheletti, who instilled in me an early love for learning and who cheered me on at every stage. I am eternally grateful for their unconditional love. I am also thankful for my son, Henry, whose smile and laughter brighten each day. Finally, I want to thank my husband, Brian, who has lived with this project nearly as long as I have. At all stages, he has offered endless assistance, from reading chapter drafts to providing child care and cooking meals, to offering much-needed encouragement. I am tremendously appreciative for all that he has done not only to help me complete this project but also to make life better in general. To him, I dedicate this book.

Searching for Scientific Womanpower

Introduction

In the January 2005 "Summersgate" debacle, Harvard University president Lawrence Summers set off a storm of protest when he linked women's underrepresentation in science and engineering to "issues of intrinsic aptitude."[1] Summers's remarks made headlines around the globe and galvanized supporters of gender equity nationwide. Mobilized by the controversy, more than 5,000 female scientists, educators, and students signed a petition imploring Congress to encourage women's participation in scientific fields. Highlighting the persistence of discriminatory practices and cultural attitudes, they called for an array of corrective measures, such as the creation of new fellowships and scholarships, expanded mentoring opportunities to assist young women, and stringent enforcement of Title IX. But the overarching thrust of their argument had less to do with promoting gender equity than it did with strengthening national security. By failing to cultivate half of its scientific talent, the petition warned, "our nation runs the risk not only of losing its technological prowess, but its national security as well."[2]

The designation of women's scientific participation as a national security measure reflects a long tradition of feminist activism that is rooted in the Second World War and early Cold War era, when anxiety about America's supply of scientific talent ran high and when open support for women's rights aroused suspicion. The mobilization and militarization of American science that took place during this period created unprecedented demand for "scientific manpower." As federal research and development expenditures rose, so did concern with the availability of this increasingly heralded national resource. Academic journals and popular publications covered the prospect of a scientific shortage at length and with varying degrees of sensationalism. Meanwhile, "manpower" experts feverishly compiled statistics on college enrollments, graduation rates, employment trends, and labor force patterns. Ad hoc committees, government agencies, philanthropic organizations, and professional societies convened conferences to address and lament the direness of the situation. It was in this context that reformers advocated "scientific womanpower" as the most obvious and efficient solution to national security woes.

Their strategy, which I have termed "technocratic feminism," represents an important but largely unexplored strand of feminist activism through which proponents tethered their own interests to broader manpower concerns. By no means a cohesive cohort, technocratic feminists were drawn largely from the ranks of professional women and a handful of male allies. Most of the technocratic feminists addressed in this book were scientists, engineers, and members of women's scientific societies; the remainder were generally college professors, government officials, and professionals in other fields. They were college-educated, and many had graduate degrees. Although a handful of African American women could be found in their ranks, the overwhelming majority were white and middle class. Their activism, therefore, very much reflected their social positions and backgrounds. They occasionally acknowledged the challenges faced by minority men and women, especially as the civil rights movement took hold, but they rarely made race central to their concerns. Instead, most technocratic feminists and the organizations of which they were a part concentrated on problems that they saw as affecting the majority of women in science.

These reformers, however, were both privileged and marginalized, especially those who made their living in the male-dominated world of science and engineering. As Margaret W. Rossiter has shown in her encyclopedic three-volume account, *Women Scientists in America*, the professionalization of American science in the late nineteenth century was accompanied by, and in many ways dependent upon, its masculinization. The designation of scientific authority as the province of university-educated men precipitated and legitimated women's exclusion.[3] Meanwhile, according to Londa Schiebinger, the folkways and customs of modern science "took form in the absence of women and . . . also in opposition to their participation." These included styles of dress, modes of interaction, hierarchies of practices and values, and "rituals of day-to-day conformity" that visibly marked women as outsiders.[4] Women who did break into science programs and professions often felt unwelcome, as their abilities were regularly questioned and their aspirations rarely encouraged. Likewise, the professional culture of science itself was structured on a male model that failed to account for the realities and responsibilities of women's lives.

The reformers who comprise the core of this study recognized and sought to remedy many of these dilemmas. Although most eschewed the feminist label for themselves, associating it narrowly with suffrage or the Equal Rights Amendment, they nevertheless espoused what can be viewed as feminist ideas. They firmly believed that women and men deserved the same opportunities for school and for work; that outmoded cultural conventions and stereotypes stymied women's intellectual and professional development; and, perhaps most important, that change was needed and possible. They realized fully that women's exclusion stemmed from a series of cultural attitudes and deliberate choices regarding who could "do" science and who could not. But, in the context of the Second World War and early Cold War years when "scientific manpower" was supposedly at a premium, they argued that this artificial and inaccurate distinction was ultimately wasteful and unpatriotic.

In an era when dissent was not only discouraged but also punished, reformers found that the language and cause of national security provided a socially acceptable and politically savvy means for promoting women's education and employment. Within this framework, encouraging women to enter engineering became a mechanism for increasing the production of scientific personnel. Providing young women with female role models in the field promised to attract new sources of "brainpower." Innovative programs enabling married women to combine scientific work with domestic life ensured the fuller utilization of female intellect. Even blatant critiques of sex-role socialization became part of a wider effort to mobilize the country's vast reserves of untapped talent.

This strategy was beneficial insofar as it enabled reformers to collaborate with government, industry, and education officials in the search for "scientific womanpower." It also helped reformers to raise awareness among parents, teachers, and the general public regarding the suitability of scientific careers for women. Moreover, it provided individual women with much-needed encouragement in an era largely hostile to their educational and professional aspirations. At the same time, however, reformers' entreaties to "utilize" female intellect and stem the "waste" of future scientists did little to challenge the persistent channeling of women into the lowest levels of education and employment. Technocratic feminism also served to bolster the broader process through which science was becoming increasingly militarized and female students increasingly marginalized.[5] Thus, national security prerogatives and scientific manpower concerns could only advance feminist interests so far. Even sympathetic allies who were willing to utilize women were not yet willing to view them as equals.

Nevertheless, these efforts are significant because they laid the groundwork for later feminist reforms in both science and society. By the time that Betty Friedan's *The Feminine Mystique* hit stands in 1963, these activists had already identified and proposed remedies for many of the dissatisfactions expressed on its pages. One of these reformers, Mary Ingraham Bunting of Douglass College and later of Radcliffe, had even considered collaborating with Friedan on the book project. Bunting had made the acquaintance of Friedan during the late 1950s through her cousin (and Friedan's Smith College classmate), Marion Ingersoll. The two women found that they had much to discuss and had even exchanged chapter drafts before ultimately parting ways. Although Bunting described their separation as amiable and Friedan acknowledged Bunting as one of the "educators valiantly fighting the feminine mystique, who gave me helpful insights," Bunting later expressed frustration with the book's notoriety. She seemed to resent that the exposé had been credited with the rebirth of organized feminism in the 1960s, and she suggested that the kind of critiques and initiatives that she had already launched had actually cultivated the climate for the book's success. Thus Bunting, who regarded *The Feminine Mystique* as more of a capstone than a catalyst, believed that Friedan "caught that tide beautifully" but did not create it.[6]

Bunting's comment encapsulates what a growing number of historians have more recently confirmed: that throughout a period known popularly as the depths of domestic complacency, there existed significant feminist activity that bridged generations of reform.[7] Nancy Gabin, Susan Hartmann, Dennis Deslippe, and Dorothy Sue Cobble have chronicled the efforts of working-class women who drew on traditions of labor organizing to combat discrimination and improve their lot.[8] The civil rights movement and the movement for peace, which provided additional outlets for feminist activism, similarly spanned generations as Susan Lynn, Harriet Alonso, Leandra Zarnow, and others have shown.[9] In these circles, the influence of left and Popular Front feminists was particularly felt.[10] Other historians, such as John D'Emilio, Allan Bérubé, Rickie Solinger, and Marcia Gallo have illuminated the protracted battles for sexual liberation and reproductive rights that took place throughout the mid-twentieth century.[11] Postwar feminism found further expression through civic groups, professional societies, educational institutions, and government commissions, which helped pave the way for later feminist initiatives.[12]

Historians have also detailed how many of these efforts were simultaneously limited and justified by national security concerns. In the context of the Cold War, the doctrine of "domestic containment" not only heightened women's family responsibilities, as Elaine Tyler May has argued, but also legitimized their involvement in public life.[13] Members of the pacifist organization Women Strike for Peace invoked their rights as mothers to oppose nuclear proliferation and the arms race.[14] Women's volunteer groups, such as those described by Laura McEnaney, fused "Cold War military ethics and idealized domesticity" in their embrace of civil defense. As McEnaney argues, they "saw in home protection an opportunity to articulate essentially feminist aspirations," such as equal representation on planning boards.[15] Anticommunism provided another tool for some activists, even as it raised suspicions about many in their ranks. One example can be seen in the civil rights movement, where activists routinely invoked anti-Communist appeals and other Cold War rhetoric in their struggle to end racism at home and abroad.[16] Joanne Meyerowitz has observed similar developments in the burgeoning movement for gay liberation. One of the main homophile publications, the *Mattachine Review*, for example, adopted what she calls "an unequivocally anti-communist stance." It also, according to Meyerowitz, "at least occasionally printed arguments about national security and wasted national resources."[17] This tactic was likewise pursued at various times by some women's groups, including the National Federation of Business and Professional Women's Clubs and the American Association of University Women.[18] Other organizations, such as the National Manpower Council, the Commission on the Education of Women, and the President's Commission on the Status of Women, similarly framed women's education and employment as Cold War manpower initiatives, as Susan Hartmann, Linda Eisenmann, and Cynthia Harrison have aptly demonstrated.[19]

In no area, however, were reformers more willing and able to employ national security manpower concerns than in science and technology, where the weighty shadow of "big science" and nuclear war lent special urgency and immediacy to their arguments. The identification of science as a national security priority further bolstered these efforts. Technocratic feminists' search for "scientific womanpower," then, reveals much about the history of American feminism, the politics of national security, and the complicated relationship between the two.

As social and political landscapes shifted in the 1960s and 1970s, so did technocratic feminists' reliance on national security goals and scientific manpower concerns. The second wave of American feminism, coupled with declining public support for the war in Vietnam, led both older and younger generations of reformers to stake their claims on women's equality and explicitly feminist concerns. Yet they did not dispense entirely with older traditions of activism. Established women's scientific societies as well as newer feminist organizations continued to identify many of the same gender stereotypes, cultural conventions, and discriminatory practices that mid-twentieth-century reformers had previously recognized as obstacles to women's scientific success. They also carried forward various initiatives already under way, such as creating scholarships, writing guidance materials, mentoring younger women, and assisting married women in balancing work and home life. Moreover, reformers periodically resorted to technocratic feminism, despite the limitations of this approach. This was especially the case as conservative opposition to the gains of the women's movement rose and federal outlays for scientific research and development resumed their upward climb, thereby reestablishing science and scientific manpower as national security priorities.

By taking a long view of the subject, I seek to illuminate the history of feminist interest in science before feminism's second wave and to trace continuities between early and later efforts. In doing so, I build on the work of historians of science such as Margaret Rossiter, Londa Schiebinger, Amy Sue Bix, Ruth Oldenziel, Pamela Mack, and Sally Gregory Kohlstedt, who have ably documented the struggles of female scientists to gain acceptance within their fields.[20] An extended treatment of reformers' use of scientific manpower concerns and national security prerogatives will expand our understanding of the problems and possibilities that they encountered along the way. I also aim to enrich the growing body of scholarship on mid-twentieth-century feminism, or what Dorothy Sue Cobble calls "the missing wave."[21] My focus on women in science provides a new perspective on the range of activism taking place in this era. Additionally, I seek to respond to the call placed by Nancy Hewitt, Kathleen Laughlin, Jacqueline Castledine, and others to recognize continuities in feminist movements over time.[22] As this book shows, feminist interest in science did not simply surge from the social movements of the 1960s and 1970s. Rather, it ebbed and flowed in overlapping currents and ripples of reform. That these can still be seen today provides additional evidence of what has become known as a "long women's movement" that not only predated feminism's second wave but also weathered the antifeminist backlash of the 1980s.[23]

In tracing these developments, I draw heavily on a vast collection of published and unpublished primary sources, such as organizational records, newsletters, conference proceedings, personal correspondence, and oral histories. These include the papers and publications of government agencies, manpower commissions, and professional organizations, which reveal much about national security priorities and anxieties. The most interesting and informative accounts, however, come from the papers of those reformers who actively worked to expand and improve women's participation in the sciences. Their letters, oral histories, and publications constitute an invaluable resource that, ironically, has been woefully underutilized by most scholars.

The organization of this book proceeds chronologically. Chapter 1 examines how the mobilization and militarization of American science during the Second World War facilitated the expansion of opportunities to women in scientific fields. The identification of scientific manpower as a national security priority, coupled with the drafting of college-aged men, enabled reformers to promote the education and employment of female scientists. The chapter also investigates women's wartime experiences as scientists, engineers, and technical aides, paying particular attention to the continued resistance that they faced as well as the postwar backlash that they encountered.

Chapter 2 examines the problems and possibilities of the postwar period. The dawn of the atomic age and the emerging Cold War resulted in a precarious peace that demanded perpetual preparedness in all areas of society. This development resulted in a new iteration of technocratic feminism that was based on an expanded definition of national security and an increasingly entrenched national security state. The chapter explores efforts to expand women's education and employment amid new national security concerns, international crises, and a broader surge of interest in "scientific womanpower." Particularly important are the activities and outreach efforts of the newly created Society of Women Engineers, which emerged as a principal proponent of technocratic feminism.

Chapter 3 investigates the national security anxieties arising from the launch of the Soviet Sputniks in 1957, focusing on efforts to increase women's scientific participation throughout the early 1960s. During this period, which marked the heyday of technocratic feminism, a growing number of reformers situated women's education and employment within an increasingly diffuse national security state. By examining women's scientific societies such as Sigma Delta Epsilon and individuals such as Mary Bunting, it also uncovers innovative efforts to enable married women to combine scientific and domestic work.

Chapter 4 focuses on efforts to expand women's participation in scientific fields amid the second wave of American feminism and changing national security concerns. In addition to addressing how older organizations for women modified their work, it also examines the formation of new women's scientific societies. The chapter pays particular attention to how many of the activities carried out by this generation of reformers extended, altered, and adapted earlier advocates' core ideas. While emboldened to take a more explicitly feminist approach, second-wave activists targeted many of the same obstacles to women's scientific participation. Also important is the fact that both generations periodically resorted to the assumptions and strategies of "technocratic feminism," thereby illuminating important threads of continuity with the past.

Finally, the epilogue summarizes the problems and possibilities of technocratic feminism, tracing the surprising persistence of this strategy, given the emergence of more radical feminist critiques. While the end of the Cold War, an increasingly global marketplace, and the current "war on terror" have led policymakers to redefine national security priorities, science has retained a privileged position within the national security state. Consequently, the identification of "scientific womanpower" as an invaluable national resource continues to inform feminist approaches to science, despite the inherent limitations of this approach. The dilemma at the heart of this strategy—how to balance feminist interests with national prerogatives—remains a weighty one even today.

CHAPTER ONE

The War of "Trained Brains"

In March 1942, less than four months after the bombing of Pearl Harbor, Barnard College dean Virginia Gildersleeve published an article in the *New York Times Magazine* surveying recent wartime developments. She warned that "a shortage is becoming apparent which is far more serious than the shortage of sugar, or even the shortage of rubber: this is the shortage of trained brains."[1] By "brains," Gildersleeve was referring to college-educated professionals upon whose expertise, she believed, the outcome of the Second World War would hinge. Of particular concern were those in scientific and technical fields with direct military applications. With her office located just yards from Columbia University's Pupin Physics Laboratories, home to some of the earliest atomic experiments in the United States and where the Manhattan Project was being born, Gildersleeve suspected that the "hush-hush work across Broadway" and in labs across the country would be instrumental to winning the war.[2] Thus, she argued, "it is now of the utmost importance for schools and colleges and the population generally to realize that good brains, trained, or capable of being trained, are among the most precious assets of the nation." Given the drafting of young men, however, Gildersleeve concluded that "this ominous national shortage of trained brains" must be filled by women.[3]

Gildersleeve's identification of female "brains" as an invaluable national resource was informed by the recent mobilization of American science in preparation for war. Beginning in the late 1930s, a small group of scientists, engineers, and policymakers helped redefine the relationship between science and national security. They called on the federal government to sponsor and coordinate militarily important research not only in government laboratories and the armed forces, as was customary, but also in industries and universities across the country. Their efforts resulted in unprecedented federal spending for scientific research and development and the creation of a diffuse contract system through which significant numbers of civilian scientists engaged in government-sponsored defense research, often for the first time. As research budgets spiraled and scientific employment opportunities grew, so did concern with the country's ability to staff its projects.

What followed was a surge of interest in "scientific manpower" as a critical and quantifiable wartime resource.

These developments undergirded the activism of Virginia Gildersleeve and other technocratic feminists during the Second World War. Gildersleeve's generation of reformers consisted largely of professional women born in the late nineteenth century. Their experiences in college, graduate school, and the professions had taught them much about sex-based discrimination, which they fought both individually and collectively through a wide range of associations and affiliations. While few claimed the feminist label, most had ties to large, feminist-oriented women's organizations, such as the American Association of University Women (AAUW) and the National Federation of Business and Professional Women's Clubs (BPW). Some were also active in professional societies, such as the American Council on Education. Only a handful, however, were scientists or engineers themselves. What brought them together in the search for "scientific womanpower," then, was their perception that the exclusion of women from male-dominated fields impeded women's progress more generally.

As the story of these reformers reveals, the wartime mobilization of scientific womanpower did not come about immediately or easily. The gradual decision to recruit, train, and employ women scientists was the product of numerous debates that took place among reformers, educators, industrialists, and government bureaucrats. Paradoxically, the wartime demand for "trained brains" and the national security prerogatives that surrounded it would justify new opportunities for women in science but also limit the nature of their participation.

Science Mobilizes for War

While science and technology had long contributed to the outcome of armed conflicts, significant scientific discoveries during the 1930s and 1940s ushered in a new phase of science and combat.[4] The early 1930s saw key developments in what would later be known as "radar," the radio detection and ranging system used to detect enemy aircraft and confuse enemy signals. Advances in German rocketry also highlighted the importance of science in war. But perhaps the most remarkable scientific feat was the discovery of nuclear fission, which struck both awe and fear in the heart of the international scientific community. Following the 1939 announcement of this achievement, scientists around the world turned their attention to the possibilities of generating and harnessing atomic energy.[5]

Amid these developments and mounting tensions in Europe, a small but influential group of American scientists and engineers began mobilizing the country's scientific community for war. At the helm of these efforts was Vannevar Bush, the Massachusetts Institute of Technology engineer and then president of the Carnegie Institution of Washington. Bush was convinced not only that American involvement in the Second World War was inevitable but also that the war itself "would be a highly technical struggle [and] that we were by no means prepared in this regard."[6] In June 1940 he met with President Franklin Roosevelt to propose the creation of the National Defense Research Committee (NDRC) to coordinate nearly all areas of weapons research. Roosevelt quickly approved the plan, appointed Bush to head the committee, and made available to the NDRC virtually unlimited access to presidential emergency funds.[7] As the committee embarked on its work, it relied on what one of its members called the "revolutionary" approach of issuing contracts to research universities and industrial laboratories.[8] Although research contracts had been used previously by other organizations (most notably the National Advisory Committee for Aeronautics, which Bush also chaired), the scale on which they were employed by the NDRC was new. Within six months, the NDRC had already authorized 126 contracts to 32 academic institutions and 19 industrial firms and was on its way to creating a national network of universities and industries engaged in government-sponsored defense research.[9]

As the NDRC grew, so did Bush's interest in further strengthening wartime science. In response to Bush's prodding, Roosevelt issued an executive order establishing the Office of Scientific Research and Development (OSRD) in June 1941. As reflected in its name, the new agency oversaw not only research, as had the NDRC, but also the development of production prototypes. It was thus here that research and development, or R&D, were "coupled in a union that was to become standard in government terminology."[10] Additionally, the OSRD, which would be headed by Bush, subsumed the NDRC and established a second committee under its purview that focused on medical research. Instead of relying on presidential emergency funds, however, the OSRD received direct congressional appropriations along with funds transferred from the army and the navy. This change in financial policy resulted in an explosion of federal monies for research and development: in contrast to the $6.5 million that the NDRC had been allocated in 1940–41, the OSRD's total budget for the war years amounted to nearly half a billion dollars.[11] By the end of 1945, the office had let more than 2,000 defense contracts to 465 institutions and was playing a pivotal role in building what one *New York Times* reporter termed "the greatest war machine the world has ever known."[12]

While the OSRD was generally considered the most prestigious of the scientific agencies during World War II, it was not the only institution engaged in wartime science and technology. Federal agencies such as the National Advisory Committee for Aeronautics, the technical branches of the armed services, and the scientific bureaus of the government carried out defense research as well. The new women's military reserves, such as the U.S. Navy's Women Accepted for Voluntary Emergency Service, or WAVES, also made notable contributions, although only a small percentage of their recruits worked in scientific fields. Meanwhile, industry bore primary responsibility for the production of goods already researched and developed. This stage, which demanded varying levels of scientific and technical proficiency, was coordinated on a large scale through federal agencies, such as the War Production Board, that awarded procurement contracts for finished products.[13] Wartime mobilization especially benefited such newer industries as aviation and synthetic rubber, which were financed almost entirely by government capital. The aircraft industry went from being the country's forty-first largest industry in 1939 (smaller than the American candy industry) to the first largest in 1944. More generally, manufacturing output doubled between 1940 and 1943, while the production of weapons, warships, and planes increased exponentially as defense spending rose.[14]

As scientists and engineers across the country turned their attention to defense projects ranging from bombs to blood substitutes, it became apparent that manpower and not money presented the most serious obstacle to their success.[15] Recognizing this difficulty, government officials, educators, and industrialists all embarked on measures to assist in the identification and recruitment of "trained brains." In the summer of 1940, President Roosevelt approved the creation of the National Roster of Scientific and Specialized Personnel, which was made available to defense contractors and government agencies seeking to fill job openings.[16] While the roster was still getting off the ground, the NDRC arranged for the formation of the Office of Scientific Personnel, to be housed under the National Research Council, which would assist government agencies and the military in locating scientific talent.[17] Later, in 1942, the OSRD created its own Committee on Scientific Personnel in order to study these problems further.[18] Meanwhile, the U.S. Office of Education and individual corporations sponsored short-term, college-level training programs in scientific and technical fields. These free courses, open to the public, were frequently accompanied by or tied to employment in defense industries after completion.[19] Also pertinent is the Science Talent Search, the annual scholarship competition funded by Westinghouse and administered by the Science Service in an effort to identify young people with scientific aptitude. As part of the inaugural competition in 1942, thousands of high school students submitted essays on the timely theme "How Science Can Help Win the War," thus reinforcing the broader importance of science to the war effort.[20]

Although Bush regarded many features of wartime science as temporary— most notably the NDRC and OSRD themselves—they would have long-lasting effects. They brought scientific personnel into the sprawling defense matrix with unprecedented speed and scope and forged new alliances among civilian scientists, military brass, and government officials. Scientists enjoyed an expanded degree of influence in military decision making and even became advisors at the top echelons of government. The federal government's heavy reliance on the research contract also facilitated closer and often lasting collaboration among the government, industry, and academia. In general, the massive federal sponsorship of science and technology, the resulting growth of these sectors in the name of national security, and the mounting preoccupation with scientific manpower were important developments that would not be reversed easily.[21] Moreover, they served as the basis for technocratic feminism both during the war and for many years to come.

Turning to Technocratic Feminism

Virginia Gildersleeve's proclaimed interest in "trained brains" was very much rooted in her commitment to the education and advancement of women, a commitment that is best understood in the context of her own history. She was born in New York City in 1877 to Judge Henry Alger and Virginia Crocheron Gildersleeve, with whom she shared her name. Along with her two older brothers, she grew up in a townhouse on West 48th Street, near Fifth Avenue, where she lived for the first thirty-five years of her life. She was introduced at a young age to intellectual pursuits through such activities as watching her brother Alger conduct chemistry experiments on the fourth floor of their home and sitting in the courtroom on the bench beside her father while he heard a case. Her brother Harry, a Columbia student seven years her senior, first brought her to the university library, where she was deeply impressed by the shaded green lights and endless rows of books. "My membership in Columbia University and devotion to it began that day," she later recalled.[22]

Virginia Gildersleeve at Barnard College, ca. 1945. Photograph courtesy of Barnard College Archives, Barnard College.

It was her mother, however, who had the biggest impact on Gildersleeve's intellectual development. She never bothered to instruct her daughter in cooking or housekeeping and told the young Virginia that since she had "brains and no nerves" there was no reason why she should not have as good an education as her brothers had. She saw to it that her daughter attended the Brearly School, a college preparatory for young women, and then enrolled at the recently established Barnard College in 1895. After graduating first in her class in 1899, she began graduate work at Columbia University and earned her master's degree in medieval history the following year. She spent the next five years teaching first-year composition at Barnard before enrolling in Columbia's Ph.D. program in English and earning her doctorate in 1908. Concern for her aging parents, however, led her to turn down an associate professorship at the University of Wisconsin and to look for a position closer to home. Initially, she cobbled together a string of teaching assignments at Columbia and Barnard but soon became the obvious choice for Barnard's vacant deanship. In 1911, Columbia University president Nicholas Murray Butler named Virginia Gildersleeve dean of Barnard College, a position that she would hold for nearly four decades, until her retirement in 1947.[23]

From her new platform, Gildersleeve worked vigorously to expand opportunities for women at Barnard and beyond. She insisted that women should not be restricted to marriage, nor should marriage be an obstacle to a career. While she acknowledged women's tendency to enter female-dominated professions, such as teaching, she refused to limit women to those jobs. The fact that most of Columbia's professional schools were closed to female students especially troubled her, and she embarked on a crusade to enroll women at those institutions. With relative ease, she secured a place for female students in the newly established School of Business when it opened in 1916. The new School of Journalism had been a tougher battle, but it also agreed to admit women when it opened in 1912. The stiffest resistance came from the older and more established professional schools with a long history of rejecting female applicants. The medical school had been denying admission to women since 1873 when suffrage leader Lillie Devereux Blake first petitioned the Columbia Trustees to enroll them. But Gildersleeve finally swayed the dean in 1917 to admit female students on the condition that she would personally select the first candidates and guarantee their success. She employed a similar strategy in her quest to enroll women in the law school. After a decade-long campaign, the Columbia Law School finally succumbed to "the Gildersleeve treatment" in December 1926, when it agreed to admit several Barnard graduates. Among Columbia's professional schools, only the School of Engineering continued to exclude women, a fact that would not be forgotten by Gildersleeve.[24]

Gildersleeve's interest in women's status extended to social and political realms as well. She introduced a personal hygiene course at Barnard, which included sex education, and she allowed undergraduates to smoke. She also encouraged political activism and did not interfere when her students took up controversial causes. In contrast to women's colleges that banned suffrage activity (at Vassar, students met in the local graveyard to escape the watchful eye of administrators), Barnard proudly claimed its own chapter of the Equal Suffrage League much to the dismay of some onlookers. Parents provided one source of disapproval. In her first year as dean, Gildersleeve was approached by a student's mother who implored her to forbid Barnard students from participating in a Fifth Avenue suffrage parade. The distraught woman claimed that "to march in a parade would be a shocking and shameful thing for them to do and would injure the College greatly."[25] But Gildersleeve refused to bow to such concerns, believing that it was her duty "to distinguish between acts that were ethically wrong and conduct that merely did not conform to the customs of the moment."[26] She therefore fostered her students' political participation and civic engagement, which she viewed as the responsibility of educated women.

As an educated woman herself, Gildersleeve was active in a wide range of causes and organizations. Early in her career, she served as a member of the League of Nations Association and advocated world peace through international governance. During World War II, she played an instrumental role in creating the WAVES and headed its advisory committee. After the war's end, she became the only female delegate appointed by President Roosevelt to represent the United States at the San Francisco conference that drew up the United Nations charter. In the interim, Gildersleeve's interest in internationalism shaped much of her work in the field of education. She was a long-time member of the American Council on Education, the largest and most influential group of educators in the United States, and became its first female chair in 1926. Through her involvement with the council, she became increasingly active in international study and worked to facilitate the foreign exchange of students and faculty. Her particular passion, however, was promoting international collaboration among college-educated women. An indefatigable presence within the AAUW, she chaired its first Committee on International Relations from 1918 to 1922. She also helped found the International Federation of University Women in 1919 and served as its president for two terms, first from 1924 to 1926 and later from 1936 to 1939.[27]

Although Gildersleeve worked tirelessly to secure educational, economic, and political opportunities for women at home and abroad, she harbored mixed feelings toward organized feminism and never claimed the label for herself.[28] Instead, she sought to distance herself from those "militant feminists" known for their shocking tactics, flamboyant protests, and headlining arrests. Frequently the lone woman on university councils and professional committees, Gildersleeve believed that because she "was not battering at the doors from without, but working from within, it was important to avoid as far as possible creating antagonisms." Experience, however, had taught her that many of her male colleagues "had to be handled rather gently" and "dread the prospect of having a woman around." As a result, she devised her own strategy, which she called "boring from within." "If [a woman] is to gain any influence," Gildersleeve explained, "she must establish herself as a pleasant, amiable, but intelligent human being, no trouble but rather a help. The men can then turn to her in any puzzling questions involving women, perhaps enjoy her protection in warding off attacks by militant feminists from outside, and in time will lend an attentive ear to her own projects."[29]

Gildersleeve's preference for "boring from within," as opposed to more confrontational approaches, helps explain her reliance on technocratic feminism. By the time the Second World War began, she had almost thirty years of experience navigating the male preserves of Columbia University and the professional world. She was proactive but patient, persistent but pleasant, and certainly politically savvy. She had her finger on the pulse of wartime developments and was very much aware of the demand for "trained brains" in a variety of professional fields. Although she was not a scientist herself, she followed the activities of Vannevar Bush's OSRD with particular interest and realized the manifold implications of its contract system, which benefited Columbia University greatly. She was hopeful that Barnard would profit from that relationship, as it would be more closely integrated into the war effort than most colleges for women and could very well become the center for training "front line young war scientists."[30] Her expansive professional connections also brought her into close contact with outside individuals and organizations charged with the recruitment of scientific talent. While genuinely concerned with the war's outcome, her desire to assist in this endeavor was largely motivated by her own interest in women's education and employment, as well as her keen awareness of masculine privilege. Embracing wartime prerogatives would enable Gildersleeve and other technocratic feminists to advance their long-standing goals as unobtrusively as possible.

Even before the bombing of Pearl Harbor, Gildersleeve began thinking about how to marshal female intellect in the name of national preparedness. Some of her earliest efforts were carried out under the auspices of the Committee on Women in College and Defense, which had been established in the fall of 1940 as part of the National Committee on Education and Defense.[31] Chaired by Meta Glass, president of Sweet Briar College and former president of the AAUW, the committee brought together representatives from institutions of higher education as well as the American Council on Education.[32] In this capacity, Gildersleeve worked with other educators, such as Kansas State College dean and biochemist Margaret Justin, Bennett College president Willa Player, and Wellesley College president and future director of the WAVES Mildred McAfee, to plan for the mobilization of college-educated "womanpower" at the national level.[33]

Also included in this group was the esteemed industrial engineer and psychologist Lillian Moller Gilbreth. The much sought-out efficiency expert was familiar not only with the challenges facing women in scientific and technical fields but also with the importance of maximizing their contributions to the defense effort. Just one year younger than Gildersleeve, Gilbreth was born in 1878 to one of Oakland, California's most prominent families. Her father, William Moller, was a partner in a large retail hardware business, while her mother, Annie, was the daughter of a wealthy real estate developer. The oldest child in a home of three boys and five girls, the young Lillie, as she was called then, was tutored at home by her mother until she entered public school at the age of nine. By her own admission, she was a shy child who loved studying and had a special fondness for poetry and music. Her mother's frequent pregnancies and recurring illnesses, however, required that she balance her academic interests with helping to care for the younger children in the house, a skill that would long stay with her.[34]

Despite her family obligations, Gilbreth excelled academically and gradually gained in self-confidence as well. She was particularly influenced by her high school English teacher, Elsie Lee Turner, whom she called "the kind of person that a studious quiet girl would like to be."[35] The fashionable young instructor, who married while Gilbreth was in school, seemed to provide living proof that bookish girls were not doomed to lives of spinsterhood, as her mother had led her to fear. But when Gilbreth decided that she, too, should attend college, her father initially refused, claiming that women of her social class and position belonged in the home. Eventually, he capitulated, and in the fall of 1896, she enrolled at the University of California in nearby Berkeley. When she graduated four years later with a Bachelor of Literature and as the first woman to serve as a commencement speaker, she moved to New York City to pursue a master's degree in English at Columbia University, where Virginia Gildersleeve was also studying at the time. Although it does not appear that they knew each other, Gilbreth did meet the psychologist Edward Thorndike, whose views on people's abilities to learn new skills would profoundly influence her later work. They remained in touch for much of the next four decades, but their relationship in New York was rather brief. Homesick after a short stay, Gilbreth returned to California to resume her studies at Berkeley, where she earned her degree in 1902.[36]

After graduation, she began studying for a doctorate but took a break in 1903 in order to tour Europe. Just days before departing, she was introduced to Frank Bunker Gilbreth, a cousin of her chaperone and a prominent building contractor known for his use of work simplification techniques in the field of construction. When the couple married the following year, they forged a relationship that was not only personal but also professional. Lillian regularly advised Frank on business matters and later became a partner in their scientific management consulting firm. Their work brought them into the inner circles of the industrial engineering community, a relatively new field aimed at improving organizational and industrial efficiency. Lillian's insistence on the need to integrate the study of thought processes into engineering work won her particular acclaim, as can be seen in the reception of her *Psychology of Management*, which appeared in serial form in the *Industrial Engineering and Engineering Digest* in 1912 and 1913 before being published as a book in 1914. Building on her interest in combining the human and mechanical aspects of engineering, Lillian Gilbreth then went on to become the first person to earn a Ph.D. in industrial psychology from Brown University, which she received in 1915.[37] The Gilbreths were perhaps best known, however, for their pioneering work in time and motion studies through which they documented discrete movements in order to streamline work processes and increase productivity. To promote their ideas, they lectured widely, published prolifically, and held summer workshops for management professionals. They even applied time and motion principles to raising their eleven surviving children, as later popularized in the 1948 book *Cheaper by the Dozen*.[38]

Following Frank's untimely death in 1924, Lillian Gilbreth quickly encountered the limits of acceptance for women in industrial engineering. Despite her accolades, she discovered that few factory owners wanted to hire her and several even canceled the contracts that they had placed with her husband. After losing their three biggest clients, she sought out new ways to keep the family business afloat, which she did, to some degree, by embracing gender stereotypes. She frequently played up her responsibilities as widowed mother of a large family in order to generate interest in her work. She also supplemented income from the firm with teaching, an acceptable field for women, by establishing a motion study school in her home. This endeavor soon opened new avenues for Gilbreth, as it became apparent that many of her students were eager to use motion study principles in their businesses to train women workers and cater to women consumers. Home economists were similarly attracted to the potential of scientific management to transform domestic spaces. Consequently, a growing share of her research and consulting work became geared toward these subjects. Throughout the 1920s and early 1930s, Gilbreth carried out such projects as streamlining department store operations, marketing sanitary napkins, and designing efficient kitchens. She also established herself as an expert in household management and authored numerous publications on the subject, including her 1927 *The Home-Maker and Her Job*.[39] Gilbreth's nonconfrontational strategy was much in line with the one increasingly adopted by other female scientists and engineers during the Great Depression. To avoid direct competition with men for the few jobs available, they frequently counseled each other to embrace scientific "women's work" in fields such as home economics, nutrition, botany, and new hybrid positions in the chemical industry (such as chemical librarians and secretaries). Although these jobs commanded less pay and prestige than positions reserved for men, they also provided a safety net in hard times.[40]

For Gilbreth, however, this new direction did more than simply allow her to tread water: it helped make her one of the best-known women in America. In 1930 she appeared on the journalist and former muckraker Ida Tarbell's list of the "fifty foremost women of the United States," along with Jane Addams, Helen Keller, Margaret Sanger, Amelia Earhart, and Mary McLeod Bethune. She was also included in a *Good Housekeeping* readership poll to discover the country's "greatest living women." Top politicians took notice of her as well, and that same year, fellow engineer and president Herbert Hoover named her to head the women's section of his Emergency Committee for Employment, which brought her into contact with hundreds of women's organizations. Although her official duties ended the following April, her interest in women's employment prospects did not. In 1935 she accepted a faculty position at Purdue University, where she became a professor of management in the School of Engineering and later a career counselor for women. With the outbreak of World War II, she reduced her commitments there in order to be closer to the defense industries, which she frequently advised on efficiency matters. She also spent some time in Washington, D.C., where she served on several wartime mobilization committees, such as the advisory group for the WAVES. Although, like Gildersleeve and many women of her generation, Gilbreth frequently claimed that she was not a feminist, she belonged to a wide range of activist organizations that advocated on behalf of women's education and employment. These included the BPW, the AAUW, and the Committee on Women in College and Defense, which she joined in 1941.[41]

At Gilbreth's first meeting of the group in September of that year, the committee set out to assess the degree to which new training opportunities for college women were needed for the defense effort. Early reports from a gathering of university and government officials held that summer had suggested that "there is a very great need for men—and an increased need for women—with specialized training."[42] Committee members were disappointed to learn, however, that those demands had not fully materialized. Their inquiries to the National Roster of Scientific and Specialized Personnel and other government agencies, moreover, elicited vague responses and revealed only that "women would probably be needed in greater numbers as men were called from work they are now doing."[43] In general, the committee found its initial efforts stymied by a lack of information regarding projected trends, and even years later, Virginia Gildersleeve bristled when recalling how "from our government we got almost no light and leading."[44]

Committee members encountered similar frustrations when they reconvened in January 1942, this time in Baltimore, to take part in an emergency meeting of college and university presidents. The two-day Baltimore Conference, as it became known, drew more than 1,000 attendees and was the largest gathering of higher education leaders assembled to that date. Speakers covered an array of topics, ranging from accelerated coursework to preinduction training. Yet while the program was broad in scope, it was far from comprehensive and focused on the schooling of young men. When women were mentioned, it was generally in the context of such traditionally feminine roles as teachers or USO hostesses. Only U.S. Civil Service commissioner Arthur S. Flemming explicitly addressed a need for female engineers, chemists, and physicists.[45]

At the end of the conference's first day, several members of the Committee on Women in College and Defense joined others interested in women's education for a special "sectional meeting" that was chaired by Meta Glass. There they discussed the glaring lack of attention to women in both the program panels and the conference resolutions that the organizers had asked them to approve. For nearly four hours, they debated how best to include female students in the war effort, drafted amendments to the proposed resolutions, and designated Glass to bring to the attention of the government and other relevant agencies "the fact that the 'manpower' of the nation includes also woman power, and that the ignoring of this fact will result in wasting a large part of the resources of the nation." They also stressed the need "to urge upon the authorities the importance of using this woman power in an orderly, systematic and intelligent manner, as they are endeavoring to use men."[46] Members of the group were pleased to see their concerns reflected in the final resolutions that were adopted by the conference the following day. Although many of the statements remained focused on men (five of the sixteen dealt with the selective service alone), the group's influence is obvious. The Baltimore assembly resolved that institutions of higher education and government agencies should cooperate in determining "the immediate needs of man power and woman power for the essential branches of national service—military, industrial, and civilian" and in ensuring "a continuous and adequate supply of men and women trained in technical and professional skills."[47] Thus, by presenting manpower concerns as the basis for their grievances, the sectional group achieved some moderate success.

As the country became further embroiled in the war effort, reformers became increasingly determined to situate womanpower at the center of policy debates and recommendations. In March 1942, several members of the Committee on Women in College and Defense traveled to Washington, D.C., to take part in a two-day conference titled "War Demands for Trained Personnel," held by the Institute of Women's Professional Relations. Many members of the committee, including Lillian Gilbreth and Virginia Gildersleeve, were already well acquainted with the institute, which had been established in 1928 to survey and expand opportunities for women in professional and nontraditional fields.[48] Its founder, Catherine Filene Dodd (later Shouse), was the daughter of Lincoln Filene, the prominent Boston merchant and philanthropist known for his advocacy of a minimum wage for female workers. His interest in issues affecting working women influenced young Catherine and was reflected in her own education and employment. As a junior at Wheaton College, she directed the school's Bureau of Vocational Opportunities and organized its first intercollegiate conference on opportunities for college women in 1917. After graduation, she accepted a position as assistant to the chief of the Women's Division of the U.S. Employment Service of the Department of Labor in Washington, D.C. She returned to Massachusetts in 1919, enrolled at Radcliffe for graduate work, and transferred to the Harvard Graduate School of Education when it opened in 1920. During this time, she was also commissioned by Houghton Mifflin to edit *Careers for Women*, a vocational handbook containing short descriptions of various occupations. Published in 1920, the influential anthology included numerous entries under the section "Scientific Work" as well as candid assessments by top women in the field. Eight years later, with the endorsement of the AAUW, she established the Institute of Women's Professional Relations and named Chase Going Woodhouse as director.[49]

Woodhouse shared with Dodd an ongoing interest in the professional and economic status of women. Her father, a railroad developer, believed that women should be able to earn their own way, and her mother, a teacher, was the first woman in the family to hold a full-time job outside of the home. Her maternal grandmother also shaped her political consciousness by taking her at a young age to polling places each election day to protest women's inability to vote. Woodhouse vividly recalled how her grandmother drove angrily in the family carriage, walked as far as she was permitted, and loudly asserted, "Gentlemen, as a taxpayer I regret I will have no say in how my taxes are spent."[50] These experiences stayed with Woodhouse as she embarked on her education and career. In 1908 she enrolled at McGill University in Montreal, Canada, where she earned her B.A. in 1912 and her M.A. in economics the following year. She then pursued a Ph.D. in political economy, first at the University of Berlin and later, when the First World War cut her studies short, at the University of Chicago. After marrying in 1917, she accepted a position at Smith College, where she taught from 1917 to 1925 before moving to Washington, D.C., to work as a senior economist for the home economics bureau of the U.S. Department of Agriculture. Woodhouse returned to academia in 1928, this time as vocational director at North Carolina College for Women, where she and Dodd would house the institute.[51]

Woodhouse and Dodd faced an uphill battle: hardly a year after the institute's founding, the Great Depression swept the nation and decimated opportunities for professional women. Throughout the 1930s, they arranged several conferences to evaluate women's employment prospects, including a special forum on women in chemistry, which was held in April 1939. As other female scientists had done throughout the 1930s, they found that most attendees recommended hybrid positions combining science and secretarial work and indicated that they might serve as an "entering wedge" to higher paid jobs. Not all participants agreed, however. The New York Times reported that chemistry Ph.D. Ruth O'Brien of the federal Department of Agriculture "rose in something closely approximating wrath" upon hearing this suggestion. O'Brien believed that "for a really able woman chemist bent on maintaining her professional dignity, it is definitely derogatory to permit herself to have anything to do with a typing job," citing "an octopus-tendency of the type-writer to wrap its arms around her and refuse to let her rise above it." But O'Brien held the minority view, and most participants felt that work as a chemical secretary represented an attractive alternative to unemployment. For the time being at least, as the New York Times headline announced, "Sidelines [Were] Stressed for Girl Chemists."[52]

The outlook for female scientists appeared to brighten, however, as the United States mobilized its scientific resources for the Second World War. The wartime expansion of science and industry, as well as the emerging call for "trained brains," must have seemed rife with opportunity to Woodhouse and the recently remarried Catherine Filene Shouse. In early March 1942,

Shouse reported considerable clamoring for women in scientific fields, a welcome change from the Depression era. Later that month, the Institute for Women's Professional Relations explored this development further at its "War Demands for Trained Personnel" conference. Along with members of the Committee on Women in College and Defense, more than 100 educators, industrialists, and government officials were in attendance, both to offer advice and to receive direction.[53] Civil Service commissioner Arthur Flemming, who had been the only presenter at the Baltimore Conference to signal a specific need for female scientists and engineers, spoke at this conference as well. His message—that "the largest untapped scientific resource in the country lies with the professionally trained women"—was now echoed by many others. The director of the National Research Council's Office of Scientific Personnel, Joseph Morris, reported an "appallingly acute shortage" in physics and electronics and urged colleges to consider preparing women in those fields. Various government agencies and the military indicated a willingness to employ female chemists, engineers, and metallurgists. George Bailey of the OSRD even promised immediate placement of women with scientific training. After all, he explained, "This war is not exclusively a soldier's war: it is a civilian's war; it is a scientist's war; it is a woman's war. Woman has a very definite part, and she must be trained to do that part. To do it most effectively, she must be trained especially as a scientist; a physicist, an engineer, or a technician."[54]

Also present was Leonard Carmichael, the director of the National Roster of Scientific and Specialized Personnel, who similarly stressed the importance of women to the war program. He delineated his staff's efforts to identify the nation's "trained brains," which involved surveying individuals regarding their expertise, cataloging their responses, and compiling lists of available personnel. The fact that women comprised just 4 percent of the resulting roster in 1941, however, led some audience members to question the amount of effort that was actually made in locating them.[55] Kathryn McHale, the general director of the AAUW, confronted Carmichael in front of the assembly, charging, "I still am skeptical of your belief in the available resources. I don't think that you have really tapped them in a nation-wide sense. It is inconceivable, with the higher education of women having gone on nearly three periods of twenty-five years each, that you have tapped the supply available in my own Association alone."[56] She then recommended establishing a central clearinghouse and using existing venues, such as alumnae publications and AAUW's own journal, to identify and truly exhaust the available supply of female talent.[57]

Given McHale's position as the head of the country's principal organiza-tion of college-educated women, her frustration with Carmichael is not sur-prising. Nor is her willingness to enlarge the influence of the AAUW, which she had directed since 1929. Like Woodhouse and Shouse, McHale had spent the previous decade helping college-trained women eke out what-ever careers they could amid the ongoing economic crisis. She was well known for her advocacy of women's issues, and it was under her leadership that the AAUW's agenda expanded significantly to focus on the economic and political status of women. In her exchange with Leonard Carmichael, however, she did not mention barriers to women's advancement or the prejudice that she obviously sensed. Rather, she framed her invective and subsequent recommendations in familiar manpower rhetoric.[58]

McHale's stated concern with Carmichael's failure to identify female "brains" appears to have had an impact. Just several weeks later, in early April 1942, his National Roster of Scientific and Specialized Personnel tapped Chase Going Woodhouse to serve in its newly created position of consultant in the field of women. To assist her in her work, Woodhouse quickly assembled a committee consisting of McHale and Helen Hosp, an associate at the AAUW national headquarters and the executive secretary of the Committee on Women in College and Defense. As one of their first orders of business, they devised a four-part work plan that involved col-lecting data on scientific shortages, enlisting the support of colleges and universities in contacting alumnae, promoting women's enrollment in shortage subjects, and establishing advisory placement committees to use scientifically trained women in their own cities or regions. To this end, the committee helped establish "War Work Information" centers in major cit-ies to collect, assess, and distribute information regarding employment op-portunities. By the fall of 1942, these centers were up and running in Bos-ton, New Haven, Philadelphia, and New York, the latter one being located at Columbia University. Over the next several months, additional centers were added in St. Louis, Minneapolis, Dallas, and Cleveland.[59] Woodhouse touted these initiatives as eagerly anticipated solutions for long-standing problems faced by professional women. The National Roster, she claimed, provided "a dual opportunity—helping to meet the war manpower short-ages and helping college alumnae to find a useful place for themselves in the world of work."[60]

Woodhouse's committee cooperated closely with the Committee on Women in College and Defense, which, by the fall of 1942, had been re-configured as the Committee on College Women Students and the War.[61]

The committee's new chair, Pembroke College dean and former AAUW president Margaret Morriss, began looking for help from other educators in increasing women's representation on the National Roster and in scientific fields more generally. In January 1943, Morriss published an article in the American Council on Education's *Educational Record* proposing that all female students with even modest scientific or mathematical abilities be directed toward those subjects in light of the international situation. She added, "The colleges themselves are responsible for securing all the women scientists they can," suggesting that the war's outcome depended on it.[62]

Morriss's advocacy of scientific womanpower as a vital war measure captured the essence of technocratic feminism. It also reflected the ongoing efforts of her colleagues, not only in their shared committee work but also at their individual home institutions. At Barnard, Virginia Gildersleeve began early on to identify meaningful ways in which her students could contribute to the defense program and, in 1940, established the National Service Committee to assist in this task. One of the committee's projects was creating "war majors" and "war minors" that stressed the study of militarily important subjects, such as physics, chemistry, and mathematics.[63] By June 1941, she noted that Barnard's Occupation Bureau had already experienced an increased call volume for women trained in these disciplines, and she predicted that there would soon be a shortage of physicians and bacteriologists as well. "It is true," Gildersleeve argued, "that a reluctance to employ women, developed during the depression, still lingers. But we hope departments and employers will hasten to realize that it is better to appoint a first rate woman than a mediocre man. Soon even the mediocre man will not be available, and they will be forced to employ women. . . . A more speedy realization of the advantages of doing so will help our national efficiency."[64]

It was in the name of national efficiency that the National Service Committee also designed several short-term extracurricular courses to prepare Barnard students for defense work. Among these was a course in engineering drafting that was taught by faculty in Columbia's School of Engineering. This arrangement, Gildersleeve believed, "was the turn of the lock preliminary to the opening of this great School to women."[65] The School of Engineering was, after all, the last of Columbia's professional schools to exclude female students. Its policy of refusing women admission had been formalized by university trustees in the 1890s and reaffirmed in 1911, the same year that Gildersleeve became dean of Barnard.[66] Although Gildersleeve had successfully convinced Columbia's medical and law schools to admit women by promising to hand-pick the first applicants, she found the School of Engineering to be a much tougher battle. She later reflected that "for a good many years I felt that if a really tip-top candidate appeared, I might be able to insert her into the School, but no one did. Then the Second World War changed the situation drastically."[67]

The war presented Gildersleeve with an opportunity to pursue her long-standing goal of opening the School of Engineering to women, which she began advocating as a defense measure. But while the wartime demand for "trained brains" bolstered her argument for women's admission, it did not completely dissolve all resistance. Perhaps the most outspoken opponent of coeducational engineering education was the School of Engineering's associate dean, James Kip Finch, to whom the admission of women seemed neither practical nor desirable. In October 1942, he issued a seven-page memorandum to the engineering faculty imploring them to reject Gildersleeve's proposal for admitting women to the school. He warned, "We should not be stampeded into a mistaken and useless action under the impression that we are accomplishing something of value in winning the war." As an alternative to enrolling female students, he proposed that Columbia expand its short-term, nondegree offerings instead. Doing so, he suggested, would enable the school to contribute to the war effort but avoid admitting women as degree candidates.[68]

To justify the continued exclusion of female students, Finch employed a number of arguments, such as citing the small number of women in engineering as evidence of their lack of interest in the field. But rather than interrogate the reasons for women's underrepresentation, he sidestepped them almost entirely. He gestured to the subject of discrimination only once when he noted somewhat incredulously that the American Institute of Chemical Engineers had been "reported to 'discourage' applications for admission by women," using quotation marks to set off the word "discourage" from the rest of the text.[69] Finch also claimed that women's admission would negatively affect the school's finances, relations with alumni, and the operations of student organizations. Although these were all problems that Columbia's other professional schools had successfully addressed after their decisions to admit women, Finch maintained that the engineering program involved additional difficulties that were not only "peculiar" to the school but also "far more perplexing and uncertain of solution." The most significant and legitimate of these difficulties was the school's requirement that first and second year pre-engineering courses be taken at the all-male Columbia College. Since there was no indication that the college would open its pre-engineering curriculum to women, Finch noted that female applicants would have to complete their first two years of coursework elsewhere. But because, according to Finch, "no women's college in the United States does, or probably can, offer an equivalent course of study," he concluded that "there are no women today prepared to enter our School of Engineering."[70]

With characteristic savvy, Gildersleeve responded by authorizing a two-year pre-engineering course at Barnard. She also worked out an arrangement through which Barnard students could take the remaining prerequisite courses at Columbia College instead. Consequently, the School of Engineering heeded her call for "trained brains" and voted to admit female students in December 1942.[71] An official announcement of this decision explained that "the need for trained engineers is so great at present that it is hoped that a considerable number of able young women may be attracted to this important profession."[72] In the end, Gildersleeve's careful maneuvering and strategic appeal to wartime prerogatives enabled her to open the last of Columbia's professional schools to women.

Women Scientists and Engineers in a World at War

Although Gildersleeve encountered notable resistance in her crusade to open Columbia's School of Engineering to women, other institutions capitulated more readily. Dwindling male enrollment, coupled with mounting manpower concerns, resulted in women's admission to another twenty-eight all-male engineering schools.[73] The war also facilitated women's entrance into scientific and technical fields at coeducational universities and women's colleges alike. The Ohio State University revised its curricula to meet war needs by adding several "women-only" classes in physics, mathematics, and chemistry. The all-female Smith College modified its offerings to include a variety of new technical courses with wartime applications. Meanwhile, Wilson College, another women's school, revamped its science program to stress militarily important subjects such as electronics.[74]

The creation of the women's military reserves provided additional opportunities to study scientific subjects. Advanced training for WAVES officers was often given in coeducational settings at schools across the country. At the University of Chicago, they received instruction in aerological engineering, while at the Massachusetts Institute of Technology (MIT) and the University of California in Los Angeles they enrolled in radio courses. Other WAVES officers trained at the Naval Aviation Training School in Hollywood,

California, the Navy Pre-Radar School at Harvard University, and the Navy Technical Training Command School in Corpus Christi, Texas.[75]

Reformers urged female students to take advantage of these new opportunities, which they cast as beneficial to both women and the war effort. Gildersleeve explained to an assembly of Barnard students that their preparation in shortage fields was in high demand and made them "precious assets of the nation."[76] The former journalist and current consultant to the War Manpower Commission Eva Hansl told female graduate students at Catholic University that "all scientific work, from anthropology to zoology, is becoming increasingly important to the war program." Consequently, "you young women graduating into the labor market . . . constitute the largest untapped reservoir of technical labor in the country."[77] At a careers convocation for college women held at the University of Cincinnati, Margaret Hickey, who chaired the Women's Advisory Committee of the War Manpower Commission and served as the vice president of the BPW, similarly urged students to consider enrolling in defense-related fields. "Even if you don't want a degree in chemistry or medicine," she said, "the country wants it for you."[78]

Whether it was at the explicit urging of reformers, a more general response to wartime recruitment campaigns, or some combination of the two, female students did in fact enter wartime science in increasing numbers. By January 1943, chemistry enrollments at Smith College had increased 68 percent, while physics had gained 38 percent and mathematics 33 percent. More than a quarter of all Vassar students declared majors in the sciences during the war years.[79] At New Jersey College for Women, its 1944 yearbook editors observed, "Science has had a war boom [here] as well as everywhere else. Freshman chem classes are swollen to an unbelievable size and the same interest holds in biology, physics, math, and the other sciences."[80] Chemistry even surpassed home economics as the most popular major among "NJC" women.[81] Nationwide, the biggest percentage increase in women's enrollment was in the field of engineering, which jumped by 75 percent during the war. In absolute numbers, 181 women earned undergraduate engineering degrees between 1940 and 1945, reflecting significant growth when compared with previous periods.[82]

While women's wartime enrollment in engineering degree programs was remarkable, it paled in comparison to the number of women participating in short-term, nondegree programs sponsored by the federal government and defense industries. The largest of these was the government-funded Engineering, Science, and Management War Training (ESMWT) program, which enrolled more than 282,000 women between 1940 and 1945.[83] Established by Congress in 1940, the ESMWT program was one of the first large-scale federal efforts to recruit and train scientific "manpower," both in general and regardless of race or sex (it even included a nondiscrimination clause to this end). The program offered free college-level courses in engineering, physics, chemistry, and other defense-related fields. It also included several courses specifically designed for women, such as junior engineering, engineering drawing, and electrical principles and measurements. By the end of the war, ESMWT courses were given at 227 institutions of higher education, including numerous women's colleges. All-female schools such as Vassar, Smith, Wilson, Wellesley, Bryn Mawr, Hunter, and Simmons provided not only courses for current students but also "refresher" classes for alumnae. In response to these measures, women's enrollment increased from less than 1 percent of participants in the program's first year to 21.8 percent in 1943–44.[84]

Defense industries feeling the pinch for trained personnel developed similar short-term programs, either in conjunction with ESMWT or on their own. One aircraft company sponsored a forty-eight-week engineering course for women at Bucknell University, North Carolina State College, and the Universities of Michigan, Connecticut, and New Hampshire. At Purdue University, the Radio Corporation of America established a ten-month program to train women in engineering basics. The participants, most of whom had completed at least one year of college, received a small salary, lodging, and tuition.[85] Similarly, Vought-Sikorsky Aircraft established a program for women in aeronautical engineering at New York University's Daniel Guggenheim School of Aeronautics at the College of Engineering. In 1943, forty "Chance Vought Scholars" drawn from across the country received eight months of specialized training, along with tuition, room, board, and fifty dollars per month.[86]

The largest industrial program was sponsored by the Curtiss-Wright Corporation. In December 1942, the aircraft manufacturer announced that it would pay to train 800 college women at eight engineering schools across the country and then employ the "engineering cadettes" in its factories. As with the other programs, the corporation assumed responsibility for financial costs and arranged to pay each participating school for the women's room, board, and tuition. It also paid cadettes ten dollars per week for the duration of the ten-month curriculum. Inquiries flooded in, and in less than one month, Curtiss-Wright had received 4,000 applications from women in forty-four states. After a series of interviews and aptitude tests, more than 700 cadettes began their training in February 1943, when they flocked to Cornell, Purdue, Iowa State, Texas, Penn State, Minnesota, and Rensselaer.[87]

For many young women interested in science and technology, wartime programs such as these helped provide much-needed encouragement. According to one cadette, enrolling in the program meant finding "a group of other young women who were also interested in math, physics, and chemistry and I felt more accepted. Before, most of my acquaintances gave me the impression that my desires were a little odd for a woman."[88] Another cadette noted that "I wanted to study engineering but my family insisted it was not a job for a girl. . . . [The cadette program] was a great opportunity to do what I'd always wanted to do."[89] Many others, such as Mary Glover, who participated in the Curtiss-Wright program at Penn State, similarly viewed their involvement as a welcome chance to become proficient in a field that was previously off-limits.[90]

To recruit female students, these wartime programs advertised widely in newspapers, women's magazines, and radio broadcasts. They also relied heavily on the assistance of individual women and women's organizations. The Curtiss-Wright Corporation directly contacted deans of women to help identify potential participants, while other programs approached women's professional organizations and civic groups.[91] Technocratic feminists generally relished these requests insofar as they meshed with their own interests in women's education and employment. Indeed, some were so eager to expand women's participation that they looked for ways to do so before being asked. In October 1942, the national federation of the BPW took the initiative in writing ESMWT officials to offer its help. Gladys F. Gove, who headed the BPW's vocational service, explained that the recruitment of women for ESMWT "is very much in line with the Federation's War Program, in its undertaking to see that women are given training and employment opportunities that will enable them to make their maximum contribution."[92]

The Committee on Women in College and Defense and its successor, the Committee on College Women Students and the War, provided another source of support for these short-term programs. In addition to publicizing existing courses, the committee also promoted the establishment of new ones.[93] Some members even had a personal hand in creating them. Virginia Gildersleeve and Lillian Gilbreth, for instance, worked closely with the Stevens Institute of Technology and ESMWT to arrange a course for women in engineering.[94] Gildersleeve also advised officials at Columbia

Lillian Gilbreth, 1940s. Courtesy of Purdue University Libraries, Karnes Archives and Special Collections.

University and Grumman Aircraft, who established a similar program for women in New York City. Meanwhile, Gilbreth assisted the Radio Corporation of America in setting up its program at Purdue.[95]

Even as they worked to establish and promote these short-term programs, however, Gilbreth and Gildersleeve harbored mixed feelings toward them. On the upside, they viewed them as mechanisms for introducing women to nontraditional fields while at the same time supporting wartime needs. But they also recognized that these programs failed to prepare women as full-fledged members of the scientific community or professional life. Nor did they intend to. In the eyes of most government and industry officials, these programs, which primarily trained women as subprofessional aides or assistants, were designed to release men for more challenging and prestigious assignments.[96] The Curtiss-Wright Corporation readily admitted that its cadettes would "perform the lower category of engineering work and thus permit the up-grading of [male] graduate engineers."[97] The General Electric Company's Turbine Department recruited female math majors "to relieve [male] engineers of as much calculating work as possible, and thus permit them to concentrate on the more involved problems for which their specialized training has fit them." Although these women took over much of the work carried out by male engineers, a GE representative clearly pointed out that they "are not engineers and do not supplant engineers."[98]

Elsie Eaves, an accomplished engineer with more than twenty years of experience, was quick to point out these shortcomings. In an article that she penned for the BPW magazine *Independent Woman*, she warned that most of the calls for women engineers were for positions which "occupy the bottom rungs on the professional ladder."[99] She also expressed frustration that most media attention and recruiting campaigns focused on these lower-level jobs. Although she predicted that work as an engineering aide or technician could serve as a stepping stone or proving ground for women hoping to become professional engineers one day, she urged readers to recognize the difference between the two categories of employment.

Eaves would have agreed with Gildersleeve and Gilbreth that college women already studying engineering, or any other militarily important science, would be served better in the long run by completing their degree programs before taking a war job (many schools offered accelerated coursework to make this possible).[100] To some extent, they were right. Female graduates generally did fare better in terms of their work assignments and were certainly in high demand. In January and February 1942, recruiters from various chemical companies toured the women's colleges to sign up graduating seniors before they had an opportunity to seek other work.[101] New Jersey College for Women placement director Fredericka Belknap reported in March 1942 that the number of calls for majors in physics, mathematics, and chemistry to work in chemical plants and munitions factories was "enormous." The largest request to date had come that very afternoon when the nearby Raritan Arsenal phoned for fifty women with scientific or mathematical backgrounds to replace male section leaders. Similar requests poured in daily from various war plants not only in New Jersey but also in Massachusetts, Delaware, Maryland, and Connecticut. According to Belknap, "Senior mathematics majors were considering anywhere from one to three jobs, wondering which to take," and "there were about ten possibilities for every chemistry major."[102]

Few women, however, found positions equivalent to those occupied by their male counterparts. Although Gloria Brooks Reinish, the first woman to graduate from Columbia's School of Engineering, finished second in her class, she had trouble gaining work commensurate with her talents. She later recalled, "I was quite annoyed by the fact that Bell Labs, which was a prestigious place to work, offered me a job as a TA, that's a technical assistant." She continued: "In those days, they only had two categories of employees, MTS, which was member of technical staff, and the TA, which was technical assistant. And engineers were normally hired as members of technical staff, but this was male engineers [*sic*]. They didn't have any female engineers. But they were hiring some mathematicians and physicists who were female, and they were giving them the status of technical assistant rather than member of technical staff. So this is what they offered me, technical assistant."[103] Although Reinish managed to negotiate a higher-ranking position for herself as member of technical staff, most women in her situation were less successful.

Many women with graduate degrees faced similar disappointments. Marion Crenshall Monet, who earned her master's in chemical engineering from MIT in 1943, was hired as a "junior engineer" when she joined DuPont after graduation. When chemist and Harvard University doctoral candidate Lilli Hornig arrived at Los Alamos, she was asked to take a typing test. And mathematics Ph.D. Mina Rees, who would become the only woman scientist at the OSRD to move into a major policy position after the war, was listed as a "technical aide" and "executive assistant" in 1943–46.[104]

In reality, most high-ranking positions in wartime science were occupied by men. The famed OSRD, for example, staffed both its office and projects using "old-boy" networks.[105] According to the agency's official history, "Those charged with recruiting chemists and physicists for OSRD and its contractors knew the outstanding men in each field already and through them got in touch with many young men of brilliant promise."[106] Consequently, the number of women assigned to these projects was relatively small, and the number of women in positions of authority even smaller. Only three women seem to have supervised OSRD projects during the war, and of them, none managed large teams of researchers (as was standard practice) but instead worked alone.[107]

Neither the shortage of scientific manpower nor the efforts of technocratic feminists reversed the persistent preference for male scientists and engineers. When, for the first time in its 116 years of operation, Rensselaer Polytechnic Institute agreed to admit women, school officials were careful to stipulate that they would only accept a limited number after the total male enrollment was known.[108] In December 1942, Chase Going Woodhouse similarly observed of her work with the National Roster that most government offices seemed reluctant to place trained women and that they preferred men whenever they were available.[109] Several weeks later, in January 1943, she reported to the Women's Advisory Committee of the

War Manpower Commission that the number of requests for female engineers, physicists, and chemists had recently increased. But many of them expressed ongoing hesitance, as indicated by the fact that they began with the statement, "We find that we are obliged to employ women."[110] Bertha Nienburg, the chief economist for the Women's Bureau of the U.S. Department of Labor, also pointed out that the number of women being recruited for the better-paying scientific jobs was relatively small.[111] Shedding light on these trends, an employment officer at the Naval Research Laboratory later admitted a widespread belief among many of his (presumably male) colleagues that "women could be used most successfully in a scientific organization only when their total number did not exceed 10% of the working group."[112]

The failure of the government and industry to utilize women effectively came under attack by some reformers, such as Lillian Gilbreth. In a speech entitled "Women's Colleges as Reservoirs for Employment" that she delivered at a 1943 AAUW conference on "College Women and War Industry," Gilbreth called attention to what she saw as inefficiencies in the war effort by raising questions about the placement of women, their opportunities for advancement, and whether some might be released for higher-level positions by bringing in assistants or aides, as was commonly done for men.[113] BPW president Minnie Maffett shared similar concerns in a wartime address where she demanded to know why more women "are not in big posts, working side by side with men in the direction of scientific problems in this all-out war that affects everyone." According to Maffett, "Failure to use our ablest womanpower in this way is a shortsighted and suicidal policy."[114]

Despite their frustrations, however, both Maffett and Gilbreth were generally proud of their own wartime efforts as well as the women who entered scientific fields. Reflecting on the BPW's recent activities, Maffett stated, "I feel that . . . we have made progress—that women are taking up many more unusual professions, especially in the fields of science, and that they are making good in their new jobs."[115] Gilbreth seemed equally impressed with women engineers and commended them for their adroitness in meeting wartime demands.[116] This sense of accomplishment was shared by many female scientists themselves and often translated into an optimism about their postwar employment prospects. One engineering cadette proudly announced in 1943 that she and her female classmates "have picked up a course with a useful and rosy future."[117] Marjorie Crawford, the national secretary of the women's chemistry honor society, Iota Sigma Pi, expected that "with so many men unable to continue their studies, women with advanced training will be more valuable than ever, both for the war effort and for the postwar period."[118] Meanwhile, the engineer Elsie Eaves, who had characterized wartime training programs as a "stepping stone to professional advancement," claimed that women would find ample outlets for their skills as industries reconverted to meet the needs of a vigorous postwar consumer economy.[119]

Many others' predictions were equally positive. Evelyn Steele, who published several vocational guidance booklets for young women, observed in her 1943 *Careers for Girls in Science and Engineering* that "while it took a war to create the opportunities for training and experience which were not easily available to women before, there can be no doubt about the future. Women are being called upon to serve now; when the war is won those who have excelled will continue to serve."[120] At a 1944 vocational conference hosted by the Institute of Women's Professional Relations, chemist Walter Murphy stated, "I am confident opportunities for women in chemistry in the postwar world will be bright. Their immediate status will be governed somewhat by what women have proved themselves capable of doing in the emergency period, particularly in jobs not heretofore open to women. The ever-widening horizons in chemistry are sure to bring with them new fields for women."[121] Margaret Hickey similarly anticipated that "the engineering field will continue to offer great numbers of job opportunities" to postwar women.[122]

Not everyone, however, shared this optimism. Chase Going Woodhouse sounded an early warning bell in 1943 when she raised the question, "Is a chemist a chemist or do we have sex in chemistry, with one sex qualified to hold jobs in an emergency only?"[123] Likewise, Virginia Gildersleeve, who had fought so zealously for women's admission to Columbia's School of Engineering, now pondered the fate of those first female students. In a series of exchanges with *Woman's Home Companion* editor Esther Bien, she agreed with Bien's assessment of the manpower shortage and the opportunities it had opened for women in scientific fields. But she questioned the accuracy of Bien's prediction that these developments would result in permanent jobs for scientifically trained women. In March 1943, Gildersleeve wrote to Bien, "I do not think you are warranted in saying so positively that these types of work are going to offer life-time careers for women when the war is over." "Possibly they will," Gildersleeve conceded, "but you cannot know definitely."[124]

In spite of her uncertainty (and in an attempt to avoid undoing her own wartime work), Gildersleeve continued to stress publicly the immediate demand for "trained brains." In 1944 she issued a revised version of her vocational guidance pamphlet "Educating Girls for the War and the Post-War World," which read, "So great and urgent is the need for mathematicians and scientists that any aptitude in these directions should certainly be encouraged." Yet even as she predicted that "the scope of women's professional activities will probably remain permanently enlarged" after the war, she did admit that "it seems likely that the number of women physicists and mathematicians required will fall off rather sharply," thus revealing her emerging skepticism about the postwar period.[125]

Postwar Realities and the Lessons of War

Gildersleeve's suspicions turned out to be well founded. In the months following the end of the war, Columbia University reported a precipitous drop in the number of employers calling for scientifically trained women.[126] The same occurred in schools across the country. Amid the return of male veterans, female scientists frequently found themselves displaced and demoted. Many of the same universities and industries that had clamored for women in the not-so-distant past now shunted them to the side or dismissed them entirely. The wartime contributions of female scientists were also eclipsed by the postwar resurgence of domesticity, which denigrated women's professional aspirations in favor of family togetherness.[127]

Many of these developments were exacerbated by the GI Bill. The monumental piece of legislation enabled more than two million returning veterans to pursue higher education at government expense.[128] But while the GI Bill has been lauded for democratizing higher education, it primarily benefited men. Women made up less than 3 percent of veterans and used GI benefits less frequently than their male counterparts.[129] Moreover, the rapid influx of male GIs threatened the place of those female students who had been recruited and encouraged during the war. The wartime demand for women gave way to a pronounced preference for returning veterans, whose arrival on college campuses swelled enrollments and taxed school resources, such as housing, classrooms, teaching staff, and counseling services. Many universities, pressed for dormitory space, even converted women's residence halls into housing for male veterans. As University of Michigan dean of women Alice C. Lloyd observed, the GIs "have come in larger numbers and more quickly than anyone anticipated, and their inevitable and unchallenged rights are threatening other college groups on many coeducational campuses. The group most often endangered is that group which has never been too secure in its rights and privileges in the educational world—the women." "There is grave danger," Lloyd continued, "that the women if not actually excluded, may be neglected and relegated very definitely to second place."[130]

By 1946, as Lloyd suspected, educators across the country began curtailing women's admission. From Syracuse to Stanford, thousands of qualified women were turned away from higher education in an effort to accommodate veterans' needs. State universities such as Michigan and Wisconsin, where female students had made up 64 percent and 70 percent of wartime enrollments, respectively, now banned nearly all out-of-state women. Meanwhile, Cornell issued an announcement in January 1946 that unapologetically explained, "The dozen fraternity houses under lease to the university as 'cottages' will not be available next fall, so the number of women students will inescapably have to be reduced."[131] Although women had constituted a majority of Cornell's student body during the war years, the administration cut back their postwar enrollments to the prewar norm of 20 percent. Even women's colleges felt pressure to accommodate veterans, and many—including Vassar, Finch, and Sarah Lawrence—admitted male students for the first time.[132] Graduate programs suffered a similar fate. The Radcliffe Graduate School (the women's division of the Harvard Graduate School of Arts and Sciences) slashed its enrollment from 400 in 1945–46 to less than 300 in 1946. Meanwhile, female graduate enrollment at Johns Hopkins hovered between 21 percent and 25 percent from 1946 to 1951.[133] Although several leading women's organizations such as the BPW and the AAUW publicly expressed concern with these developments, they were not successful in offsetting the general public's overwhelming eagerness to assist veterans at this time.[134]

But gaining admission to the postwar college was only the first in a long line of obstacles encountered by women. Female students—both newly admitted ones and those who carried on from wartime days—often faced a hostile climate once on campus. Phyllis Pollock Magat, who enrolled in MIT's chemistry Ph.D. program in the fall of 1944, recalls the sharp contrast between the war years and the immediate postwar period: "Our entering class in the chemistry grad school in 1944 was small (about eight) and were mostly women. The professors were amazed but soon got over any prejudice. The problems due to being a woman disappeared during the war, but reemerged with a vengeance after the war when veterans returned to schools."[135]

One concrete example can be viewed in the distribution of financial aid, as female students who had been funded during the war frequently lost their scholarships to returning GIs. Other women daring to enter graduate programs also found that schools preferred to fund returning GIs and civilian men. As chemist Geraldine Lynch Krueger observed, "The GI Bill has enabled huge numbers of men to go on in graduate study, but relatively few women. Competition for space to do research and for departmental assistantships has never been more keen."[136] As returning veterans reclaimed their places in science and engineering programs, women's presence became even more marginal.

The GI Bill helped revive traditional social attitudes in other ways as well. The influx of married veterans, in particular, introduced what historian Barbara Miller Solomon calls "new patterns of collegiate domesticity."[137] At schools across the country, "Vetsvilles" sprouted up to house veterans and their families. There, a soldier and his wife might huddle over dinner in their Quonset hut or bundle up the children for a stroll across campus. Images such as these proliferated in newspapers and yearbooks and, before long, became typical representations of college life.[138] Many college women recall the postwar surge in "collegiate domesticity" as a powerful force and one that spread beyond the confines of "Vetsvilles." One women's college graduate in the class of 1946 explained that "marriage was in the air and everyone was doing it—it was hard to resist."[139] Some women, who chose to marry while still in college, actually benefited from newer policies designed to accommodate married students. (In earlier years, married women might have been asked to leave school.) In this regard, the GI Bill expanded the notion of who could benefit from college and, in doing so, eased the way for older, married students. But it also limited women's roles on campus and beyond, as most were regarded as wives or future wives, whether they were or not.[140]

The postwar emphasis on domesticity and traditional gender roles also shaped attitudes toward women's employment. Irene Peden, who graduated from the University of Colorado's engineering program in 1947, remembers the stiff resistance that she faced when seeking out her first job. According to Peden, "It was a very family oriented time, when people had four children, baked their own bread. The only meaningful kind of leadership position that would have been socially acceptable was to run the P.T.A. And here I was, you know, trying to get a job as an engineer, to work as one."[141] Consequently, she recalls, "I simply pounded the pavement . . . I didn't have a choice." Peden remembered that employers "would simply tell me, 'We've never hired a woman before, and we're not going to talk to you,' and shut the door." "I had a lot of that to deal with," she added.[142]

Juliette Moran encountered similar difficulties when trying to obtain a postwar position, despite her qualifications and experience. During the war, the class of 1939 chemistry major worked for the General Aniline & Film Corporation while completing a part-time master's degree program in chemistry at New York University. But when war production subsided and the company made plans to transfer Moran's division, she began looking for another position. After sending letters to the top ten chemical companies in the Northeast to inquire about work, she was disappointed when seven of the companies did not reply at all. The other two, she explained, replied that they did not have any openings, while the last one, DuPont, said that it might have an opening for a librarian. In other words, Moran lamented, "There [was] not a single job for a female with my scanty credentials as the men have come back."[143]

Women with distinguished reputations, such as applied mathematician Hilda Geiringer von Mises, found the postwar period formidable as well. When searching for an academic position, she learned about a vacancy at Tufts and asked a friend with contacts there to inquire on her behalf. In the fall of 1947, her friend relayed a terse reply from a Tufts professor, who wrote, "I am quite sure that President Carmichael will not approve of a woman. . . . We have Wm. Graustein's widow on our staff, and Ralph Boas' wife, so it is not merely prejudice against women, yet it is partly that, for we do not want to bring in more if we can get men."[144] That von Mises was one of the more accomplished experts in her field seemed not to matter to Carmichael, who was, incidentally, the same Leonard Carmichael who had directed the National Roster of Scientific and Specialized Personnel during the war.[145] His obvious and ongoing reluctance to employ women in responsible positions highlights the limits of both wartime changes and technocratic feminism.

As demonstrated in this chapter, the search for scientific womanpower was both justified and limited by national security prerogatives. The postwar backlash made especially apparent the limits of tethering women's education and employment to short-term national security goals. Wartime recruitment campaigns for scientific personnel were, after all, predicated on immediate wartime needs that were expected to subside with the resumption of peace. The fact that some of the primary vehicles for mobilizing wartime science, such as the OSRD and the ESMWT program, were slated to close at the end of the war underscores this perception. By adopting national security rhetoric, then, technocratic feminists automatically if accidentally advanced the dominant view of female scientists as temporary workers.

Many of the challenges that technocratic feminists faced when seeking to fold women into wartime science were, moreover, products of wartime science itself. While the rapid expansion of defense research, development, and production seemed promising, most of the actual growth occurred at the lower levels, where women would be concentrated. A study conducted by the National Research Council reveals that between 1940 and 1946, the staffs of industrial research laboratories increased by 50 percent in the area of professional personnel, 110 percent in the area of technical personnel, and 160 percent in the area of supporting personnel.[146] Many of these lower-level positions, and especially those for which women were disproportionately recruited, were designed in large part to release men for more difficult and prestigious assignments. The overall swelling of the scientific and technical workforce meant that the notable growth in women's participation was outstripped by the even larger influx of men. The ESMWT program, which enrolled more than a quarter of a million women, trained nearly six times as many men. And while the National Roster's attempts to locate scientifically trained women resulted in a doubling of their numbers, their overall overrepresentation increased only from 4.0 percent in 1941 to 4.1 percent in 1945, owing to the fact that men's representation had also doubled.[147] In the end, efforts to recruit scientific manpower not only justified women's participation but also reinforced their marginalization.

Few technocratic feminists, however, saw anything contradictory in their embrace of national security prerogatives. Even those who were critical of the continuous challenges and setbacks faced by women generally celebrated their inclusion in wartime science. Most viewed women's movement into male-dominated disciplines, however slow and occasionally stunted, as part of an ongoing and necessary struggle to improve their status and to gain professional acceptance. To this end, reformers brought scientific womanpower to the attention of government, industry, and education officials whenever possible. They also worked to include women in wartime training programs and gain them access to previously closed institutions. In doing so, they helped not only to expand the overall population of female scientists and engineers but also to create a new generation of scientifically trained women. Together, these efforts paved the way for continued activism in the postwar and early Cold War period, when reformers encountered new national security anxieties and renewed scientific manpower concerns.

CHAPTER TWO

Endless Frontiers
for Scientific Womanpower

In their 1946 *Journal of the American Association of University Women* article, "Science Out of Petticoats," chemists Eleanor Horsey and Donna Price surveyed the status of women in postwar science. Compared with their own experiences as graduate students during the Great Depression, Horsey and Price agreed that prejudice against female scientists had noticeably decreased. Yet opposition to their education and employment remained "very general and very large," as evidenced by such persistent obstacles as unequal pay, occupational segregation, and skepticism toward married women's career commitments. The marginalization of female scientists, the lack of support for their goals, and their continued underrepresentation were glaringly apparent to Horsey and Price, who suggested that these phenomena now posed particular problems for postwar science and security.[1]

Their assertion found footing in broader debates regarding the evolving relationship between science and the state. Although the federal government had mobilized and funded scientific research and development on an unprecedented scale during the war, it was not immediately clear what role it would or should play in the years ahead. Policymakers, scientific administrators, and military officials took up this question even before the war had ended. Despite their differences regarding the desired size and shape of government involvement, most agreed that science must remain a national priority and that American influence in the postwar world depended on continued scientific progress. Military readiness, economic prosperity, and the fate of the nation more generally, it seemed, would rest in the hands of both science and scientists.

This view was expressed most famously by Vannevar Bush, chief architect of wartime science and director of the OSRD, in his 1945 report, *Science, the Endless Frontier*. Commissioned by Franklin Roosevelt in November 1944 and delivered to Harry Truman in July 1945, the nearly 200-page document firmly established science as central to national security and advocated federal support through such mechanisms as a national research foundation and a permanent science advisory board. It also called for what Bush termed the "renewal of our scientific talent," which had been visibly depleted by the Second World War. By Bush's calculations (which were informed by the sixteen-man committee he put on this task), the war had interrupted the education of approximately 150,000 undergraduates and 17,000 graduate students who would have otherwise earned degrees in scientific and technical fields. This "accumulating deficit," Bush warned, threatened the future of postwar science and security since "the real ceiling on our productivity of new scientific knowledge . . . is the number of trained scientists available."[2]

Horsey and Price agreed with Bush's ominous assessment, reiterated his findings, and suggested that the looming shortage that he described would be remedied only "when women are encouraged to enter scientific professions, and when they no longer encounter the obstacles we have mentioned." To this end, they advocated providing government support to women as well as to men and promised that this action would double the number of scientists available. According to Horsey and Price, women constituted not only "one practically untapped source of scientists" but also a particularly important one "in view of the current demand for increased scientific personnel."[3]

By yoking the plight of female scientists to national security concerns, Horsey and Price put forward a compelling argument for improving women's participation in scientific fields. In doing so, they built on the tradition of technocratic feminism as employed by Virginia Gildersleeve and other reformers during the Second War World. In the postwar period, these efforts were buoyed by an enlarged population of scientifically trained women who knew firsthand the problems and possibilities of wartime science. While mindful of formal obstacles, however, these technocratic feminists generally focused their energies on what they viewed as equally detrimental social conventions and stereotypes. Those who were most successful in advancing their interests drew on national security anxieties not only in a rhetorical sense but also in actively encouraging scientific womanpower through their outreach efforts.

Instead of framing women's education and employment as defense measures intended largely for the duration, these reformers foresaw no clearly defined end to postwar planning along science's seemingly "endless frontier." The dawn of the atomic age and the emerging Cold War had resulted in a precarious peace that demanded ongoing preparedness in all areas of society. This development both allowed and required a new iteration of technocratic feminism, one that was based on an expanded definition of national security and an increasingly entrenched national security state.

National Security in Postwar America

The Second World War had fundamentally altered Americans' conceptions of what it meant to be secure. The bombing of Pearl Harbor, along with wartime developments in science and technology, seemed to shrink the dimensions of the globe and rendered obsolete the sense of protection previously provided by the expanse of two oceans. The war's dramatic end, marked by the detonation of two atomic bombs over Japan, further heightened this feeling of vulnerability by introducing a level of death and destruction formerly unknown. As relations with the Soviet Union deteriorated, so too did confidence that the United States could return easily to its prewar isolationism. Efforts to stave off Soviet influence and to protect American interests called for continued vigilance and military readiness amid a burgeoning Cold War.[4] As President Truman explained to a joint session of Congress in the fall of 1945, "Our geographical security is now gone," as was "the luxury of time with which to arm ourselves."[5] Consequently, peacetime preparations became paramount to national security.

It was evident from early on that science would enjoy special consideration in postwar planning. In January 1945, Vannevar Bush appeared before the House Committee on Postwar Military Policy to urge continued scientific preparedness in the years to come. According to Bush's testimony:

> The speed and surprise with which great damage could be done to our fleet at Pearl Harbor is only a mild warning of what might happen in the future. The new German flying bombs and rocket bombs, our own B-29, and the many electronic devices now in use which were unknown five years ago, are merely the forerunners of weapons which might possess overwhelming power, the ability to strike suddenly, without warning, and without any adequate means of protection or retaliation. I do not mean that some methods of protection or retaliation could not be developed. I mean only that we might not be given sufficient time within which to develop those means, once hostilities had begun, before disaster overtook us. It is imperative, therefore, that we begin at once to prepare intelligently

for the type of modern war which may confront us with great sud-
denness some time in the future.[6]

The following month, the secretaries of war and the navy took up many
of these same themes in a joint letter issued to the National Academy of Sciences, in which they called for postwar coordination of scientific research.
They explained, "To insure continued preparedness along far-sighted technical lines, the research scientists of the country must be called upon to
continue in peacetime some substantial portion of those types of contribution to national security which they have made so effectively during the
stress of the present war."[7] Brigadier General and Radio Corporation of
America president David Sarnoff hammered these points home in a widely
read article published in the *New York Times* the day after the bombing of
Nagasaki. In the age of atomic weaponry, Sarnoff warned, a third world
war would be cataclysmic. Hence, "America must recognize that adequate
preparedness in science is the best insurance we can provide against the
future. Our national security depends upon it."[8]

The recognition of science's role in postwar security and the quest for
ongoing preparedness resulted in efforts to extend and make permanent
several characteristics of wartime science. Principal among these were
large-scale federal support for research and development, the facilitation of
partnerships between civilian scientists and the military, a diffuse contract
system, and concerted efforts to identify, recruit, and train scientific "manpower." Although many wartime mechanisms for coordinating science,
such as the OSRD, were eventually dismantled after the war, much of the
defense matrix that they had helped build by linking industry, academia,
and the federal government remained largely in place.[9] In the postwar period, these wartime legacies, along with the priority accorded to militarily
important science more generally, became increasingly institutionalized in
the national security state.

When discussing this development, several organizations are important
to note. First, the National Institute of Health (established as such in 1930
but later renamed the National Institutes of Health in 1948) became the
peacetime successor to the OSRD's Committee on Medical Research when
fifty of the committee's outlying contracts were transferred to it after the
war. Newly flush with funds, the institute expanded its offering of research
fellowships in an effort to remedy the perceived shortage of medical researchers. It also established its own grants research office in 1946. The
funding of medical research proved immensely popular in the postwar

period as reflected in congressional appropriations, which increased from under $3 million in 1945 to over $52 million in 1950. In both fellowships and research grants, the institute pioneered in providing government funding to investigators across the country and became the principal source of federal support for medical research.[10]

The Atomic Energy Commission, which was established in August 1946 under the Atomic Energy Act, became another major patron of postwar science. The civilian agency, which included a powerful military liaison committee, inherited the operations of the Manhattan Project and responsibility for the nation's atomic program. Although it frequently highlighted its interest in peaceful uses of the atom, such as anticancer treatments, the commission increasingly funneled its resources into weapons research and development as the Cold War intensified. Overseeing a broad network of government laboratories, it relied heavily on contractual arrangements with universities and industries to carry out its research agenda. In January 1948, the commission also created a graduate and postdoctoral fellowship program for students in physics, biology, and medicine and made almost 500 awards in 1948 and 1949, quickly becoming the largest program for advanced science education to date. In terms of expenditures for basic research, the commission's activities were dwarfed only by the military services.[11]

The most influential of these was the U.S. Navy, whose Office of Naval Research became the primary patron of academic science in the immediate postwar period. Formally created by Congress in August 1946, the office aimed "to plan, foster, and encourage scientific research in recognition of its paramount importance as related to the maintenance of future naval power, and the preservation of national security."[12] To that end, it supported scientific research not only in its own branch but also in civilian laboratories across the country through the use of research contracts. By the close of the decade, it was sponsoring nearly 1,200 projects in almost 200 universities and assisting roughly 2,500 science students in earning their Ph.D.s.[13] Although the office funded research in a wide range of disciplines, including chemistry, mathematics, and electronics, its influence on the field of physics was particularly apparent: in 1948, nearly 80 percent of the papers presented at the American Physical Society meetings were said to have received support from the Office of Naval Research.[14]

The military's research activities, however, were by no means limited to the office—or to the navy for that matter. The War Department also funded a wide range of research projects through contracts with industry and academia, which comprised approximately four-fifths of the department's research budget in 1947 (a comparable distribution was true for the navy).[15] To avoid duplication of their efforts, the two departments turned to another new agency, the Joint Research and Development Board, which had been formed the previous year to coordinate their research activities and to maintain the military's close ties with civilian scientists. With the passage of the 1947 National Security Act, however, the board and its goals were absorbed by the Research and Development Board that was created as part of the new National Military Establishment (later renamed the Department of Defense in 1949). Drawing together military leaders and chaired by a civilian, the Research and Development Board boasted a full-time secretariat, a staff of more than 200 employees, and some 1,500 university and industrial consultants. Although it lacked the authority, clout, and overall effectiveness of the OSRD, the new board nevertheless became the highest level R&D management unit in the Pentagon.[16]

As these agencies staked out their places in what historian Roger Geiger terms "the postwar federal research economy," debates raged in Congress over the creation of a national science foundation.[17] Key proponents included Vannevar Bush, who in *Science, the Endless Frontier* advocated for an "agency devoted to the support of scientific research and scientific education" as critical to peacetime preparedness.[18] With the help of his aides, Bush's vision became the basis for a bill introduced by Senator Warren Magnuson (D-Washington) on July 19, 1945, the same day that Bush's *Science, the Endless Frontier* was released to the public. Four days later, Senator Harley Kilgore (D–West Virginia) introduced a rival bill that contained many of the same aims but also allowed for, among other things, greater executive control of the agency through a presidentially appointed director, which Truman favored. Despite widespread support for a national science foundation in general, as evidenced by the joint hearings held in October where 99 out of 100 witnesses endorsed such a plan, these differences proved too divisive for swift congressional action. Although the compromise bill that Kilgore introduced in February 1946 eventually passed the Senate, it died in the House that summer.[19]

Frustrated by the impasse and eager to muster support for a foundation more accountable to his office, Truman established the President's Scientific Research Board in the fall of 1946. Chaired by John R. Steelman, then director of the Office of War Mobilization and Reconversion and later assistant to the president, the board was tasked with studying the nation's scientific research, development, and training activities in an effort to guide national science policy.[20] Its findings appeared ten months later with the first of five volumes entitled *Science and Public Policy*, which was released in August 1947. Among the principal recommendations contained in the "Steelman Report," as the document became known, were to increase significantly federal expenditures for scientific research and development (with the target of at least 1 percent of the national income devoted to such matters by 1957); create a federal program of scholarships and fellowships for undergraduate and graduate science students; place heavier emphasis on basic and medical research, particularly in universities and nonprofit research institutions; and establish a national science foundation with a director appointed by and responsible to the president.[21] Underlying these proposals and the board's work more generally was a recognition of the relationship between Cold War science and security. Although "it is unfortunate that any part of the case for Federal support of science should rest upon its military importance," the report conceded that "no responsible person can fail to recognize the uneasy character of the present peace."[22]

While the report helped justify the need for increased science spending and led to a flurry of new bills promoting a national science foundation, it took another three years before Congress passed compromise legislation that Truman found satisfactory. In May 1950, the president finally signed the National Science Foundation Act, claiming that "the fact that the world has not found post-war security . . . underscores this need."[23] The newly established foundation, which aimed "to promote the progress of science; to advance the national health, prosperity, and welfare; [and] to secure the national defense," was authorized to support basic research and education through the use of contracts, grants, scholarships, and fellowships.[24] It also possessed the power to initiate and support defense research at the request of the secretary of defense. Additionally, the agency bore responsibility for maintaining the World War II–era National Roster of Scientific and Specialized Personnel (which was reconfigured as the National Scientific Register in 1950 before becoming the National Register of Scientific and Technical Personnel at the end of 1952). Thus, even though the final version had been stripped of its national defense division, largely owing to competition from the military and militarily relevant agencies such as the Office of Naval Research and the Atomic Energy Commission, the National Science Foundation still had a clear national security mandate.[25]

The proliferation of federal research agencies in the immediate postwar period and early Cold War era became an important feature of the new national security state, as did the growth of federal funding for research and development, the expansion of scientific manpower initiatives, and the incidence of collaboration between civilian scientists and the military that they frequently forged. But just as these developments, and the integration of science into the national security state more generally, brought institutional support and financial benefits, they also posed an array of challenges. While widely regarded as a necessary, legitimate, and even welcome source of funding by most scientists, the predominance of government patronage concerned some who worried that it would redirect their research priorities. Others feared that the use of security restrictions limiting the free exchange of ideas threatened the very foundations of scientific inquiry. Although some scientists had previously experienced the classification of their research, the compartmentalization of their findings, and the requirement of security clearances during World War II, these measures were considerably and surprisingly tightened in the postwar period. In 1947–48, publication restrictions were imposed on three out of every four research reports produced in Atomic Energy Commission laboratories. In 1949, Atomic Energy Commission fellowship applicants were also subjected to scrutiny when Congress mandated that they undergo a loyalty screening by the Federal Bureau of Investigation, regardless of whether their work required access to secret information. Even high-profile scientists found their loyalty questioned in the postwar period. Physicist and National Bureau of Standards director Edward U. Condon was denounced by the House Un-American Activities Committee as "one of the weakest links in our atomic security." J. Robert Oppenheimer, the "father of the atomic bomb" and first chair of the Atomic Energy Commission's General Advisory Committee of top nuclear scientists, had his security clearance suspended by the Eisenhower administration due largely to his alleged Communist and left-wing sympathies.[26]

Underlying these measures was a fierce anticommunism and important corollary to the national security state. As the United States redirected its resources to containing Soviet influence abroad, so too did it turn toward rooting out subversives at home. The resulting "Second Red Scare" engendered a culture of fear in which dissent equaled disloyalty. In this atmosphere, advocates of causes that challenged the status quo became easy targets for anti-Communist crusaders. Race-baiting and Red-baiting frequently went hand in hand.[27] So too did anticommunism and antifeminism, as historian Landon Storrs has argued. Female reformers, especially with those with ties to civil rights, labor, pacifism, and the New Deal, increasingly found their loyalty questioned. This was particularly true of women attempting to exercise political power and remedy social inequalities. Dorothy Kenyon, the New York judge, former representative to the United Nation's Commission on the Status of Women, and member of such organizations as the American Association of University Women and the American Civil Liberties Union, became the lead case in Senator Joseph McCarthy's infamous attack on the State Department. Although she was cleared, she received no more political appointments. Historian and New Dealer Caroline Ware also came under scrutiny and was denied government consulting work while being investigated during the 1950s. Among the notations found in her file were that she was "rumored to be a Leftist" and that she "uses single name yet has been married for several years. Known to defy conventions."[28] Dorothy Bailey, a highly paid training supervisor at the U.S. Employment Service and union leader, found that her efforts to challenge sex and race-based discrimination by her employer became an issue in her loyalty case. Anti-Communist smear campaigns also helped defeat the electoral bids of several Democratic congresswomen, such as California's Helen Gahagan Douglas in 1950.[29]

The Second Red Scare affected not only individual women but women's organizations as well. In 1950, Senator McCarthy suggested that the American Association of University Women was controlled by Communists. The allegations did not stop there, however, and the association found itself under attack again in 1954 when the *National Republic* ran an article charging that "the Pink Ladies of the AAUW," as well as other national women's organizations, promoted communism in their study groups, publications, and legislative agendas.[30] In 1958, the right-wing magazine *American Mercury* similarly denounced the National Federation of Business and Professional Women's Clubs as being "notoriously infiltrated with socialistic and international activists."[31] The National Council of Jewish Women also encountered charges of being left-leaning, as did the National Council of Negro Women.[32]

Not surprisingly, national security prerogatives put a damper on many women's organizing and activist efforts. As Leila Rupp and Verta Taylor have argued, "The hostile environment reinforced organizations' tendencies to withdraw into themselves, distrust outsiders, including potential new members, and shun coalitions."[33] The same female networks that had previously served as sources of strength now posed potential liabilities. Fearful of Red-baiting, some activists even went so far as to sever their ties to progressive causes and the Left.[34]

But while the preoccupation with national security clearly discouraged dissent, it did not completely destroy female reform. Rather, many women's organizations continued their activities and embarked on new ones while consciously adapting their demands to mesh with national security concerns. By embracing the language of preparedness, technocratic feminists presented the education, employment, and advancement of women as paramount to Cold War manpower needs.[35] In no area was this more pronounced than in the fields of science and technology, due largely to their privileged position within the national security state.

Postwar Possibilities

Eleanor Horsey and Donna Price were hardly alone in their efforts to advance scientific womanpower under the guise of national security. Another example of technocratic feminism in the postwar era can be seen with Marguerite Wykoff Zapoleon, who headed the Employment Opportunities Section of the U.S. Department of Labor's Women's Bureau. Born in 1907, Zapoleon attended college during the 1920s and earned an undergraduate degree in engineering from the University of Cincinnati in 1928. She also studied at the Geneva School of International Studies and the New York School of Social Work before beginning a career as a vocational guidance counselor in the Cincinnati public schools. There, she worked with the psychologist Helen Thompson Woolley, who, as a graduate student at the University of Chicago several decades earlier, had produced a groundbreaking study of sex differences, attributing them to social environment and training as opposed to biological factors. Woolley's influence had a lasting impact on Zapoleon and her approach to counseling.[36]

After moving to Washington, D.C., in 1935, Zapoleon continued to work in vocational guidance at a number of government agencies before joining the Women's Bureau in 1944. As the Second World War drew to a close, she embarked on a study of recent changes, current developments, and projected trends in careers for female scientists. She and her staff spent several years collecting information from an astonishingly wide array of sources. In addition to consulting more than 800 books, pamphlets, and articles (including Horsey and Price's "Science Out of Petticoats"), they surveyed professional organizations, employers, educators, and women in the field. Additionally, they gleaned information from such sources as the 1940 census and the National Roster of Scientific and Specialized Personnel. The project was finally published in 1949 as a series of bulletins addressing opportunities for women in chemistry, biological sciences, mathematics and statistics, architecture and engineering, physics and astronomy, geology, geography, meteorology, and the somewhat vague "occupations related to science."[37]

Zapoleon deliberately linked her study to national security concerns, which were undoubtedly heightened when the Soviet Union detonated its first atomic bomb later that year. In her introductory bulletin, *The Outlook for Women in Science*, she raised the question, "Is our Nation finding and developing all its potentially great scientists?" and suggested that it was not. Indeed, women were underrepresented in every scientific field that she had surveyed.[38] Zapoleon then went on to identify her series as the bureau's "initial contribution both to the increasing number of women who want to train for scientific work and to those who are concerned with the present and potential use of a relatively unmined source of scientific talent."[39] In doing so, she appealed to women interested in science as well as educators, industrialists, and government officials preoccupied with scientific manpower needs.

Zapoleon was obviously familiar with current debates surrounding postwar science and security. Not only had she read *Science, the Endless Frontier* and the Steelman report, but she also quoted them verbatim in her bulletins. References to scientific shortages surfaced throughout Zapoleon's work, as she eagerly applied the findings of scientific manpower experts to women. Adopting their language and chief concerns, she included in her *Outlook for Women in Science* such chapters as "The Supply of Scientific Personnel," in which she discussed obstacles affecting the recruitment of women. According to Zapoleon, the considerable commitment of time and money required to pursue a university degree disproportionately discouraged female students as many families preferred to invest in their sons' rather than their daughters' education. Later in life, women found that their marital status and domestic responsibilities disrupted their careers in ways that they did not for men.[40] Although much of her focus was on white women, she also identified subsets of the overall population, such as older women, African American women, and disabled women, who faced additional challenges and even fewer opportunities. In all of these cases, the decision to pursue scientific study was not arrived at easily and required substantial professional and financial encouragement. Consequently, she insisted that "parents, counselors, teachers, employers and others whose advice may be sought by young women interested in science should be wary of discouraging the development of a talent that may be rare."[41]

One of Zapoleon's main recommendations regarded the provision of adequate guidance at the high school level. Like other individuals and organizations interested in solving scientific shortages, she pinpointed high school as a critical stage in young scientists' career trajectories. But, she warned, "it is at this stage that so many girls are diverted from establishing a foundation upon which a scientific specialization can be built."[42] Zapoleon observed that boys were often urged by their parents and counselors to take science and several years of mathematics, whereas girls were generally steered toward languages, history, or electives. As a result, relatively few female students entered college with four years of preparation in math or science. Although Zapoleon thought it was unlikely that women and men would enroll in science classes in equal numbers, she maintained that "it is undoubtedly true that more qualified young women would take these subjects if they were not discouraged from doing so."[43]

But encouraging women's scientific talent went beyond the classroom. Zapoleon also advocated involvement in extracurricular activities, such as science clubs, science fairs, and national science competitions.[44] One example that she described in detail was the annual Science Talent Search that had been created by the Westinghouse Corporation during the Second World War. In the postwar period, the competition continued to offer opportunities for young women to involve and distinguish themselves in scientific fields. For Zapoleon, the Science Talent Search was significant not only for the professional encouragement that it provided but also for its monetary support. Each year, the talent search awarded forty high school students all-expense-paid trips to Washington, D.C., where they competed for scholarships. Because the percentage of female students selected for the Washington trip corresponded with the percentage entering the competition, women represented between a quarter to a third of Washington, D.C., finalists. They also made up half of grand prize winners, since the talent search reserved one of its two $2,400 scholarships for a female contestant.[45]

Zapoleon regarded financial aid as critical to expanding the "potential supply of women scientists" and noted gladly that Westinghouse was one of many industries that had taken an interest in helping science students. In 1946, she reported, more than 300 companies awarded 1,800 fellowships, scholarships, or grants for scientific research. Loan funds and part-time work further expanded the range of assistance. She also identified more than 600 awards in science, mathematics, or engineering that were available through individual universities, colleges, and organizations. The doctoral and postdoctoral fellowship programs sponsored by such agencies as the National Institutes of Health and the National Research Council (which administered the Atomic Energy Commission fellowships) seemed to promise another source of support. Zapoleon also eagerly eyed the National Science Foundation proposals currently being debated in Congress and suggested that a national science scholarship program would help expand opportunities for women.[46]

Zapoleon would have been pleased to find that the National Science Foundation did go on to become an important source of funding for female scientists. By 1972, women were taking home nearly 20 percent of its fellowship awards. But when the foundation first granted predoctoral fellowships in 1952, it selected only 36 women, who made up 6.33 percent of the 569 recipients. The following year, women received just 23, or 4.14 percent, of 556 awards.[47] Similar patterns emerged at other agencies as well. The Atomic Energy Commission fellowship competition, which had been established to increase the supply of scientific personnel in radiation fields, made only 5.76 percent of its awards to women by 1953.[48] Thus, much like during World War II, women did benefit from federal manpower initiatives but were also marginalized by them. Women's presence among award winners was once again overshadowed by the much larger number of men.

As this example illustrates, the fact that federal agencies and other institutions allowed women to compete for their fellowships did not ensure an equitable outcome. Preference for male students persisted, as did the assumption that women scientists were bad investments because they might leave the workforce after marriage. Faced with this reality, women's organizations seemed to offer the most consistent and steady sources of funding. Zapoleon recognized two in particular, the AAUW and Sigma Delta Epsilon, a national women's scientific fraternity, for their outstanding support of female scientists.[49]

Zapoleon's observation was not lost on these women's organizations, which were well aware that they had a special role to play in the postwar period. Sigma Delta Epsilon president Mary Willard fully realized that her organization's graduate fellowship, which had been awarded since 1941, would take on even greater significance as the return of male veterans intensified competition for funding. Remarking on these developments, she noted, "Here is where our Fellowship comes in and where we are going to need more."[50] The much larger and older AAUW fellowship program, which dated to the late nineteenth century, served a similar function. (Although AAUW fellowships were not limited to women in science, as Sigma Delta Epsilon's were, female scientists were well represented among its award winners.)[51] For women in male-dominated fields, AAUW support became especially important amid the postwar backlash. It is no coincidence that in a survey of AAUW fellows conducted in the mid-1950s, those from the late 1940s reported encountering the most obstacles due to their sex. As AAUW member Ruth Tryon observed when interpreting these results for her history of the fellowship program, "Perhaps the competition of returned service men in this period, reversing the wartime demand for women's services, gave a sharp jolt to those who had not been conscious of discrimination."[52]

A "sharp jolt" appears to have struck other women scientists as well, who increasingly organized themselves throughout the immediate postwar period. Membership in women's scientific societies, such as Sigma Delta Epsilon and the women's chemistry society, Iota Sigma Pi, swelled after the war. Both old members and recent recruits keenly felt the disconnect between wartime rhetoric and postwar reality. The discrimination and hostility that they encountered, after having been lured and lauded just several years earlier, was undeniable. They recognized the unique resources and support that women's organizations could provide and flocked to them in growing numbers.[53]

In addition to the growth of existing women's scientific societies, the postwar period also saw the creation of new ones, especially in engineering. They were bolstered by women's record-breaking participation in engineering degree programs across the country, as former "engineering aides," eager to continue their training and upgrade their status, joined female students who had entered during the war. Although their percentage of total enrollments remained small, the absolute number of female engineering students rose precipitously: between 1946 and 1950, 646 women earned undergraduate degrees in engineering, a significant increase from the previous period (1940–45), when this number peaked at 181.[54]

This development was part of a larger trend in women's higher education, which expanded throughout much of the postwar period. While women's proportion of collegiate enrollments dropped from its wartime high of 49.8 percent to 28.8 percent in 1948 and then hovered at around a third for much of the 1950s, their total enrollments roughly doubled, jumping from 661,000 in 1946 to 1,339,337 in 1960.[55] The expansion of women's higher education was accompanied by the expansion of women's employment. Despite the postwar emphasis on domesticity, women increasingly worked outside of the home. Married women's workforce participation, in particular, rose steadily from 13.8 percent in 1940 to 21.6 percent in 1950 to 30.6 percent in 1960. This shift was especially marked for married white women. Although they remained less likely than married nonwhite women to work outside of the home, their labor force participation saw the highest rate of increase.[56]

Women's employment in engineering reflected many of these trends. Between 1940 and 1950, the number of women employed as engineers rose from under 1,000 to over 6,600.[57] But as their participation increased, so did the resistance that they encountered, especially amid the return of male veterans and the resurgence of traditional gender roles. Women engineers were keenly aware of these postwar paradoxes. Consequently, in an effort to improve their condition, women engineers banded together in Iowa, Indiana, Pennsylvania, New York, Massachusetts, and Washington, D.C.[58] Although many of these groups formed independently and evidently without knowledge of one another, their decision to organize when they did reflected broader phenomena particular to that historical moment.

In 1946, one of the earliest groups formed at the Drexel Institute of Technology in Philadelphia. Shortly thereafter, the Women Engineers of Drexel surveyed universities across the country for information regarding female engineering students. The findings were "encouraging" and pointed to a need for organizing undergraduate women on a larger scale. In response, the organization arranged a conference, to be held at Drexel in early April 1949, in order "to more clearly define the problems of women in engineering," "to search for their solutions," and "to investigate the feasibility of joining forces" with other female students in the field.[59] More than seventy undergraduates representing nineteen institutions attended the Philadelphia meeting, where they heard a keynote address by Lillian Gilbreth. It was also at that meeting that they formed a regional student organization that they named the Society of Women Engineers.[60]

At roughly the same time, women engineers in New York City were also organizing themselves. On March 27, 1949, one week before the Philadelphia gathering, a group of metropolitan area women engineers assembled at the Hotel Edison to establish an organization for college graduates and professional women. Many of the attendees, who had come into contact with each other through various personal and professional networks, had been meeting informally for several years. As one participant explained, "It might have been something as simple as having a cup of coffee, and seeing if we had something in common." Others were recent graduates who had joined women's engineering societies while in college, such as the Society of Women Engineers that area students formed at the City College of New York in March 1948. Both the newly minted professionals and the more established engineers believed that by organizing they could better facilitate women's professional advancement. At the Hotel Edison meeting, the attendees emphasized the importance of educating the public on the need for female engineers, encouraging women who demonstrated interest in the field, and disseminating information about job openings. They established an employment committee, set up a constitution committee, resolved to issue a publication, and elected temporary officers. Finally, they selected a name for their new association: the Society of Women Engineers.[61]

The fact that many of these groups chose the same name for themselves seems to have been coincidental; the postwar proliferation of such groups, however, was not. As Lillian Murad, who earned her bachelor's degree in chemical engineering in 1947, recalled, "At this time, there were sufficient numbers of undergraduates in college (women) to dream up a society which would embrace all the engineering professions, and help the women in the engineering schools in their work and later on in their jobs."[62] As they set out to expand opportunities for female engineers, they found that the Cold War climate limited the range of acceptable protest. But it also offered new justifications for educating and employing women in the field. Key developments in the Cold War, the further integration of science into the national security state, and a broad upsurge of interest in scientific womanpower would be critical to their efforts and eventual embrace of technocratic feminism.

Renewed Support for Scientific Womanpower

The Cold War entered a new phase in 1950. In January, President Truman announced that he had directed the Atomic Energy Commission to continue its work on all atomic weapons, including a hydrogen bomb, or super bomb, that would be many times more powerful than anything before.[63] The underlying push for preparedness also manifested itself in NSC-68, which was issued by the National Security Council in April and called for massive rearmament, military buildup, and permanent mobilization. But it was not until the summer of 1950 that the Cold War turned hot. After the Communist-controlled North Korean army invaded South Korea in June 1950, the United States deployed troops there to help repel the advance. American involvement in the Korean War spurred defense spending, and by 1953, national security expenditures accounted for two-thirds of the federal budget.[64] "In short order," according to historian Daniel Kevles, "the defense research and development budget followed the overall defense budget into the stratosphere."[65] In fiscal year 1951, defense R&D spending doubled to roughly $1.3 billion and then doubled again, to $3.1 billion, in fiscal year 1953. Department of Defense and Atomic Energy Commission contracts accounted for nearly 40 percent of all money spent on industrial and academic research. That roughly two-thirds of the country's scientists and engineers were engaged in defense research further illustrates the expansive nature of the defense matrix and national security state.[66]

Against this backdrop, government officials, industry representatives, scientists, and educators speculated widely and loudly about the impending shortage of scientific personnel.[67] They increasingly sought out ways to expand the country's manpower supply, and by the fall of 1950, they had begun recommending the use of women to alleviate the situation. In October, the academic vice president of the University of Minnesota, Malcolm Wiley, made this suggestion at a meeting of midwestern college administrators. "If there are not enough males to provide us the necessary flow of trained engineers," Wiley stated, "then the only solution is the utilization of womanpower in that profession."[68] Later in the month, the Smith College newspaper ran the cover story "Market for Science Majors Up, Demand Outruns the Supply," which outlined job opportunities for women in the field. And in November, the aeronautical division of the General Electric Company ran in the *Philadelphia Bulletin* an oversized classified ad for "Women Engineers."[69]

After Truman declared a state of national emergency in December 1950, the call for womanpower became even more pronounced and widespread. This growing interest came from a variety of organizations and individuals, such as University of Illinois biophysicist, Manhattan Project veteran, and *Bulletin of Atomic Scientists* editor Eugene Rabinowitch. Rabinowitch's February 1951 editorial, aptly entitled "Scientific Womanpower," identified women as the "one—and only one—large reservoir of potential scientific, medical, and engineering 'manpower,' which is as yet almost entirely untapped."[70] He called for the encouragement of women in those fields as well as the provision of government aid. The idea of recruiting female scientists received additional attention at the end of the month when *Newsweek* printed an article declaring, "Help Wanted: Women." The September issue of *Scientific American*, which was devoted to "The Human Resources of the United States," further publicized this view. It contained a report by the newly established Office of Defense Mobilization's Arthur Flemming, who similarly insisted that women were needed as scientists and engineers.[71]

Flemming's advocacy of women in scientific fields is important to note because of the consistency with which he supported them, as well as the degree to which he would collaborate with reform-minded women and women's organizations throughout the Cold War.[72] Trained in law, he began his government career in 1939 when Franklin Roosevelt appointed him to the three-member Civil Service Commission. The thirty-four-year-old Flemming became the youngest Civil Service commissioner to serve since 1889, when Theodore Roosevelt took office at the age of thirty. During his tenure there, which lasted until 1948, Flemming became increasingly interested in manpower issues, particularly as they related to national defense. During the Second World War, he served in several government posts, such as the War Manpower Commission, and spoke at numerous conferences where he continually urged the "utilization" of women and minorities.[73] Many times, he stood alone, as was the case at the January 1942 Baltimore Conference discussed in Chapter 1, when he was the only speaker to address explicitly the need for women in scientific fields.[74]

Although Flemming resigned from the Civil Service Commission in 1948 to assume the presidency of his alma mater, Ohio Wesleyan University, he found himself back in Washington, D.C., just a few years later. In 1951, he was appointed to the Office of Defense Mobilization in the Executive Office of the President where he oversaw the nation's manpower program. As assistant to the director, and later as director himself, Flemming held a special interest in the mobilization of scientific personnel. He believed that women should be used fully in all defense preparations, and he repeatedly urged the education and employment of female scientists and engineers. In his speeches, correspondence, and policy recommendations, Flemming continually drove home this theme. "Although the shortage is greatest and the demand most pressing in engineering," he argued, "all of the sciences are in need of womanpower."[75]

Flemming's concern with scientific womanpower was significant but not singular. The early Cold War era saw an explosion of manpower organizations, conferences, publications, and studies that resulted in what historian Margaret Rossiter has termed a wave of "ambivalent encouragement" for female scientists. One important example was the 1954 report *America's Resources of Specialized Talent*, which had been funded by the Rockefeller Foundation and written by Dael Wolfle. The noted psychologist and manpower expert was serving as the executive secretary of the American Psychological Association when he was tapped by the foundation to head the project. Wolfle was chosen after a lengthy search, and it is likely that his experience as a scientific administrator both made him a strong candidate and informed his approach toward the job. During World War II, he had served on the OSRD's applied psychology panel, where he was responsible for overseeing contracts with psychologists working on personnel, training, and equipment problems. Afterward, he worked behind the scenes to help establish the National Science Foundation.[76] It is not surprising, then, to find many of the themes in Vannevar Bush's *Science, the Endless Frontier* reiterated in Wolfle's report, which he began working on in the fall of 1950.[77]

Although the Korean War had concluded by the time that *America's Resources of Specialized Talent* was published in 1954, the 300-page document was nevertheless hailed as an invaluable contribution to the study of current and future manpower needs. Like Flemming, Wolfle identified women as an untapped source of talent. Despite the fact that they were more likely than men to graduate from high school, he explained, women were less likely to attend or graduate from college. Many of those who did, moreover, could only find employment in jobs beneath their education and aspirations, a fact that Wolfle attributed largely to discrimination. He observed that when women were employed in specialized fields, such as chemistry, they frequently occupied positions "of lesser responsibility, opportunity, and remuneration . . . than men."[78] He also recognized that a broader shift in attitudes toward men's and women's work was needed, but only went so far as to suggest that the larger question of "occupational equality" be taken up elsewhere, as "it is of too sweeping importance to be covered adequately in a discussion of specialized manpower problems."[79]

Building on some of Wolfle's findings, the National Science Foundation initiated a study of the loss of scientific talent between high school and college. The project was carried out under the auspices of the College Entrance Examination Board and headed by Charles C. Cole Jr., a historian and assistant dean at Columbia College. In January 1955, Cole reported that he had secured the assistance of MIT physics Ph.D. Jane Blizard and Yale-educated attorney Allaire Karzon to conduct research "on ways in which effective scientific womanpower could be increased" and "to explore possible solutions which might make science careers more manageable and more attractive to more women of superior ability."[80] Their submissions constituted the basis for Cole's discussion of female scientists, which appeared intermittently throughout his final report, *Encouraging Scientific Talent*, when it was published in 1956.

The report made clear that "the waste of talent among girls is greater than among boys," even though "there appear to be no sex differences in the distribution of ability."[81] To explain this phenomenon, Cole cited a number of social and cultural obstacles, such as the broader perception that advanced scientific training was unfeminine. Other reasons included the lack of parental encouragement, inadequate guidance, and financial concerns.[82] In line with Blizard's and Karzon's recommendations, he urged the preparation of vocational guidance materials to entice women into scientific careers and noted that "it is particularly important that girls realize the need for their talents in scientific and engineering lines."[83]

The most innovative recommendation, however, came directly from Karzon, whose "tax revision proposal to encourage women into careers" was included as an appendix. Karzon advocated that women, regardless of income or marital status, be allowed to deduct up to $1,800 in child care expenses or one-half their gross income on their federal tax returns. (While Section 214 of the new Internal Revenue Code of 1954 had recently reclassified child care expenses as business, as opposed to personal expenses that were in fact deductible, the deduction was capped at $600 and was further reduced based on income, making the deduction nearly negligible for dual-career households.) Although Karzon's proposal reinforced the notion that women were the ones primarily responsible for children, it also recognized how the responsibilities of working mothers differed from those of their male counterparts.[84]

Despite the fact that Karzon's proposal was designed to increase the supply of "scientific womanpower," it failed to attract much support from proclaimed manpower experts, such as the President's Committee on Scientists and Engineers, which snubbed the plan. Perhaps this is not surprising, given the committee's track record. The committee was established by President Dwight Eisenhower in April 1956 to serve as a clearinghouse for nongovernmental scientific manpower initiatives. Initially, however, it included no female members, a likely disappointment to Arthur Flemming, who had urged Eisenhower to establish the committee in the first place. Although Marguerite Zapoleon of the U.S. Department of Labor's Women's Bureau was eventually hired as a consultant, she did not share members' decision-making powers, nor did the two female presidents of the National Education Association, who served as ex officio members. Their marginal presence on the committee thus reflected women's marginal place in science more generally.[85]

Wider support for womanpower came from the National Manpower Council, though not immediately. Established in 1951 at Columbia University, the council brought together prominent educators, industrialists, and government officials in an effort "to stimulate the improved utilization of the nation's manpower resources during this period of national crisis and increasing military and economic mobilization."[86] From the outset, the council highlighted the importance of scientific personnel and other skilled workers. But its initial study, which focused on military deferments for college men, not surprisingly ignored the subject of women. The council's next undertaking, a four-part study of "scientific and professional manpower," nominally included women in its identification of potential engineers, physicians, and physicists. In line with traditional gender conventions, however, women received the fullest treatment in its discussion of teaching.[87] Gradually, the council began to explore other aspects of womanpower and, at the urging of Columbia economist and business school professor, Eli Ginzberg, decided to carry out a full-fledged investigation of the topic.

Ginzberg, who headed the project, had a long-standing interest in womanpower. In a later interview, he dated this interest to an experience in 1936, when he discovered that some of his best students were women. Concerned that their undergraduate training in French and art had prepared them poorly for the business world, Ginzberg began urging women's college administrators to steer their students toward math and science courses instead. He left the business school temporarily during World War II, when he headed to Washington, D.C., to work on wartime manpower problems. There, he learned of British women's participation in the defense effort and proposed that the United States register its women for the draft. Although he was "laughed out of the room," he remained interested in womanpower issues and would continue to pursue them once back at Columbia. But bringing the National Manpower Council on board was not as easy as he might have hoped. Ginzberg recalled that the decision to conduct the womanpower project was "the only time in the ten-year history of the Manpower Council that a theme had to be voted on." In the end, it was adopted by a single vote.[88]

By 1955, the womanpower project was well under way, and over the next two years, the National Manpower Council sponsored sixteen conferences across the United States where representatives from industry, government, the armed forces, civilian agencies, labor unions, and women's organizations met to discuss issues related to women's employment. These conferences became the basis for the council's 350-page treatise, simply entitled *Womanpower*, which aimed "to contribute to a fuller understanding of the nation's manpower resources by illuminating the present role of women."[89] On March 13, 1957, several male members of the council presented the final

Womanpower report to President Eisenhower at a White House ceremony. (Ironically, neither of the council's two female members was in attendance.) Both the ceremony and the report, which was released to the public later that day, received immediate and widespread publicity. By the beginning of May, 552 newspapers in 47 states (as well as Hawaii and the District of Columbia) had covered the *Womanpower* study. Approximately 250 editorials had commented on the publication, as did popular magazines and professional journals. Television and radio stations devoted air time to it and even featured interviews with some of its authors. Thus, in less than two months, *Womanpower* had already attracted more media attention than any of the council's previous publications.[90]

Womanpower's overarching argument was that "women constitute not only an essential, but also a distinctive part of our manpower resources."[91] This compendium of both new and old studies recalled women's contributions during World War II, identified the postwar "revolution" in women's employment, uncovered various forms of discrimination against women, and deplored the nation's failure to utilize female talent fully.[92] It also criticized manpower proposals that assumed there would be no change in the gender composition of the workplace, or "that the shortages of nurses and engineers . . . will be alleviated primarily by encouraging more young women, in the first instance, and more young men, in the second."[93] Consequently, the *Womanpower* authors did suggest that women might be "utilized" in science and engineering. They regarded the recent increase in the number of women engineers as "striking" and as evidence that women could succeed in those fields.[94] In order to change dominant ideas about suitable work for women, they recommended improved vocational guidance for female students. They did so cautiously, however, noting that a large increase in the number of women scientists and engineers might seriously reduce the supply of teachers.[95]

Although their actual support for scientific womanpower varied, the findings of Cold War manpower experts are nevertheless significant. In part, they helped spotlight the supposedly dire nature of scientific shortages and to identify them as national security priorities. The "waste" and "underutilization" of scientific talent became buzz words for politicians, educators, and industrialists eager to safeguard America's position in the new Cold War world. Manpower studies also illuminated changes in women's education and employment patterns and put forward concrete recommendations for better integrating women into scientific fields. Some of the most often repeated ones highlighted the need for general encouragement, vocational guidance, and financial aid. Most important, these studies and the broader Cold War concern with scientific manpower bolstered the activities of reformers, such as the newly created national Society of Women Engineers (SWE), which would emerge as one of the principal proponents of technocratic feminism. Throughout the postwar period, the society not only drew on manpower studies in a rhetorical sense but also worked to put their recommendations into action.

The National Society of Women Engineers

The national SWE was established in May 1950, when more than sixty women converged on Cooper Union's Green Engineering Camp with suitcases in tow. Among those who traveled to the woods of Ringwood, New Jersey, that day were engineering students, aspiring professionals, and established engineers. After locating their sleeping quarters on the second floor of a converted barn, the women headed to the adjacent lodge in anticipation of the weekend's events. The purpose of the gathering was to create a national organization to support and promote women's participation in engineering. After two days of discussion and debate, the group had succeeded in its goal.[96]

The decision to form a national organization reflected attendees' determination to coordinate and extend the work they had been doing at the local and regional levels. As one early member remarked, "It may seem a contradiction that women seeking equality and acceptance as engineers on the basis of merit, women fighting against prejudice, should band together in a society exclusively for women engineers. But until women are accepted as engineers as readily as they are as voters today, there is need for such a cooperative effort."[97] Most of the "Camp Green" attendees represented the small women's engineering societies that had sprung up in various parts of the United States during the late 1940s. Members of the student organization formed at Drexel and the graduate organization formed at the Hotel Edison made up the nucleus of the Camp Green contingent. A handful of older women also attended, including Elsie Eaves and Hilda Counts Edgecomb, who had unsuccessfully attempted to form a women's engineering society while undergraduates at the University of Colorado in 1919. During World War II, Eaves had helped popularize the demand for female engineers, and at Camp Green, she found herself in the presence of many women who had taken advantage of wartime opportunities. Remarking on that meeting, she observed, "There was a sprinkling of 'old timers' with

Founding meeting of the national Society of Women Engineers, held at the Cooper Union's Green Engineering Camp in New Jersey, May 1950. Courtesy of Society of Women Engineers National Records, Walter P. Reuther Library, Wayne State University.

careers well established but the spark and drive came from the graduates with brand new engineering degrees."[98]

As Eaves suggested, the bulk of the Camp Green attendees represented a new generation of female engineers and activists. Most had not even been born when Eaves graduated from college in 1920. They were children or teenagers during the Great Depression and they embarked on their own educational and career paths as the Second World War loomed. As a result, they came of age, professionally speaking, amid much clamoring for scientific womanpower and were keenly aware of the role that science had to play in the defense effort. Many had benefited from wartime shortages, as schools and industries scrambled to fill desks and laboratories. And some had even benefited personally from the efforts of earlier reformers such as Virginia Gildersleeve and Lillian Gilbreth, whose work they now carried on. Evelyn Vernick Fowler, for example, had gotten her start through the engineering aide program that Gildersleeve and Gilbreth had helped establish at the Stevens Institute of Technology. After working for a while as a drafter, Fowler reenrolled at the Pratt Institute, where she had previously studied art, and earned her B.S. in chemical engineering in 1948.[99] Similarly, Anna Kazanjian Longobardo enrolled in the Barnard-Columbia engineering program that had been formed at Gildersleeve's urging, and in 1949, she became the first woman to receive a B.S. in mechanical engineering from Columbia University.[100]

In contrast to World War II–era reformers who had focused on open-ing previously closed doors, however, this younger generation that walked through them now turned their attention to dismantling the subtle stereo-types and social conventions hindering women's participation in scientific fields. As a consequence, SWE's interest in expanding women's represen-tation went far beyond breaking down formal barriers to women's educa-tion and employment. As its certificate of incorporation would later state, SWE aimed "to foster a favorable attitude in industry toward women en-gineers," "to contribute to their professional advancement," "to encourage young women with suitable aptitudes and interests to enter the engineering profession," and "to guide them in their educational programs."[101] At Camp Green, they laid the groundwork for these initiatives by instituting dues to sustain the organization, adopting temporary rules to govern its operations, and approving an emblem to signify its presence. They also held on-site elec-tions and chose as their first president, thirty-one-year-old Beatrice Hicks.[102]

Like the majority of SWE members, Hicks had gotten her first big break during the Second World War. But her interest in engineering went back much further. The New Jersey native first encountered engineering through her father, a chemical engineer. She often told people that she decided to become an engineer at the age of thirteen, after admiring the Empire State Building and the George Washington Bridge with her father and learning that engineers designed those structures. Hicks attended high school during the early 1930s and found that her ambition was met with resistance from both classmates and teachers who viewed engineering as an inappropriate field for women. Determined, she enrolled at the New-ark College of Engineering (now the New Jersey Institute of Technology), where she would earn her bachelor's degree in chemical engineering in 1939. Following graduation, Hicks worked at the college as a research assis-tant until wartime labor shortages facilitated her employment in industry. In 1942, she joined Western Electric, a subsidiary of Bell Telephone and defense contractor, and later became its first female engineer. In addition to working on long-distance telephone technology, she developed a crys-tal oscillator (a device used in aircraft communications to generate radio frequencies) and enrolled in several graduate engineering courses. At the end of the war, Hicks worked as a consultant until her father died in 1946, at which point she became vice president and chief engineer of her family's business, the Newark Controls Company. In the meantime, she continued her graduate work at the Stevens Institute of Technology and received her master's degree in physics in 1949.[103]

After accepting the SWE presidency at the Camp Green meeting, Hicks outlined her plans for the new organization. She set up separate committees to deal with various logistical matters such as conventions, publicity, and awards. Other highlights of the gathering included reports given by members on fostering congenial relationships among women in engineering, helping undergraduates find their place in industry, and promoting laws favorable to women engineers. Before adjourning, the group also voted to recognize Lillian Gilbreth as its first honorary member.[104] Although Gilbreth, who was now in her seventies, was not in attendance at the Camp Green meeting, she would become a staunch supporter of the organization. She regularly counseled officers, delivered addresses at SWE conventions and banquets, and provided financial support (including the royalties from her biography of her late husband, Frank). It is also significant that Gilbreth was someone with experience mobilizing "scientific womanpower."[105]

In the summer of 1950, just weeks after the meeting at Camp Green, Hicks announced, "I am convinced we are going to grow into a large and powerful organization."[106] On the surface, her optimism might seem premature, given the infancy of the national organization. But it is important to note that her proclamation coincided with the beginning of the Korean War. As defense spending soared and manpower studies proliferated, so did SWE's efforts to promote the education and employment of scientific womanpower under the guise of national security. The Cold War concern with perpetual preparedness, moreover, bolstered SWE's activities even after the immediate conflict subsided. Although federal research and development expenditures dropped slightly when the Korean War ended in 1953, they soon resumed their upward climb and increased by 35 percent between 1954 and 1957. Defense projects accounted for more than 50 percent of total expenditures for industrial research in 1956, and by the end of the decade, the military provided more than a third of federal research and development funds allocated to universities.[107] The ongoing relationship between science and security was accompanied by continued concern about the availability of scientific manpower. SWE clearly understood the implications of these developments both in general and for the group's activist efforts. As one SWE member remarked, "The present shortage of engineers affords us a wonderful opportunity to bring to the attention of the public the possibility of alleviating the shortage by encouraging girls to become engineers."[108]

Although SWE could not predict the extent of the Korean crisis or the degree to which industry and government actually intended to recruit women, it publicly embraced the prospect of an engineering shortage. At its March 1951 convention, which was attended by more than 100 members and guests, the society held a panel titled "The Effect of the Current Emergency on Women in Engineering," where participants forecasted expanding educational and vocational opportunities. The discussion was moderated by John Russell, a professor of electrical engineering at Columbia University. Members most likely found his opening remarks uplifting, as he predicted that the Cold War shortage of engineers would result in far greater opportunities for women than at any previous time, including World War II. Elsie Eaves was also featured on the panel and similarly called attention to the growing need for engineers. In addition, she urged members to be persistent in their activism, explaining, "It isn't the war itself that makes the jobs, but our willingness to exert ourselves more on future planning when war is on the horizon."[109]

Advocating womanpower became a popular theme in SWE's work, and the group repeatedly looked to tether its interests to broader manpower concerns. At the convention's business meeting, the Awards Committee announced that it would soon confer the first SWE award on an established woman engineer in order to recognize and publicize women's professional contributions. At this point, other SWE members advocated presenting awards to high school girls and college women with demonstrated aptitude for engineering as a way to encourage their participation in the field. Additionally, SWE president Beatrice Hicks suggested establishing a committee to study the feasibility of sending members to high schools, colleges, and universities to talk to female students.[110] Although national security concerns were recorded nowhere in this discussion, Hicks made sure to raise them publicly. In her address where she announced the new award, she related its importance to "the present desperate shortage of trained people" and the reality that "the needed personnel will be drawn from those having engineering aptitudes, whether men or women."[111] Hicks and other members of SWE clearly recognized that the specter of emergency lent urgency to their activities.

SWE members found national security rhetoric a particularly useful tool when dealing with government officials, educators, industrialists, and the general public insofar as it offered a common language and seemingly shared goals. One example can be seen in the society's efforts to raise money for scholarships. In December 1951, corresponding secretary Phyllis Evans Miller drafted a letter for donors where she not only thanked them for their interest in the society but also emphasized that "if women are to help overcome the present shortage of trained engineers, it is first necessary that they receive the proper schooling" and "help in their financial problems."[112] Society members also invoked the language and cause of national security when advocating for improved working conditions. In a letter to the editor of the *New York Times* that was published in September 1951, Beatrice Hicks referred to the current shortage of engineers as "a long-term deficiency of grave concern to the defense mobilization effort" and suggested that eliminating "industry's 'double standard' in pay scales and advancement opportunity" would serve as a "necessary inducement to attract women."[113] Hicks urged the encouragement of female engineers more generally in letters to manpower experts such as M. H. Trytten, who had directed the National Research Council's Office of Scientific Personnel since the Second World War. In August 1951, Hicks informed Trytten that SWE recognized the shortage of engineers and, to that end, was working to encourage young women to enter the field. She closed by offering to assist his office "in any way we can help to alleviate the technical manpower shortage."[114] Hicks wrote a similar letter to Arthur Flemming that same day, lauding him for his identification of women as "the richest additional source of technical manpower" and saying that the society would be happy to help him in his mobilization efforts.[115]

Government officials responded favorably to SWE and frequently enlisted the society's support in recruiting scientific womanpower. In 1951, George Hickman, the placement officer for the U.S. Navy's department of civilian personnel, wrote to SWE for assistance in finding scientists and engineers to staff its projects. He explained, "You no doubt know the Navy is presently engaged in an expansive research and development program vital to the future security and progress of our Nation. As a result, there are a number of employment opportunities for persons who are trained in the fields of engineering, physics, electronics, and related sciences."[116] Hickman's letter became the first job ad published by SWE, reproduced in its September journal under the heading "Employment Opportunity."[117] Additionally, SWE announced in January 1952 that it would be collaborating with the U.S. Office of Education and the new National Science Foundation in gathering information for the National Scientific Register. SWE members seemed pleased with what they regarded as a sign of the government's willingness to identify and utilize female engineers.[118]

Another way that SWE attempted to demonstrate its usefulness to manpower concerns was through participating in conferences on the subject. In November 1951, Hicks represented the society at the Thomas Alva Edison

Foundation's Institute for Science Teachers, held at the late inventor's home. The two-day conference, which was offered in cooperation with the U.S. Office of Education and the National Science Teachers Association, focused on current and projected shortages of scientific and technical personnel.[119] The event attracted more than sixty teachers, counselors, industry executives, scientists, engineers, government officials, and manpower experts, including M. H. Trytten and Dael Wolfle. After considering a number of proposals for increasing the supply of scientific talent, the group advocated improved vocational guidance in the high schools, careful analysis of engineering school dropout rates, and education of the general public about the work of scientists and engineers. In her notes on the conference, Hicks agreed with these recommendations and linked them back to SWE's own goals, remarking that "the Society of Women Engineers is keenly aware of the world's dependence on technical manpower, and the manifold responsibilities of a society such as ours."[120]

In addition to embracing national security concerns rhetorically, SWE also worked to put manpower recommendations into action. Of particular interest to the society was the demonstrated need for vocational guidance and general encouragement. Engineering had traditionally been considered a field for men only, and the continued marginality of women seemed to validate this claim. Female engineers, if not altogether invisible, conjured images of lonely, unattractive career women wearing thick spectacles and "sturdy brown shoes," as one member lamented.[121] The perceived incompatibility of engineering and womanhood (particularly femininity, marriage, and motherhood) presented yet another challenge to the recruitment of female students. SWE recognized that enlisting scientific womanpower required recasting the field as a suitable one for women and, to this end, advised not only female students but also individuals who played a significant role in their educational and vocational decisions. These were mainly parents, teachers, and guidance counselors, many of whom were either unaware or unaccepting of women entering engineering. SWE recognized the cultural constraints facing women in the field and sought to dismantle them through a broad program of education and example.

The society believed that the depiction of women engineers in educational and vocational literature deserved particular attention. Distributed to counselors, teachers, students, and parents, guidance materials enjoyed widespread readership and potential influence. Often, however, these materials either ignored or discouraged engineering as a profession for women. Such was the case with the 1942 booklet issued by the prominent

Engineers' Council for Professional Development (ECPD), the accrediting agency for engineering programs. As suggested by its title, *Engineering as a Career: A Message to Young Men, Teachers, and Parents*, the publication promulgated a highly masculine image of the field. It included just one paragraph on "women in engineering," which stated that physical strength requirements excluded women from most engineering fields and that those women who did succeed in engineering generally possessed "unusual ability" and "extraordinary . . . skills."[122] Still in circulation nearly a decade after publication, the booklet was brought to the attention of SWE president Beatrice Hicks, who promptly contacted the ECPD regarding its inaccuracies and inadequacies. Hicks contested the ECPD's assertion regarding the physical requirements of engineering, noting that few present-day engineers handle heavy objects. She also argued that the ECPD's statement about women engineers' exceptional qualifications bolstered separate standards of achievement for men and women. The requirements of engineering work, she added, should not vary by sex.[123]

Hicks then elaborated on the broader implications and cultural obstacles presented by the kind of information contained in the publication. She explained, "Many women who have the basic aptitudes to become excellent engineers never enter the profession because they have not recognized engineering as a possible career or because they have been discouraged by teachers, parents, or by untutored professional counselors." After pointing to the shortage of qualified personnel, Hicks identified women as "the richest unused source of engineering ability" and called on the council to revise the booklet with these manpower objectives in mind. "It is my belief," Hicks wrote, "that the Engineers' Council for Professional Development could make a worthwhile contribution through a special effort to encourage and help young women to analyze their aptitudes and obtain the necessary education to enter engineering." She concluded her letter by offering to assist the ECPD with revisions and enclosed a copy of the *Journal of the Society of Women Engineers*.[124]

After several rounds of follow-up correspondence with Hicks, the ECPD issued a revised version of the publication in 1953. In addition to dropping the word "men" from the title, the booklet (now called *Engineering: A Creative Profession*) noted recent changes in the field that facilitated the employment of women, namely, the move away from strenuous physical labor. The publication also excerpted from one of Hicks's letters a list of subfields that frequently employed women engineers.[125] This victory, however, was a limited one for SWE insofar as references to women remained infrequent and problematic. Even though the ECPD had expanded its discussion of women engineers from one paragraph to three, the revised version took up only one-third of one page. Moreover, the booklet featured no pictures of female engineers. While images of male engineers abounded, only three scenes even included women: one depicted a secretary taking notes for her boss, a male engineer; one showcased a woman working at a food-processing facility while a male engineer tended to machinery in the background; and the third featured a woman wearing high heels and vacuuming her spotless, modern kitchen above the caption "Today—Engineers' application of scientific principles have [*sic*] released many of us from daily drudgery."[126] In spite of the ECPD's concessions to Hicks's remarks, the revised publication reinforced traditional gender roles, upheld the image of engineering as a masculine enterprise, and provided little actual encouragement for female engineers.

The scarcity of information on engineering as a profession for women led SWE to conduct a survey of its members and women on its mailing list. The results, SWE believed, would reveal a more nuanced picture of women engineers than could be found in publications such as the ECPD's. In 1953, the new SWE president, Lillian Murad, announced that the society had secured the assistance of the Women's Bureau of the U.S. Department of Labor, which agreed to tabulate the survey results and would later publicize the findings in its 1954 bulletin, *Employment Opportunities for Women in Professional Engineering*.[127] SWE must have viewed the Women's Bureau as a logical ally, especially in light of the study carried out by Marguerite Zapoleon in the late 1940s. But the bureau's eagerness to work with SWE on this particular survey also reflected its own preoccupation with manpower issues and changes within the bureau itself.

In 1953 and at the height of McCarthyism, President Eisenhower appointed Republican stalwart Alice Leopold to replace labor activist Frieda Miller as director of the Women's Bureau. Under Leopold's control and in the context of the Cold War, the bureau increasingly shifted its base of support from working-class women and the labor movement to professional women's groups. Additionally, the bureau deemphasized legislative advocacy in favor of a commitment to job placement and employment initiatives. Following the lead of its parent agency, the Department of Labor, the bureau also began functioning primarily as a data collection facility whose aim was to assist the federal government in mobilizing the available labor force. As historian Alice Kessler-Harris has observed, "From its original position of helping women who happened to hold jobs, the

Bureau had now shifted to a stance of helping a nation decide how to use women better."[128]

Amid these changes, the bureau agreed to collaborate with SWE in an effort to glean information about the available pool of female engineering talent. What their study showed was that engineering was not entirely or especially incompatible with marriage and motherhood, as was commonly assumed. When asked about their marital status, 37 percent of employed respondents reported being married, 51 percent were single, and 12 percent were either widowed, divorced, or separated. Of those employed women who were married or who had been married previously, one-third had children. The authors of the bulletin suggested, however, that the relative youthfulness of the sample set probably skewed these findings somewhat.[129] This observation was confirmed when a follow-up survey was conducted in the spring of 1955 and revealed that while the median age of employed respondents had crept up slightly (corresponding with the lag time between the two surveys), so did their rate of marriage. More specifically, the second survey showed that respondents were almost equally divided between single (46 percent) and married (45 percent), with less than a tenth reporting as widowed, divorced, or separated. The second survey also revealed a higher percentage (two-fifths) of respondents with children.[130] In both cases, these patterns were relatively similar to those of other female professionals in the workforce.[131]

In reporting these findings in its *Employment Opportunities for Women in Professional Engineering*, the Women's Bureau made repeated reference to national security anxieties. The title page featured a statement from President Eisenhower lauding the contributions of engineers to both the national economy and what he termed the "military preparedness program."[132] Likewise, the first chapter, "Engineering Manpower and Women's Prospects," opened with a recent quotation from Arthur Flemming advocating the use of women to ease the engineering shortage.[133] Drawing on such high-ranking officials within the national security state underscored the importance of both the survey results and the use of womanpower more generally.

National security concerns also surfaced in the society's own report, *Women in Engineering*, which was edited by SWE member Patricia Brown and released in 1955 in another effort to reshape public perceptions of female engineers. Intended as a resource for students, teachers, counselors, employers, and SWE itself, the forty-page document included a list of scholarships for women, a directory of accredited engineering curricula, prerequisites for engineering programs, statistics on women in the field, and suggestions for further reading. The bulk of the booklet consisted of articles written by SWE members, such as Katharine Stinson (SWE president, 1953–55) and Lois Graham McDowell (SWE president, 1955–56), who argued that the current shortage of engineers demanded the recruitment of women. To this end, they called attention to the need for improved counseling and provided concrete suggestions for identifying, advising, and encouraging female students. They also included quotations from Arthur Flemming to help substantiate their points regarding the need to combat "the present and potential shortages" in engineering by enrolling larger numbers of women.[134] Beatrice Hicks's essay, "Our Untapped Source of Engineering Talent," reiterated many of these themes and denounced the "waste of graduating less than 100 women engineers per year in all of the United States." But she also predicted that because of the shortage and because of SWE's efforts, "[women's] engineering talent will not long remain dormant."[135]

The society distributed *Women in Engineering* to colleges, industrial corporations, government committees, engineering societies, and 455 high schools throughout the country.[136] The response was overwhelmingly enthusiastic. Letters poured in thanking SWE for the booklet, proclaiming its usefulness, and requesting additional copies. Among those lauding the publication were high school and college guidance counselors, deans of engineering, the U.S. chief for engineering education, the President's Committee on Education Beyond the High School, and defense contractors such as the Sperry Rand Corporation, DuPont, and General Motors.[137] Vida Grace Hildyard, the educational counseling chair and only female member of the Wichita Council of Technical Societies, could hardly believe the positive response that she received from her male colleagues when she shared the booklet with them and recommended that they encourage female students. She wrote, "This suggestion was received with enthusiasm far surpassing my wildest expectations. In fact, the men all thought every counselor in each of our members' societies should have a supply of booklets, so that he might not only have them to pass on to our five high schools and the girls he might be counseling, but also for his own information. They requested me to ask if it would be possible to obtain 200 of the booklets at once, and I hope that is only a start!"[138] Before long, the demand for the booklet had outrun the supply, and in February 1957, SWE announced that it would release a revised edition in 1958.[139]

Most of the work behind *Women in Engineering* had been conducted by SWE's Professional Guidance and Education Committee. Announced in 1951–52, the committee served as one of the primary vehicles through which SWE carried out its mission. As indicated in its title, the committee concerned itself with advising female students, working with parents and schools, and educating the public about engineering as a career for women.[140] On the national level, the Professional Guidance and Education Committee undertook projects, such as the *Women in Engineering* booklet, that were aimed at the broad dissemination of educational and vocational information. In 1953, the committee compiled and distributed a list of coeducational engineering colleges and technical schools where women could enroll. The Cleveland Board of Education's director of guidance and placement, Mildred Hickman, was so thrilled about receiving the information that she wrote to SWE requesting additional copies for each of the district's twelve high schools. The Professional Guidance and Education Committee also created a centralized Speaker's Bureau that schools, clubs, and event organizers could contact when looking for someone to talk about women engineers. Additionally, the committee fielded and directed hundreds of inquiries from students, parents, advisors, educators, and the general public regarding women in engineering.[141]

The majority of the committee's activities, which involved making contact with female students, their parents, their teachers, and their guidance counselors, were carried out through local chapters, or sections, which had their own Professional Guidance and Education Committees. Recognizing the importance of personal encouragement, many of these initiatives aimed to celebrate and reward individual women's academic accomplishments. One particularly popular activity carried out by sections across the country was judging science fairs in their communities and awarding female winners with special certificates or prize money.[142] Other examples of providing personal recognition can be seen in the efforts of the Detroit section's Professional Guidance and Education Committee. After securing the necessary information from the University of Detroit's dean of engineering, local SWE members wrote letters of commendation to female students with high engineering aptitude scores. The Detroit section also presented corsages to high school girls being recognized at the Engineering Society of Detroit's annual dinner for students achieving high marks in science and mathematics.[143] In addition to supporting individual women with demonstrated interest and ability, this strategy enabled SWE to showcase scientific womanpower.

Many Professional Guidance and Education Committee activities served the dual purpose of calling attention to the engineering shortage and projecting a positive image of women engineers. In April 1952, the Professional

Guidance and Education Committee of SWE's Pittsburgh section sponsored a symposium for high school girls, their parents, and student counselors. The committee mailed notices to about 150 schools within thirty miles of Pittsburgh. Held at the Mellon Institute, the symposium featured addresses by SWE members as well as representatives from Westinghouse Electric Corporation and the University of Pittsburgh and featured such presentations as "The Engineering Shortage and the Place of Women in the Engineering Field," "The Success of Prominent Women in Engineering," and "Why I Am Glad I Studied Engineering." In addition to sharing their experiences and presenting themselves as desirable role models, SWE members informed the audience about course requirements and the availability of scholarships. Afterward, the conveners learned with satisfaction that several of the women who attended the symposium subsequently enrolled in engineering colleges.[144]

Similar outreach efforts took place across the country. Houston members regularly addressed audiences of high school girls on "women in engineering" and "engineering as a career for women."[145] In Los Angeles, Professional Guidance and Education Committee member Marie Scully gave the keynote speech at a 1956 luncheon attended by seventy female students and professionals in the field. That same year, she took part in a half-hour NBC-TV panel show designed to interest high school and college students in technical careers.[146] Additionally, almost all SWE sections participated in the panel discussions held for high school students as part of Engineers Week, which itself was a Cold War creation. Established in 1951 by the National Society of Professional Engineers, Engineers Week typically included meetings, public addresses, and proclamations lauding engineers' contributions to American society, lamenting the engineering shortage, and urging the recruitment of bright students to the field.[147] Similarly, SWE members in Detroit participated in the semiannual engineering and science vocational meetings that the Engineering Society of Detroit held in conjunction with local high schools. Through these events, SWE members met personally with female students. In 1956, the Detroit section reported advising almost fifty interested young women in that year alone.[148] Margaret Eller, a member of SWE's Detroit section and chair of the Professional Guidance and Education Committee, later recalled of these gatherings, "That's how we got girls to go into engineering."[149]

SWE members realized that they were often the first and perhaps only female engineers with whom teachers, counselors, parents, and students would come into contact. They also believed that they had a unique, self-imposed responsibility to recast engineering as a suitable field for women. As one member recounted, "No male engineer can really do this job for us—we represent the living, breathing evidence when we go before a high school audience, a PTA meeting, or a counselors' conference."[150] In addition to making themselves visible examples of successful women in the field, SWE members both understood and articulated the cultural deterrents to women's engineering achievement. Whether judging science fairs or writing guidance literature, SWE members sought to dismantle these obstacles and encourage female students. Their activities attracted the most interest and support, however, when couched in the language of national security.

Taking Stock of SWE

In February 1957, SWE president Miriam "Mickey" Gerla (1956–58) asked members to "[take] stock of SWE." "But how do we measure the extent to which we are fulfilling our aims?" she asked. "Are we encouraging women with suitable aptitudes and interests to enter the engineering profession, and guiding them in their educational program? . . . And how do we know whether our Professional Guidance and Education programs have specifically contributed to the increased enrollment in the colleges—now numbering over 500 women?" "There is much to be done in this area," she admitted, "but we should ask ourselves if we have progressed from where we were two or five or seven years ago, rather than be disturbed because there is so much still undone."[151]

Using these criteria, most SWE members would have responded favorably to Gerla's inquiries. The small group that gathered at Camp Green had already grown to more than 500 members. The society had expanded geographically as well, and sections could be found across the country in such places as Los Angeles, Chicago, Houston, Atlanta, New York, Washington, D.C., Boston, and the Pacific Northwest. Although less tangible, the encouragement provided by members to girls and women in the field was another source of pride. As one member recounted, "I know from my own experience that our organization can be of great help to wavering girls who meet with discouragement at home as well as at school."[152] Another member remarked of the society's early activities that "we believe that we should be satisfied this year if we do nothing more than increase the knocking on the local college doors by women who indicate increased engineering interests."[153] SWE members were also generally pleased with the recognition that they received from other engineering and scientific societies, most of which were significantly older and male-dominated. By invitation, SWE took its place alongside these groups at such events as the 1952 "Centennial of Engineering" and the seventy-fifth anniversary of the American Society of Mechanical Engineers held three years later. SWE's inclusion signified to members a new level of acceptance among their male colleagues.[154]

Still, these examples of progress existed alongside the reality that SWE members and other female engineers remained roughly 1 percent of the profession, both despite and because of the growth of Cold War science.[155] As had been the case during World War II, the majority of opportunities for women tended to be in the least prestigious and most poorly paid positions. Industries usually hired women for specific jobs, but rarely promoted them. Frequently, women found themselves employed as assistants to higher-ranking men. This practice became increasingly common in academia with the postwar proliferation of "research associate" positions. Made possible by burgeoning science budgets, these appointments enabled faculty members to enlist research assistance and for universities to accommodate dual-career couples in an era of fierce antinepotism laws. In most cases, however, it was the wife and not the husband hired as a research associate, enjoying little recognition or job security.[156]

Not surprisingly, male students and scientists were also the primary beneficiaries of most scientific manpower initiatives. The modest gains in women's enrollments during the postwar period and early Cold War era were dwarfed by the surge of male students. New postwar and Cold War manpower programs, such as the National Science Foundation fellowship program, largely followed these trends. Between 1952 and 1961, only one woman was included among the program's 749 graduate fellows in engineering, for example.[157] Consequently, women continued to be sorely underrepresented in scientific fields, where they remained at the margins. As SWE president Patricia Brown (1961–63) would later remark of the 1952 Centennial of Engineering, "We were accepted and yet not quite accepted. . . . [W]e were off in our own little group most of the time."[158]

The tenacity of gender conventions and stereotypes, moreover, proved particularly troublesome for SWE. From the outset, SWE recognized that it would have to show not only that women could be engineers but also that engineers could be women (and womanly). While challenging and improving public perceptions of female engineers comprised a critical part of SWE's efforts to recruit scientific womanpower, it also took up more time than the society would have liked. This constant battle was fought on a number of fronts. Sometimes it involved visual cues such as wearing lipstick, dainty heels, and figure-flattering frocks. In other instances, it required written or spoken statements proclaiming engineering's compatibility with womanhood. Several sections even distributed talking points and stock answers to which SWE members could easily refer when addressing anxious audiences. One Professional Guidance and Education Committee handout reminded members to "assure the girls, and particularly their parents, that engineering is a perfectly respectable occupation for a woman." Not only is engineering "a nice clean office job," but "a woman can be an engineer, take time out to raise her family, and return to engineering." The SWE member who penned this document readily admitted, "Yes, some of these items were written with tongue-in-cheek." "But," she added, "take another look. Don't you agree that these represent questions which need to be answered, parental fears which need to be allayed, self-evident (to us) truths which need to be iterated?"[159] For SWE, projecting a positive image of women engineers required accepting, on the surface at least, dominant notions of femininity.

SWE's insistence on the compatibility of engineering and womanhood sometimes attracted too much attention. While the society seemed generally pleased with the growing publicity given to the organization and to women in the field, public interest often focused more on members' qualifications as women rather than as engineers. In 1952, SWE member Margaret Kearney wrote to Beatrice Hicks, "I have detected a note of flippancy . . . in the attitude of the supervising principals who have phoned for program speakers. It is obvious to date that they are interested in knowing whether the engineer is blonde or brunette, rather than if her degree is Chemical or Electrical."[160] Hicks herself also faced similar challenges. Although her feminine qualities provided evidence of the compatibility of womanhood and engineering, they also drew disproportionate attention from the public and the press alike. One reporter even exclaimed, "Honestly, you'd never know it (that she was an engineer) to look at her. . . . She wears flowers and earrings and polka-dot linen pumps."[161] Although comments such as these reinforced SWE's conviction that engineers could be women and that women could be engineers, they also served to belittle women in the field and to cast them as curiosities.

The Cold War climate, as well as technocratic feminism more generally, limited the extent to which SWE could openly attack gender conventions and the condition of women. In this era of Communist "witch hunts" and Red-baiting, the society exercised much caution in crafting its public image. At the January 1951 board of directors meeting, Phyllis Evans Miller announced that several prospective members in the Pittsburgh area had asked for assurance that none of the society's activities could be considered subversive. In response to this question and under the advice of its lawyer, SWE decided to include in its certificate of incorporation and bylaws a nonpolitical affiliation clause renouncing the society's ability to lobby for legislative change and to endorse political programs.[162] According to Hicks, "There are many reasons for this, all of which are to protect the members and the society. . . . Each member of the Society automatically becomes identified with any position taken by the Society and in legislation this can be a professional handicap particularly on controversial questions."[163] Although Hicks acknowledged that while there were certainly legislative issues regarding women where SWE members "have a material interest and would like to be effective," she added that the group "cannot afford to relinquish our 'safe' position."[164] As a result, SWE's broader interests in the advancement of women were quietly subsumed under the rubric of national security.

As McCarthyism waned, some members raised concerns about this stance. In March 1957, Olive Mayer of San Francisco wrote to SWE president Mickey Gerla questioning the functionality of the organization "if we cannot democratically participate as a group in formulating the laws which govern us as engineers and as women workers as other organizations do."[165] She noted that the Equal Rights Amendment (ERA) had been endorsed by more than 100 women's organizations, such as the American Medical Women's Association, the National Association of Women Lawyers, and the National Federation of Business and Professional Women's Clubs, and lamented that SWE had not done the same. She also charged that the decision to restrict the society's activities barred SWE from working with other engineering groups on legislative matters, much to the detriment of them all. Mayer then listed the "many issues which directly affect our members as women and as engineers" and that SWE might want to engage. These ranged from national science scholarships and scientific research appropriations to equal pay laws and nursery schools for working mothers. Cold War caution, however, prevented SWE from issuing formal declarations on these topics or working with other organizations to effect change.[166]

Mayer raised her concerns again in a letter to the editor of the *SWE Newsletter*, which appeared that same month. Here, she was even more outspoken in her advocacy of the ERA and asked explicitly, "Shouldn't we add our support and opinions to the campaign now being organized for the grand slam push?"[167] She also suggested collaborating with other women's groups on such matters as equal pay and highlighting these matters at the SWE national convention each year.[168] Although many members likely shared Mayer's concern with the status of female engineers, few were willing to adopt a bolder approach at this time. In August 1957, Margaret Kipilo of the Pittsburgh section responded openly to Mayer in her own letter to the editor. Kipilo supported the idea of organizing the annual convention with a theme in mind, such as "overcoming prejudice," but also suggested that the group had already made significant progress in this area through its publicity efforts. She explained that "when it is known that certain women are doing engineering tasks that heretofore were done by men only, the prejudice loses its foundation. This seems to me the best method on this."[169] Kipilo also conceded that equal pay was a subject with which SWE should be concerned but did not go so far as to advocate collaborating with other women's organizations. Rather, she suggested working with the male-dominated National Society of Professional Engineers, claiming that "a man will fight for equal pay when he realizes that a company will hire a woman engineer instead of him if it can pay her less for the same work."[170] Despite the fact that this group clearly did not have women's interests at heart, Kipilo seemed to believe that its assistance might provide a level of professional legitimacy that most women's organizations could not.

SWE's status as a tax-exempt nonprofit organization further complicated matters, as IRS regulations restricted such groups' political activities. When the IRS attempted to rescind that status in January 1960, a move that would have negatively affected the society's fund-raising efforts, SWE modified its certificate of incorporation to bring it more visibly in line with tax regulations. The new provisions defined the society as an "exclusively educational" organization that would devote "no substantial part of its activities [to] carrying on propaganda."[171] As SWE vice president and soon-to-be president Patricia Brown explained in a March 1961 newsletter article, compliance with IRS guidelines meant that the society "cannot actively work toward influencing legislation affecting engineers or women. The Society certainly could not work for such projects as . . . free nursery schools for working mothers, licensing requirements for engineers, or modifications in state labor laws for women." She did add, however, that any member "is free to engage in all such work as an individual, but not in the name of the Society."[172]

In the few times that SWE did take a stand on legal issues, it did so quietly and without drawing much attention to itself. When the 1957 convention committee arranged to hold the annual gathering in Houston that March, it confirmed ahead of time with the Shamrock-Hilton Hotel that its African American members would be accommodated. Upon arrival, however, Yvonne Clark, a class of 1951 Howard University graduate and mechanical engineer, found that the hotel would not honor her reservation. The convention chair argued with the clerk, unsuccessfully, and Clark wound up staying with in-town relatives instead. The hotel reluctantly agreed that she could still attend the convention as long as she was met at the door and escorted at all times by a white person. Although Clark accepted these terms and participated in the conference in the end, SWE vowed that none of its members should be subjected to such mistreatment again. It quietly resolved to stop holding conventions in states where public assembly laws prohibited integrated meetings and canceled plans for the upcoming convention in Atlanta.[173] But it was not so bold as to draw media attention to the Houston incident or to lobby for legislative change.

While the Cold War climate clearly limited SWE's activities and affiliations, however, it also bolstered them, as this chapter has demonstrated. National security anxieties helped legitimize SWE's efforts to improve the condition of female engineers and to lessen the prejudice that they faced. Shared "manpower" concerns enabled SWE to collaborate with government agencies, industrialists, and educators who were themselves entangled in the defense matrix. And while SWE generally shunned affiliation with other women's organizations at this time, national security anxieties did allow it to collaborate with other technocratic feminists, such as those at the Women's Bureau, which had itself adopted manpower rhetoric in an effort to justify its own activities. That the bureau's Marguerite Zapoleon was featured as a speaker at SWE's 1956 regional conference provides further evidence of this collaboration.[174]

Throughout the 1950s, SWE's outlook was optimistic and for seemingly good reason. The integration of science into the national security state and the proliferation of manpower studies had resulted in significant clamoring for scientific talent. Although women's participation expanded slowly and unevenly, the Cold War concern with "perpetual preparedness" suggested that women would not endure the same kind of backlash and retrenchment that they had experienced after World War II. Scientific manpower needs were not viewed as being for "the duration" but rather as part of science's "endless frontier." Technocratic feminism also enabled SWE to put otherwise ambivalent manpower recommendations into action, with little risk of suspicion or derision. The projected demand for scientific personnel, along with pride in their own activities, led SWE members to continue embracing national security anxieties for much of the following decade. And as new Cold War crises emerged, they would be joined by an expanding network of technocratic feminists who increasingly carried out similar efforts.

CHAPTER THREE

Scientific Womanpower
Enters the Sputnik Era

In January 1958, *Parade* ran a feature article entitled "Meet Phyllis Weber—Housewife and Satellite Engineer." The piece chronicled a day in the life of thirty-seven-year-old Weber, who was described as a wife, a mother of four, and the only woman engineer on the U.S. earth satellite program, Project Vanguard. A graduate of Purdue University's engineering school, Weber worked for the Grand Central Rocket Company, the firm responsible for developing rockets to launch the U.S. Navy's Vanguard missile. Her typical day included getting up at 6:00 A.M. to dress, preparing breakfast for her family, getting her children ready, heading to the plant, where she was responsible for computing the performance of "secret, highly complex rocket machinery," and then returning home at 5:00 P.M. to cook dinner, supervise her children's homework, and turn in for the night. She described her life as a busy but happy one. She focused not on the difficulties of such a full day but rather remarked that her routine was nothing special. "Nowadays a housewife can be a scientist, an engineer, a nuclear physicist—anything society will let her be," she explained. "All it proves," Weber stated, "is that America has been wasting its womanpower for years."[1]

Weber's concern with wasted womanpower was echoed by Women's Bureau director Alice Leopold, who wrote the accompanying article, "Wanted: More Phyllis Webers." Leopold outlined a growing need "to enlist . . . potential laboratory workers in skirts" and recommended a broad program of career guidance and public education that was very much in line with the activities carried out by the Society of Women Engineers. She called on parents and educators to teach young women that there was nothing unfeminine about scientific work and to encourage them in their studies. She similarly advised employers to overcome their reluctance to hire female scientists. Finally, she urged the general public to "realize that in this competitive technological world we need all the scientific power we can muster."[2]

The idea that "more Phyllis Webers" would bolster the place of the United States in the Cold War world was increasingly promulgated throughout the late 1950s and early 1960s by a growing number of women and women's organizations. Their invocation of scientific manpower concerns and national security prerogatives marked the heyday of technocratic feminism. As the Society of Women Engineers had done and continued to do, these activists used national security rhetoric to challenge the social and cultural obstacles to women's participation in scientific fields. Scientific manpower concerns also enabled them to expand their programs to assist established women like Phyllis Weber in juggling the day-to-day demands of family life and career. The primacy of technocratic feminism was spurred by new Cold War crises, an increasingly diffuse national security state, and a renewed surge of interest in "scientific womanpower."

The Soviets and Scientific Womanpower

On October 4, 1957, the Soviet Union triggered what would become known as "the Pearl Harbor of the Cold War" when it launched into orbit the world's first artificial satellite. The 184-pound device, dubbed "Sputnik," circled the earth once every 96 minutes, emitting short, eerie "beeps" as it flew overhead. Although the satellite itself was no bigger than a basketball, its entry into space made evident that the Soviet Union possessed the launching capacity to send nuclear missiles from one continent to another. Stunned Americans gathered around their radios and in their backyards, eager to witness this remarkable feat. One month later, the Soviet Union flexed its technological muscles again when it launched Sputnik II, a substantially heavier satellite weighing 1,120 pounds and carrying a dog wired for medical monitoring, which aroused speculation that a human would be next to orbit the earth. By escalating the threat of nuclear warfare and twice lapping the United States in the emerging space race, the Sputnik launchings generated much anxiety about the seemingly superior state of Soviet science.[3]

In the aftermath of the Soviet Sputniks, the apparent deficiency of American science attracted both interest and despair. A growing number of politicians, educators, and scientists became convinced that the United States had been outpaced by its Cold War adversary and needed desperately to "catch up." The ensuing panic fueled the creation of the National Aeronautics and Space Administration (NASA) in 1958, as well as dramatic increases in federal research and development budgets. Between 1957 and 1967, federal R&D expenditures almost quadrupled, reaching close to $15 billion. Particularly remarkable was the sizable increase in allocations to nondefense activities, which now commanded nearly the same size share as military ones. This growth was due largely to the high priority given the space program (NASA was a civilian agency), the burgeoning attention to medical research, the blurring of lines between civilian and military activities more generally, and an increasingly expansive conception of national security itself.[4] As President Eisenhower remarked in his 1958 State of the Union address, Americans "could make no more tragic mistake than merely to concentrate on military strength." According to Eisenhower, "what makes the Soviet threat unique in history is its all-inconclusiveness. Every human activity is pressed into service as a weapon of expansion. Trade, economic development, military power, arts, science, education, and the whole world of ideas—all are harnessed to this same chariot of expansion."[5] It was not entirely clear, however, how to measure success in these realms or to determine when enough was enough. Consequently, national security became more comprehensive and less comprehensible at the same time.

The amorphous struggle that ensued informed national science policy, national education policy, and reform movements. New scientific manpower concerns eased objections to federal aid to education and paved the way for the monumental National Defense Education Act (NDEA) that Congress passed in 1958. Explicitly drawing on Cold War themes, the legislation boldly proclaimed that "the security of the Nation requires the fullest development of the mental resources and technical skills of its young men and women."[6] The NDEA legislation aimed to strengthen education in "defense disciplines" such as science, math, and foreign languages, although it would eventually include other subjects as well. Some of its main provisions were funds for guidance services in secondary schools, federal loans for undergraduates, and fellowships for graduate students. Meanwhile, the National Science Foundation and other federal agencies also expanded their scientific manpower initiatives. By the end of the 1960s, one third of all science and engineering graduate students had some type of financial support from the federal government.[7]

The inclusion of women in these programs sought to offset the shortage of "scientific womanpower," which appeared especially severe when compared with Soviet society. The National Manpower Council's 1957 *Womanpower* report cited several early Cold War surveys that found that the USSR graduated some 13,000 women engineers annually.[8] Other statistics furnished by Soviet scientists (and based on current enrollments instead of graduation rates) suggested that women made up as much as one-third, or 203,000, of their country's engineering students.[9] Despite methodological discrepancies, both figures indisputably dwarfed the U.S. graduation rate of fewer than 100 women engineers per year.[10]

The Soviet Union's evident success at attracting women in scientific fields led to much public consternation. Across the country, ominous headlines claimed that "Soviets Are Ahead with Womanpower," "Women Add Much in Soviet Science," and "Red Engineering Schools Loaded with Women."[11] Another example can be seen in the January 1959 *Washington Post* article entitled "Talents of U.S. Women Being Wasted, 3 Soviet Scientists Say," which featured firsthand observations from members of a recent Soviet delegation to the United States. The *Post*'s interview with Alla Masevich, a "woman astronomer" who had coordinated the physical observations on the Sputniks, seemed to confirm that the Soviets' lead in the space race had been clinched by female talent.[12]

The insinuation that the outcome of the Cold War hinged on the utilization of women had real resonance as the post-Sputnik panic set in. The Sputnik saga dramatized the importance of scientific womanpower to national security and exposed the failure of the United States to promote women's scientific participation. It also reinforced earlier warnings issued by the Society of Women Engineers and others regarding the dangers of "wasting" female intellect. Other reformers soon took up these arguments as well and embarked on their own initiatives to encourage women and girls. In doing so, they frequently called attention to the distinct advantage enjoyed by the Soviet Union as a result of its willingness to educate and employ female scientists and engineers. As Ethaline Cortelyou of the Armour Research Foundation remarked in her June 1958 *Chemical Bulletin* article, "The successful launchings of Sputnik I and Sputnik II indicate what can happen when a people realize that brains have no sex!"[13]

This logic, however, proved tricky. Certainly, the high participation of women in Soviet science helped refute still prevalent perceptions that women lacked the ability to succeed in these fields. It also supported claims that the United States could no longer afford to discourage its women from engaging in scientific and technical pursuits. But even as they applauded the Soviet Union's "utilization" of womanpower, technocratic feminists had to avoid drawing too much attention to Soviet women themselves. Although some Soviet scientists such as Alla Masevich were deemed "attractive" by the American press, many more were depicted as tough, manly, severe, or, at best, plain—the very stereotypes that the Society of Women Engineers had struggled to dismantle.[14] Likewise, the "hard-working" nature of female Soviet scientists was generally cast as the inevitable and undesirable result of what one Connecticut woman called "frantic attempts on the part of the Soviet Government to badger the populace into record production."[15]

Thus, Soviet women's scientific servitude seemed antithetical to American values. The thought of forcing women into the workplace (scientific or otherwise) repulsed many middle-class Americans, who regarded the supposedly comfortable lifestyle of the American housewife as emblematic of their own country's affluence and cultural superiority. Nowhere was this more apparent than in the 1959 "kitchen debate" between U.S. vice president Richard Nixon and Soviet premier Nikita Khrushchev, held at the American National Exhibition in Moscow. In the model kitchen of a full-scale, six-room, ranch-style home, Khrushchev and Nixon quarreled over the symbolic merits of washing machines and electric ranges. While Nixon extolled the virtues of these time-saving devices, pointing out that they had been "designed to make things easier for our women," Khrushchev condemned that "capitalist attitude" and retaliated with pride in his country's hardworking women. That the Soviet system had little use or regard for full-time homemakers only bolstered Nixon's conviction that American superiority very much rested on Cold War domesticity and sharply defined gender roles.[16]

As an increasing number of individuals and organizations embraced technocratic feminism, they struggled to balance these competing concerns. While they urged the "utilization" of female intellect, they carefully avoided denigrating women's roles as mothers and wives. Nor did they suggest that American women give up their domestic responsibilities in order to pursue scientific careers. Instead, they attacked the broader cultural climate that devalued women's intellectual contributions, squandered female intellect, and discouraged potential "Phyllis Webers."

Expanding Support for Scientific Womanpower

Among the new proponents of technocratic feminism was Sigma Delta Epsilon, the graduate fraternity for women in science. Founded in 1921 at Cornell University by twelve female students, the organization originally aimed to combat the isolation that they experienced in their studies and social lives. They chose as their motto "United in friendship through science" and rented a house near campus, where they roomed together. When one of the members moved away to the University of Wisconsin, she found a small group of female scientists there and initiated plans for bringing them into a national organization. In March 1922, the national Sigma Delta Epsilon was chartered and incorporated the following month.[17]

One of the fraternity's first activities after its founding was holding an All Women in Science Luncheon at the annual meeting of the American Association for the Advancement of Science. These gatherings enabled female scientists from across the country to meet each other and drum up support for the new organization. The fraternity also petitioned to become an affiliate of the association and was finally recognized in 1939 when its membership was deemed sufficiently large with some 2,000 members. Sigma Delta Epsilon prided itself on the fact that it was the only women's organization affiliated with the association at the time.[18]

As the fraternity grew, it shifted its emphasis toward academic activities and sharing research findings. In that vein, Sigma Delta Epsilon established a national research fellowship in 1939 and made its first award in 1941. During World War II, however, the group curtailed much of its activity and suspended its national conventions in response to wartime rationing and travel restrictions. When members resumed meeting in the postwar period, they continued to counsel one another, share their research, and publicize their accomplishments. But their desire to achieve acceptance within the predominantly male scientific community often curbed their willingness to tackle head-on the discrimination and discouragement that many faced. Thus, while the group was particularly prominent because of its alignment with the American Association for the Advancement of Science, it was often conciliatory in tone. Invoking technocratic feminism in the wake of the Sputnik scare enabled it to become increasingly outspoken and activist in its orientation.[19]

In December 1958, Sigma Delta Epsilon teamed up with the American Association of Scientific Workers, the National Federation of Business and Professional Women's Clubs, and three other groups to hold the Conference on the Participation of Women in Science. This event would become one the first major post-Sputnik discussions of "scientific womanpower," a growing source of concern for the sponsors and society alike. Although the number of female scientists and engineers had nearly doubled in the past several years, jumping from 7,712 in 1954–55 to 12,027 in 1956–58, their overall representation had crept more slowly from 6.67 percent to 7.22 percent of the total. Much of this growth, moreover, was concentrated in the natural and behavioral sciences, fields that were considered more feminine than the so-called hard sciences such as physics and engineering, where women made fewer inroads. Women also remained concentrated in certain occupations: nearly half worked in educational institutions, while just a quarter worked in industry. Most of the rest were scattered among government agencies, nonprofit institutions, and self-employment. In nearly all these cases, they were disproportionally represented at the lowest levels.[20]

Women's "underutilization" became a major theme at the conference, which was held in conjunction with the American Association for the Advancement of Science's annual meeting in Washington, D.C. There, women and men from across the country gathered in the Congressional Room of the Willard Hotel to identify and remedy obstacles to their nation's science program. Crystallographer Elizabeth Wood of Bell Labs gave a sarcastically titled opening address, "Sugar and Spice and Everything Nice," in which she lambasted the cultural curbing of women's scientific talent. The two most insidious constraints facing women, she claimed, were the widespread assumptions that "mechanical gadgets and scientific things are the province of men" and that "the right thing to do for universal approval is to marry and have a family."[21] In a paper examining "Women's Attitudes Toward Careers," Hofstra College psychologist Anne Steinmann reported on her three-year study of fifty-one female college students and their parents, concluding that the present American mood had resulted in "an unrealistic, hysterical back-tracking" of career women into the home.[22] The University of Maryland's Annabelle Motz expounded on "The Multiple Roles of the Woman Scientist" while the panel discussions that followed revealed support among audience members for government-sponsored maternity leave, nurseries, homemaking services, and tax deductions for working mothers.[23] The highlight of the afternoon was an address by Arthur Flemming, who had been recently appointed head of the Department of Health, Education, and Welfare. Flemming denounced what he identified as a double standard in education and employment practices whereby women were denied the same encouragement and compensation as men. He warned that this phenomenon not only lacked justification but also jeopardized the national security. Flemming called for continued attention to this matter and concluded his talk by reminding audience members of their "definite obligation to keep turning the spotlight on our manpower problem."[24]

Betty Lou Raskin did precisely that in her charismatic evening address, "American Women: Unclaimed Treasures of Science." The thirty-four-year-old Raskin, who headed Plastics Research and Development at the Johns Hopkins University Radiation Laboratory, had earned her undergraduate degree in chemistry from Goucher College before earning her M.A. in the same subject from Johns Hopkins. She began her educational and professional career in the midst of World War II, and it is obvious that she regarded manpower shortages as a powerful tool for opening doors to women. She now pointed out to her audience the waste of female talent in the United States and recalled a recent conference of 2,000 plastics engineers at which she had been the only woman. "If a Russian meeting of that kind were held," Raskin noted, "more than 600 women would be present." "Thousands more female engineers are graduated in one year in the U.S.S.R. than we have graduated in our entire history!"[25]

With surprising boldness and disarming wit, Raskin issued a scathing indictment of the cultural barriers to American women's scientific success. According to Raskin, the underrepresentation of women in scientific fields "is not due to any intellectual incompetence or lack of creative ability on the part of women. It is the fault of our cultural conditioning and our poor vocational guidance."[26] She also blamed the media and advertising agencies for their role in discouraging girls and young women from entering science: "They have made the mink coat, not the lab coat, our symbol of success. They've praised beauty, not brains. They've emphasized leisure time, not hard work and originality. As a result, today's schoolgirl thinks it far more exciting to serve tea on an airplane than to foam a new light-weight plastic in the laboratory."[27] Raskin then proposed a number of tactics to challenge this perception, such as providing college-bound "girls" with booklets about scientific careers, casting a popular actress as an aeronautical engineer in a romantic comedy, showcasing a female scientist each month in a women's magazine, and using laboratory equipment as props in department store displays of women's fashions. She hoped that such measures would help the public to view science as compatible with femininity and to encourage women in those fields. Failure to do so, she warned, would have serious consequences. Raskin insisted that "the longer we continue to ignore the scientific potentialities and skills of the women in this country the more we are hurting our chances for survival."[28]

These themes received additional attention the following afternoon when Ethaline Cortelyou addressed Sigma Delta Epsilon's annual All Women in Science Luncheon. About fifteen years older than Raskin, Cortelyou had earned her bachelor's degree in chemistry from Alfred College in New York in 1932. Her marriage to a male chemistry professor both helped and hurt her search for employment during the Great Depression, when she ended up stringing together several positions in industry and teaching. After the Second World War began, she found work as a technical editor on the Manhattan Project at the University of Chicago, where she assisted in the preparation of the classified table of isotopes.[29] Perhaps owing to her experiences during the Great Depression, when many female chemists embraced similar kinds of scientific "women's work" as alternatives to unemployment, Cortelyou continued in the field of technical writing and editing after the war had ended. She also counseled other women to do the same, believing that they would encounter less resistance in these positions where "men have not become so firmly entrenched as to resent feminine competition."[30] But as the Sputnik panic set in, she quickly lost much of that Depression-era mentality and, by 1958, was publicly criticizing science teachers and departments who followed her earlier advice.[31]

One of Cortelyou's many critiques of scientific women's work can be seen in her June 1958 *Chemical Bulletin* article, "Utilizing Chemical Womanpower to Combat the Alleged Shortage of Chemists." She linked the funneling of women into technical editing and other "science-related fields" to the broader problem of "wasting" female talent. While she did not oppose women's personal decisions to take on such work, especially in the absence of other opportunities, she condemned the practice of limiting women to those positions. She also criticized employers who avoided hiring women out of fear that they would be employment risks, paid them less than their male counterparts, or assigned them to mundane laboratory tasks. "Certainly," she argued, "the prospects of 'serving as another pair of hands' for some man chemist is not sufficiently alluring to interest a girl in four years of hard work needed to obtain a bachelor's degree in chemistry."[32] Thus, the better "utilization" of female chemists would be just as important to meeting scientific shortages as the encouragement of new ones.

During the spring and summer of 1958, Cortelyou elicited much attention as she repeatedly posited that "brains have no sex." Several major newspapers, such as the *Washington Post* and *Chicago Sun-Times*, carried feature articles on her, lauding her "highly refreshing and provocative opinions of the role of women in science" as well as her "missionary zeal." As an officer of Sigma Delta Epsilon, she was also well known to members of the fraternity who agreed that she would make the perfect speaker for their December 1958 All Women in Science Luncheon and widely promoted her slated address.[33]

Cortelyou did not disappoint. Her discussion of "The Status of the American Woman Scientists" proved insightful and inspiring and helped reinforce several of the themes tackled the previous day by other speakers. Like Betty Lou Raskin, Cortelyou highlighted Soviet women's scientific participation, urged the greater encouragement of female science students in the United States, and criticized the potency of anti-intellectualism. She charged that some colleges and universities "actually try to make science courses into obstacle courses for the few girls hardy enough to attempt science majors" and demanded that they "do more than merely pay lip service to the possibility of women as a source of badly needed scientific and technical workers."[34] She also criticized the failure of industry to provide maternity leaves or other forms of support for working mothers, explaining that when female scientists left the labor force temporarily to have children, they frequently found that rapid technological advances made much of their scientific knowledge obsolete and their reentry difficult. To help women keep up with developments in their fields, Cortelyou recommended part-time education and employment opportunities, such as work that could be done in the home and refresher courses. While not ideal (refresher courses were often expensive and part-time work was usually poorly paid), these initiatives could ease women's return to full-time positions. They also promised to facilitate the labor force participation of older women and married women, whom recent manpower studies had identified as critical to the national economy and the national security.[35]

Cortelyou ended her address by stressing the importance of female solidarity. "Give other women a break when you can," she argued. "If you are in a supervisory position, hire women and do what you can to eliminate inequalities of salary. If you have a woman supervisor, support her." And when a job can be done on a part-time basis, "do what you can to have it assigned to a capable woman who would welcome such a diversion from some of the humdrum routines of housework and raising a family." In all, she concluded, "be a woman and be glad of it. Lipsticks and slipsticks are entirely compatible, and a pretty hat does not mean that the head under it is empty."[36]

Cortelyou's captivating talk nicely wrapped up the main themes and goals of the conference, a major outcome of which was the formation of the National Council on the Participation of Women in Science several months later in March 1959. Sigma Delta Epsilon was well represented in the new organization, which consisted initially of several dozen women and a handful of men. The fraternity's outgoing president and George Washington University Medical School professor of bacteriology, Mary Louise Robbins, who had been instrumental in organizing the council, served as its first chairperson. Other Sigma Delta Epsilon members also held leadership roles, both as members of the executive board and as committee chairs. They included Ethaline Cortelyou; Elizabeth Weisburger of the National Cancer Institute; Ernestine Thurman of the National Institutes of Health's Division of Research Grants; the pharmaceutical consultant Betty Lankford McLaughlin; and Harriet Boyd, a medical technologist at the University of Pennsylvania.[37] Representatives of the Women's Bureau and the American Association of University Women were also in attendance at the council's organizational meeting, as were members of the American Association of Scientific Workers.[38]

By most accounts, the council got off to a good start. In May, the council's chair, Mary Louise Robbins, reported that several high-ranking officials in government and other agencies had expressed interest in the council's work. Buoyed by their show of support, she predicted that the council would expand to a few hundred members before long.[39] The council had also been successful in securing $200 in startup funds from the American Association for the Advancement of Science, which enabled it to pursue an increasingly ambitious agenda. One idea was to sponsor a White House conference on women in science in order to publicize and dramatize the issue. The council also began planning a center dedicated to expanding women's scientific participation, improving attitudes toward female scientists, and ending discriminatory education and employment practices. To make this possible, the group requested $7,300 from the National Science Foundation and the National Institutes of Health. The plan, however, was never realized as the council's proposal was rejected on unspecified "technical grounds."[40] The decision must have seemed perplexing, if not insulting, given that one of the council's active members, Ernestine Thurman, actually worked in the grants division of the National Institutes of Health and was most certainly familiar enough with its technical regulations to help the group prepare a properly formatted proposal. This incident not only decimated the council's agenda but also revealed the fragility of support for scientific womanpower.[41]

A similarly telling exchange took place that spring when the *New York Times Magazine* published an essay by Betty Lou Raskin. Raskin's article, "Woman's Place Is in the Lab, Too," was based loosely on her conference address and reiterated many of the same themes, such as scientific shortages, wasted womanpower, and cultural deterrents. A revised conclusion touted current efforts to address these issues, such as the formation of the National Council on the Participation of Women in Science. But unlike the glowing response she had received from her largely female audience just a few months earlier, Raskin now faced both skepticism and hostility from several male readers who rejected the very idea of a scientific shortage. It is significant that when men such as Arthur Flemming made similar recommendations regarding Cold War manpower needs, they rarely encountered such opposition. Although some educators, industrialists, and government officials occasionally questioned the severity of the shortage situation, few denied it as vehemently as those men now responding to Raskin's remarks. In one letter to the editor of the *New York Times*, Arthur Kahn of New York charged that even if there was a shortage of engineers and scientists (which he doubted), "there is a much greater and more dangerous shortage . . . of women," meaning those who adhered to traditional gender roles. He blamed this phenomenon largely on "formalized and informal" education and warned that "any solution would not seem to require suggesting to girls, even indirectly, that engineering is more important and more creative than motherhood, and that the road to fulfillment involves direct competition with men."[42]

Disappointed but undaunted by these incidents, members of the National Council on the Participation of Women in Science reorganized themselves into the American Council on Women in Science in June 1959. They quickly embarked on a new fund-raising campaign and secured contributions from a variety of individuals and organizations. That fall, the council's new chair, Betty Lankford McLaughlin, reported being pleased with the "considerable interest" expressed in the council, such as a proposal from a Washington, D.C., area civic organization for help administering a $500 graduate scholarship. The scholarship, which was designed for a woman desiring "refresher courses" in order to resume a scientific career after taking time away to raise children, clearly combined the council's interest in encouraging women's scientific participation with broader manpower concerns. As McLaughlin explained when touting these initiatives, "achievement of the aims of the American Council on Women in Science will result in an increased number of women in the scientific field, with a concomitant reduction in the shortage of personnel."[43]

The council's principal undertaking was holding conferences on women's scientific participation, such as the one from which it had sprung. In December 1959, the council cosponsored with Sigma Delta Epsilon the Second Conference on Encouraging Women to Enter Science, which was held in conjunction with the American Association for the Advancement of Science's annual meeting in Chicago. Chaired by Ethaline Cortelyou,

Members of Sigma Delta Epsilon at the December 1959 All Women in Science Luncheon, Washington, D.C. Photograph by Pics Chicago. Courtesy of Sigma Delta Epsilon Records, #3605, Division of Rare and Manuscript Collections, Cornell University Library.

the conference featured a keynote address by Alan T. Waterman, the director of the National Science Foundation, who discussed "Scientific Womanpower—A Neglected Resource." Much like Arthur Flemming, Waterman was a government leader and potential ally who, publicly at least, regarded the "utilization" of women as critical to meeting overall manpower needs. In his address (which was most likely written by his female assistant, Lee Anna Embrey), Waterman offered much rhetorical support for encouraging women's scientific participation and warned that "as a nation, we cannot afford this serious waste of intellectual resources."[44] After identifying discriminatory hiring practices and cultural conventions, he lamented that "women are being wasted in science because of an immature attitude on the part of society that it is unattractive for a woman's brain to be showing."[45] Although Waterman failed to provide any real solutions or concrete directives for change, he nevertheless delighted his audience with his seemingly strong support for their goals. He also provided them with new fodder: Cortelyou and Thurman, for example, would repeatedly cite Waterman's remarks in their own addresses and articles on encouraging women's scientific talent.[46]

Thurman also chaired the third and last Conference on Encouraging Women to Enter Science, which, like its predecessor, was cosponsored by Sigma Delta Epsilon and the American Council on Women in Science. Held in December 1960 in New York City, the event featured a keynote address by Margaret Mead as well as several panels and workshops on improving women's participation in scientific fields. The opening session also included a talk entitled "Utilizing Our Scientific Womanpower," thus reinforcing the importance of the council's work to Cold War concerns. Although the conference generated much interest and enthusiasm—a testament to both the importance of the topic and the hard work of its organizers—it was the last time that Sigma Delta Epsilon and the American Council on Women in Science would collaborate. The council sponsored no additional conferences, nor did it continue its operations much after 1962.[47]

The circumstances surrounding the council's disappearance are not known, although in August 1961 the new national president of Sigma Delta Epsilon, Delaphine G. R. Wyckoff, informed Sigma Delta Epsilon secretary and former council chair Betty Lankford McLaughlin that, to her knowledge, Sigma Delta Epsilon had never officially sanctioned the council, nor the participation of Sigma Delta Epsilon officers and members in council activities. This information came as a surprise to both McLaughlin and Thurman, who not only had been instrumental in the council's organization and administration but now responded that they had been advised differently by past Sigma Delta Epsilon officers. Ultimately, however, McLaughlin conceded that Sigma Delta Epsilon had "effectively conducted" such programs long before the council's formation and that "these programs should be continued by the Fraternity."[48]

The American Council on Women in Science most likely folded, then, because its main supporters realized that they could just as easily pursue their objectives through the older and more established Sigma Delta Epsilon. Although Sigma Delta Epsilon members had helped establish the council in the first place, they probably did so with the hope that a separate organization would attract new supporters. But when the council ended up drawing most of its members and officers from Sigma Delta Epsilon, both groups must have recognized the unnecessary duplication of their efforts.

Despite its short life span, the American Council on Women in Science remains important because it reveals a growing impatience among female scientists to improve their lot. In the aftermath of the Soviet Sputniks, women who were already involved in a women's scientific society found it expedient to form a new, broader organization in the hope of expanding support for "scientific womanpower." The resistance that they faced in this endeavor is also important, as it made visible some of the ambivalence surrounding the "utilization" of female intellect. Thus, while the council's run was a brief one, it nevertheless reveals much about the opportunities and obstacles posed by space age science.[49]

Sigma Delta Epsilon and the Committee to Encourage Women to Enter Science

The American Council on Women in Science had expected to work closely with Sigma Delta Epsilon's newly formed Committee to Encourage Women to Enter Science that had been created in response to the Sputnik scare. In December 1957, just weeks after the launchings, Mary Louise Robbins, who was president-elect of Sigma Delta Epsilon at the time, directed the fraternity's attention to trends in women's scientific participation. According to Robbins, a recent National Science Foundation report had revealed a decline in the number of women entering scientific fields, especially at the graduate level. Given the international climate as well as Sigma Delta Epsilon's own interest in these issues, she inquired, "Should not our organization be thinking about this and do something about it?"[50] Sigma Delta Epsilon members answered with a resounding "yes," and with this mandate, Robbins established the Committee to Encourage Women to Enter Science in the fall of 1958.[51]

To chair the committee, Robbins selected Meta Ellis of the Aerojet-General Corporation of Sacramento, California. Ellis, who had previously worked with Ethaline Cortelyou at the Armour Research Foundation, struck Robbins as a perfect fit for the position, as she was the one who had suggested establishing such a committee in the first place. Ellis also impressed Robbins with her enthusiasm for encouraging women's scientific participation, an enthusiasm that was obviously influenced by her own experiences in the aerospace industry. As an employee of what *Time* magazine dubbed "the General Motors of U.S. Rocketry," Ellis clearly understood the significance of the Soviet feat and sought to capitalize on the recent upsurge of interest in scientific womanpower. While Ellis realized that Sigma Delta Epsilon had always been concerned with women in science, she also believed that recent developments in the space race made evident that "today, a special, urgent need is felt in this direction." She called on the organization to redouble its efforts by supporting the new committee, adding that "it is both favorable and timely that Sigma Delta Epsilon should choose to act now."[52]

The Committee to Encourage Women to Enter Science was deeply rooted in Cold War anxieties, which Ellis invoked at every turn. She eagerly revealed to other Sigma Delta Epsilon members her committee's intent "to spotlight our nation's need for increased scientific manpower resources and to suggest the wider use of scientific womanpower," as Arthur Flemming had suggested.[53] This strategy, committee members hoped, would allow them to improve women's education and employment opportunities in scientific fields. According to Ellis, they aimed "to influence public opinion by persuading students, parents, school administrators, and employers alike that women trained in science are necessary to alleviate our nation's personnel shortages." In doing so, the committee sought "to impress the public with the variety of interesting careers there are for women in the sciences" and "to lower the resistance of school administrators and employers."[54]

Although Sigma Delta Epsilon was a graduate organization, committee members realized that many women were steered away from scientific careers long before they reached that stage. As a result, much of the committee's early work targeted women in the secondary schools. By the spring of 1959, the committee had formulated a broad agenda that included providing young women with information about careers in science and encouraging female students through science fairs and career days. While some of the committee's activities were national in scope, such as its "clearinghouse" function for gathering and disseminating news stories about Sigma Delta Epsilon members, most of its work was conducted by chapters at the local level.[55] Much like the Society of Women Engineers' Professional Guidance and Education Committee, Sigma Delta Epsilon's Committee to Encourage Women to Enter Science relied heavily on individual members for what it considered its most important job: providing personal encouragement to young women.

Sigma Delta Epsilon's committee regarded science fairs as "an excellent opportunity to encourage girls of aptitude to pursue scientific careers" and urged local chapters to become involved in any way they could. Ellis suggested that members write congratulatory letters to female winners and send copies to their science teachers and high school principals. She also recommended that they invite the girls to a Sigma Delta Epsilon meeting or a gathering in their honor. These activities, Ellis believed, would provide female students with recognition of their accomplishments as well as an opportunity to meet other women in scientific fields.[56]

Individual chapters eagerly embraced Ellis's recommendations. In 1958, Penn State's Nu Chapter helped high school girls set up their science fair exhibits and awarded twenty-five dollars to the one with the best project. The chapter also feted the students at its next meeting.[57] Meanwhile, the

University of Illinois's Gamma Chapter began holding an annual breakfast to honor girls who won awards at the Westinghouse Science Talent Search. The University of Minnesota's Xi Chapter established an annual tea for blue ribbon winners, which was followed by a tour of the university laboratories "to show these young women—and perhaps future scientists—what opportunities there are."[58] The Xi Chapter also participated in regional activities, such as the 1960 Junior Minnesota Academy of Science meeting in St. Cloud, where ninety-one award-winning girls displayed their projects. After speaking with the female students to determine their specific interests, Xi representatives Agnes Hanson and Marie Berg matched them up with individual Sigma Delta Epsilon members "to sustain the girls' scientific curiosity through correspondence."[59] Other chapters participated in science fairs by sending members to judge exhibits and distribute guidance materials.[60]

Sigma Delta Epsilon members did not limit their activities to science fairs and competitions, however. In 1959 the University of Wisconsin's Beta Chapter began its high school program for female students in the Madison area. Selected by their science teachers, participants attended an evening "kickoff" event, which included a Sigma Delta Epsilon meeting, a short lecture on a scientific subject, and a "social hour" for mingling with women scientists. The next day, the students toured the university laboratories, where they learned about research in biology, chemistry, physics, and mathematics. On two separate Saturdays, they "worked" in the laboratory of their choice under the supervision of a Sigma Delta Epsilon member. "In this way," the chapter reported, "the girls can get a better understanding of a research program, have the opportunity to use some of the equipment, and . . . help with some of the demonstrations." The chapter also helped place many of its participants in summer laboratory jobs following high school graduation.[61] The program was enthusiastically received by students, many of whom went on to study science in college and graduate school. By 1965, Beta Chapter had even inducted at least one former participant as a full-fledged graduate member.[62]

Participation in "career days" was another popular activity for many chapters, whose members frequently addressed student assemblies and gave scientific demonstrations at local high schools. They also led science-related field trips for interested students, often in collaboration with other educational and professional organizations. In 1959, Ellis announced that the Northern California Section of the Instrument Society of America had solicited the participation of Sigma Delta Epsilon in its "Spend a Day in the Career of Your Choice" program for high school students. Ellis urged all local members to take part in the program and all faraway members to implement similar programs in their hometowns.[63]

Ellis also sought to extend Sigma Delta Epsilon's influence and aims through "intersociety councils" that drew together educators, counselors, scientists, and teachers from a variety of professional societies interested in science education. Although one of the oldest ones, the Mid-Hudson Science Advisory Council, had been established in 1955, these councils became increasingly popular after the Sputnik launchings and appeared in such far-flung places as New England, Washington, D.C., southern California, and Hawaii. In 1960, Ellis helped establish one such group in Sacramento, where representatives of thirteen professional societies came together to increase student interest in scientific and technical subjects. The Sacramento council, as well as similar ones nationwide, provided additional avenues for Sigma Delta Epsilon to encourage female students through career days, science fairs, and individual counseling.[64]

Although most of Sigma Delta Epsilon's vocational guidance activities targeted high school students, some did take place at the college level. Several chapters held "research days" for undergraduate women that, like the Wisconsin program for Madison-area students, were designed to encourage aspiring scientists. In 1960, members of Purdue University's Pi Chapter led laboratory tours and equipment demonstrations for undergraduate chemistry majors in an effort to promote interest in graduate study and research.[65] Other chapters, such as the University of Missouri's Delta Chapter, presented undergraduate research awards to college women. Each year, members recognized one outstanding college senior, who received a certificate, a cash prize, and the honor of having her name engraved on a permanent plaque in the library.[66]

Taken together, these activities fulfilled several functions. First and foremost, they provided young women and girls with encouragement that went well beyond the broad proclamations espoused by various government and industry officials. While Sigma Delta Epsilon members often invoked Cold War rhetoric and manpower statistics regarding the "waste" of female intellect, they agreed that much more needed to be done. In order to encourage women in meaningful ways, Sigma Delta Epsilon president Delaphine Wyckoff realized, "We need to do work on the grass roots level with high school girls, and even college undergraduates, to show them what scientific work is like."[67] At the same time, these activities afforded Sigma Delta Epsilon members the opportunity to share with younger women their own passion for scientific subjects. "As members of SDE," Wyckoff explained, "we are enthusiastic about our life work in the sciences, its opportunities, and its challenges." "The kinds of projects that some of our chapters are engaged in . . . can have a two-fold benefit. Besides showing girls what goes on in a science laboratory, our own members can have the exciting experience of presenting science as a stimulating quest for knowledge."[68] Lastly, these activities enabled Sigma Delta Epsilon to expand its influence and generate new support for its goals. Insofar as they meshed with broader manpower concerns, these activities offered a shared solution to otherwise uninterested audiences and facilitated collaboration with unlikely allies.

Confronting the Fear of "Feminine Fallout"

Even as groups such as Sigma Delta Epsilon encouraged girls and young women to enter science, they gradually incorporated other activities to assist older female scientists who had temporarily "retired" to raise children or who struggled to combine domestic and scientific pursuits. In doing so, they aimed to combat what *Wall Street Journal* reporter Arthur Lack had reproachfully dubbed "feminine fallout," or women's tendency to abandon scientific training and careers after marriage. The Cold War reference made its lexiconic debut in a January 1958 front page story, "Science Talent Hunt Faces Stiff Obstacle: Feminine Fallout," in which Lack panned current congressional proposals to fund science education. His objections were based not on the threat of federal control, as other criticisms were, but rather on the squandering of taxpayer dollars on female students. He noted with alarm that federal officials expected women to receive at least one-third of the 10,000 math and science scholarships to be offered annually under the proposed aid-to-education plan. "Hence it's inevitable," he quipped, "that some Government money will go to train scientists who experiment only with different household detergents and mathematicians who confine their work to adding up grocery bills."[69]

To illustrate the severity of "feminine fallout," Lack cited a recent AAUW survey of its fellowship recipients showing that at least one-sixth of those responding were currently unemployed. Although the survey also revealed that most planned on returning to professional work as soon as family obligations eased up, Lack nevertheless took these findings as proof that "the ladies weren't making gainful use of their advanced training."[70] He consulted several leading educators to validate his claim but must have been disappointed when they reiterated instead how many professional women who leave paid employment to raise children do in fact return once their domestic duties diminish. (Indeed, nearly every manpower study of college-educated women's workforce participation corroborated this trend.)[71]

Persisting in his skepticism, Lack turned his attention to women's education patterns and intellectual abilities. He noted with interest that "there's apparently some foundation for the widespread masculine notion that ladies are deficient in mathematics," such as women's tendency to specialize in the humanities and to score lower on college entrance exams. The contributing cultural influences seemed to escape him, even though he did acknowledge that female students generally earned better grades, made up the majority of high school honor students, and were less likely than men to drop out of the college at which they originally enrolled. Yet instead of interrogating these discrepancies, Lack held fast to his belief that federal scholarships would be wasted on women. He even suggested that restricting the number of female recipients would be desirable but suspected that doing so "would probably embroil the Government in a great controversy with the many 'equal rights' advocates among the ladies."[72]

Predictably, Lack's article caused quite a stir. Two weeks later, the *Wall Street Journal* published a letter to the editor from Susan Spaulding, inquiring "What Feminine Fallout?" Spaulding, an AAUW member and executive assistant to the president of New York University, sharply criticized Lack's "confusing barrage of extraneous statements concerning housewives and professional work, obstacles to employment, comparative performance of boys and girls in mathematics and in general scholarship, and other matters." She charged that his article "proves nothing as to the advisability of awarding scholarships to scientifically minded girls, but unfortunately contrives to give the impression that scholarships to such girls would represent a loss."[73] While Spaulding recognized that professional women often suspended their education or careers to raise children, she argued that "feminine fallout" was nowhere as insidious or insurmountable as Lack insisted.

To substantiate her claim, Spaulding provided a healthy mix of anecdotal and statistical evidence. She first related the details of her recent visit to a women's college where she learned from the male physics department chair that even when his students married, they generally continued on with science in some way. Many married other scientists, continued subscribing to scientific journals, and returned to professional work as soon as circumstances allowed.[74] Spaulding also cited statistics from her own university's Institute of Mathematical Science, which, she noted, had contracts for basic research with all branches of the Defense Department, the Atomic

Energy Commission, and the National Science Foundation. The institute's staff of 190 included twenty-three women, eleven of whom were married and seven of whom had children. One of the mothers was even on the faculty. Regardless of marriage or motherhood, Spaulding reasoned, "the trained scientific mind . . . finds it hard to stay away from the laboratory."[75]

For Spaulding then, there was little reason to fear that fellowship money would be squandered on female students, as all available evidence indicated that most women scientists would, at some point, use their training. The bigger problem was that most fellowship programs failed to account for intermittency in women's education and employment and only awarded funds to full-time or traditional-aged students. As a result, women who delayed their education or took time away from school in order to raise children were often ineligible.[76]

Recognizing this dilemma, Sigma Delta Epsilon revamped its fellowship program in 1959. The organization did away with its one large award in favor of several smaller "grants-in-aid" to assist in the continuation or completion of a specific project, with preference being given to women thirty-five years of age and older. "In this age group," explained fellowship chair Ruth Dippell, "there is frequent demand . . . but little opportunity to secure [such stipends]." Thus, "while we should encourage women to enter science, we should also consider the means by which they might be encouraged to remain in science."[77]

Sigma Delta Epsilon widely advertised the new program using the mailing lists of the National Science Foundation, the American Chemical Society, selected professional journals, and its own chapters. It sent out more than 950 announcements, with requests that they be posted in "a conspicuous place." Although the publicity costs ran significantly higher than in previous years, Sigma Delta Epsilon believed that "the new plan must be given maximum opportunity to 'sink or swim.'" The gamble paid off, and within the first week, the organization received more requests for applications than it had in either of the last two years it awarded fellowships.[78]

The new grants-in-aid program attracted not only a record number of submissions but much general interest as well. Patricia Grinager, a Ph.D. candidate and mother of four, wrote to Ruth Dippell expressing her "appreciation for the apparent philosophy of Sigma Delta Epsilon grantors." Even though Grinager was not applying since she was not in a science program, she nevertheless recognized the award's broader significance. As she explained to Dippell, she had "inched her way up past the B.S. (1956, Columbia, Anthropology) and Master's (1957, Columbia, Anthropology) toward the Doctorate (Social Foundations of Education, Stanford, hopefully 1962) against sometimes almost superhuman odds with top honors throughout." "All along the line I have felt the built-in academic blindness toward women, who, like myself, 'gave' ten years getting a family started only to discover later that these years are not considered in most scholarship age limitation statements."[79]

Most of the women selected for the grants-in-aid shared much in common with Grinager. Judith Williams, for example, struggled to combine her graduate work at Texas Christian University with her family responsibilities. "Although she is married and has two young children," the fellowship board reported, "she is anxious to continue her work." Forty-three-year-old Joy Burcham Phillips, who had earned a Ph.D. from New York University in 1954, used her award to resume her study of pituitary function. The industrious JoAnne Mueller, who held a master's degree from Indiana University, even set up a laboratory in the basement of her house. Working from home, which her award made possible, enabled Mueller to tend to her one-year-old child while still fitting in forty hours of research a week.[80]

Throughout the early 1960s, Sigma Delta Epsilon increasingly focused on combating "feminine fallout" by helping women who wanted to combine scientific work with homemaking activities. In addition to assisting a broader range of women, this enlarged mission also breathed life into nearly defunct chapters, such as the one at Cornell University. After reassessing and reformulating its goals, Cornell's Alpha Chapter was reactivated in 1964. Its officers explained that the decision to seek reinstatement stemmed from their recognition that "the need for women in science is greater than ever. The problems of adjustment to graduate study, the dual role of homemaking and a scientific career, competition for jobs—all these and others—remain."[81] The Alpha Chapter's proposed projects included not only encouraging Ithaca area high school girls to enter science but also helping married women "keep on with study for advanced degrees or hold a job in scientific work and still maintain a home and family."[82] Although it took several years to get off the ground, the Alpha Chapter finally carried out this plan by creating a job roster of trained women that employers could use when hiring people for part-time work. The "Dial a Lady Scientist" program, as it was popularly called, promptly identified more than 100 interested and available women and placed many young mothers in positions that could be combined with homemaking.[83]

Meanwhile, members looked for other ways in which the fraternity might better help wavering women and fulfill its own potential. In 1964, Alpha

Chapter member Margaret Stone took up this subject with national secretary Hazeltene Parmenter and inquired, "Should we sponsor nurseries? Are we putting pressure on colleges to accept women who wish to resume studies or bring their knowledge up to date in courses designed for this need?"[84] She noted that such measures would not only be helpful to female scientists but also resonate with the public in light of recent manpower concerns. "At last," she argued, "people have begun to think about these things as possibilities . . . as though we had just discovered that women have brains!"[85] Stone and other members recognized that Sigma Delta Epsilon had benefited from the recent upsurge of interest in scientific womanpower and hoped to sustain that momentum in the years ahead.

Mary Ingraham Bunting and the "Climate of Unexpectation"

Another new proponent of technocratic feminism was Mary "Polly" Ingraham Bunting, a microbiologist turned women's college administrator. Born in Brooklyn, New York in 1910, Bunting and her three siblings grew up in a family that placed a premium on education and activism. Her father, Henry Ingraham, was a successful Wall Street attorney with a penchant for writing, drawing, gardening, and fishing. For many years, he served as a trustee of Wesleyan University, where he had earned his bachelor's degree in 1900 before picking up his law degree from New York Law School two years later. Bunting's mother, Mary Shotwell Ingraham, was a Vassar College graduate and untiring activist. Even as she ran her household and raised four children, she threw herself into various social organizations, such as the YWCA. She first became involved with the Brooklyn branch in 1908, following her college graduation and marriage to Henry. She served as its president from 1922 until 1939, when she was elected president of the national board. For more than six years, she presided over the national YWCA and was a driving force in its decision to adopt racial integration in the 1940s.[86]

Polly Bunting developed an early interest in science and the natural world. As a child, she spent her summers at her family's country house in Northport, Long Island, where she rode horses, watched birds, and collected plant specimens. Back in Brooklyn, she attended the Packer Collegiate Institute, a private all-girls school with a rigorous science curriculum requiring much laboratory work. Her experiences there cemented her interest in the physical sciences, which she continued to study at her mother's alma mater, Vassar College. Vassar proved an ideal fit for Bunting, as its scientific course offerings rivaled those of the best men's colleges. She sampled a variety of subjects and decided to major in physics, which she regarded as fundamental to any line of scientific work. It was not until her junior year, however, that she encountered bacteriology and realized that she had found her calling. The study of microorganisms fascinated her, and she "knew very quickly that that was it."[87]

After graduating from Vassar in 1931, Bunting headed to the University of Wisconsin and earned her Ph.D. in agricultural bacteriology in 1934. There, she met her future husband, Henry Bunting, a medical student whose father had taught their pathology class. While Henry finished his medical degree at Harvard and an internship at Johns Hopkins, Polly stayed on at Wisconsin as a research assistant before becoming an instructor at Bennington College in Vermont. Because the terms of Henry's internship forbade him from marrying, the couple delayed their wedding until 1937, at which point Polly joined her husband in Baltimore and taught at Goucher College. After a year, they moved to Connecticut when Henry joined the faculty at Yale Medical School. The chair of Yale's bacteriology department arranged a research assistantship for Polly, which gave her free reign of the laboratory for her own experiments. In addition, she enjoyed the privilege of using the university libraries, auditing courses, and sharing her ideas with other scholars. Although the job paid only $600 a year (which was subtracted from her husband's salary once the university learned that she was working), it conferred on her "legitimate status" and a way to integrate herself into the Yale bacteriology department. For Polly, these perquisites more than made up for the job's low pay and prestige, and she delighted in the rather unusual opportunity to resume her own research. She realized full well that her arrangement provided what most scholars needed and what so few (especially women) had, namely, time, freedom, and support. Her experience at Yale would also greatly influence her later thinking about professional women's intellectual development.[88]

Polly Bunting continued at Yale until her first child was born in the fall of 1940. She bore three more children over the next seven years and spent most of that time at home with them. Meanwhile, she kept active in various community affairs, such as the school board. She returned to part-time teaching and research in 1946, first at Wellesley (while Henry spent a year at Harvard and MIT) and later back at Yale. But life as she knew it took an unexpected turn when her husband died suddenly from a brain tumor in 1954. Left to support four children, Bunting stayed on at Yale for another year while she looked for full-time work. The chair of the microbiology department tried to cobble together a position for her there, but with little luck. Although she had given lectures, conducted research, and published papers, Yale was unwilling to appoint her to the faculty. She later reflected that she had mixed feelings about such a situation anyway and would have been reluctant to accept a "sympathy" position. But the fact remained that she needed to find some way of sustaining herself and her family.[89]

When Bunting received an invitation to become the dean of Douglass College—the women's college at Rutgers University—she was both pleased and surprised. As a widow, she wanted very much to maintain her independence, and this position would allow her to do just that. But it would also require that she give up her scientific research and embark on a new career. She had never before considered academic administration, nor did she have any experience with it. While she viewed herself an unlikely candidate, she later learned that it was her friend and former Bennington College colleague Barbara Jones who had recommended her for the job. Jones, who was married to the president of Rutgers University, had paid Bunting a visit in the fall of 1954 under the pretense of being in the area. "It was years before I realized that she had come to see what shape I was in," Bunting later reflected, "and would I be a good person to put on the list at Douglass College."[90] Although Bunting had no idea that Douglass was looking for a dean, her interest in educational issues evidently impressed Jones, whose husband passed along Bunting's name to the search committee. Several months later, Bunting met formally with the Douglass trustees and toured the campus. When the offer arrived shortly thereafter, the job—and the financial stability it promised—seemed very attractive, even though it would involve another major life change. After much deliberation, Bunting accepted the position and in March 1955 was formally named the third dean of Douglass College.[91]

News of Bunting's appointment revealed much fascination with her status as a widowed mother of four. Publicity photos routinely featured the new dean surrounded by her children, while headlines drew attention to her multiple roles. One paper boiled down her credentials to "Yale lecturer" and "mother." Another one announced, "New [Douglass] Dean Able to Combine Raising Family and Career." And Rutgers University president Lewis Webster Jones lauded Bunting as "one of the rather rare individuals who have successfully combined a distinguished career in research and scholarship with the responsibilities of her family."[92] Bunting's ability to juggle home and professional life roused her students' interest as well, especially after she and her family moved into the stately dean's residence nestled in the heart of campus. The sight of children piling out of her tan-and-cream station wagon parked in front of the red brick mansion enthralled onlookers. So too did glimpses of the new dean on her morning walks, usually with at least one child and one dog in tow. Seniors attending her Friday night buffets had the opportunity to dine with Bunting and her family, as did other students who occasionally dropped by. Without setting out to be, Bunting quickly became a highly visible example of what her students could achieve. As the class of 1959 wrote in its yearbook dedication to her, "Mother, scientist, and educator; she may well be our pattern."[93]

This kind of attention was new to Bunting, as was the "deaning business" more generally. Indeed, the first faculty meeting over which she presided at Douglass was the first faculty meeting she had ever attended.[94] But Bunting proved to be a quick study, and she set about her job in the way that she knew best: as a scientist. She stated early on that she would make no pronouncements until she had a chance to "look and learn," and she spent the summer of 1955 actively collecting information about the college.[95] For months, she pored over reports, consulted with her predecessor, and met with trustees, faculty, students, and alumnae. By the time the academic year opened in the fall, she had already "investigated every nook and cranny of the campus," as the alumnae magazine reported.[96] In the little brown notebooks where she used to record bird sightings and beehive conditions, Bunting now dashed off thoughts about education or copied interesting passages from books. She relied on these observations to put forward ideas or "hypotheses" and launch programs that she labeled "experiments." Her empirical approach to the deanship of Douglass College not only lent her credibility in the space age but also eased her transition from scientist to administrator. Yet she never saw these two roles as entirely separate. In one of her first speeches as dean, she told the college assembly that the "supposed choice" between research and administration "is not between activities but between problems." "And the problems of higher education today seem to me at least as absorbingly interesting and challenging as the love-life of bacteria."[97]

It was the subject of education in general, rather than women's education in particular, that first captured Bunting's imagination. Necessity, after all, had landed her at Douglass, and she viewed her position in terms of self-support and service to the state. She came to the deanship with no real interest in "women's issues," although she did acknowledge early on that "anyone taking a job of this sort must obviously and necessarily believe as I do in the essential importance of higher education for young women."[98] But women's organizations made her uncomfortable, and she shied away from such groups as the National Association of Deans of Women and the AAUW. When she finally ventured onto the national scene in 1956, it was to assist the American Council on Education in setting up its Office of Statistical Information and Research. Appointed by the council's president Arthur S. Adams, Bunting served for two years on the oversight committee, which collected higher education data and established policies for the new office. Adams, whose interest in women's education was well known, urged the committee to break down its statistics by sex, which few organizations did at the time. This assignment proved "enlightening" for Bunting, who along with the rest of the committee meticulously documented and evaluated "the involvement of women in all the different levels and fields of learning."[99] Although she still resisted aligning herself with "women's issues," she became increasingly interested in quantifying them through extensive data collection and rigorous analysis.[100]

Bunting's committee experience is significant because it prompted her to view the study of women's education as a legitimate area of academic inquiry. At the same time, it introduced her to influential educators, many of whom came to know Bunting as an astute and articulate colleague. These two developments help explain why she was approached and why she agreed to participate in the American Council on Education's October 1957 invitational, "The Present Status and Prospective Trends of Research on the Education of Women," held in Rye, New York. Chaired by Bryn Mawr College president Katharine McBride, the Rye Conference, as it became known, drew together deans of women, college presidents, and other individuals interested in women's education, including Marguerite Zapoleon of the Women's Bureau. It also represented the first time that Bunting took part in such a narrowly focused event, even though she continued to express discomfort with women's issues.[101]

Despite her own misgivings, Bunting was establishing a reputation for herself as an authority in the field of women's education. She participated actively in the discussions and was both deferred to and cited by other conference participants. As one of the twelve invited speakers, she joined the ranks of such luminaries as Anna Rose Hawkes, AAUW president; Nevitt Sanford, coordinator of the Vassar study on high-achieving young women; and Kate Hevner Mueller, author of the 1954 sensation, *Educating Women for a Changing World*. In her own address, which drew on her observations at Douglass as well as her work on the statistical information committee, Bunting identified several areas in the field of women's higher education that she believed warranted further attention, such as determining motivation and sustaining intellectual momentum. She also pointed to possibilities for continuing education after college and faulted the current educational structure for making it nearly impossible for women to pursue education and family life at the same time. Although she did not advocate any clear-cut solutions, the questions that she raised at Rye would influence her later initiatives in the field of women's higher education.[102]

The Rye Conference brought Bunting into the inner circle of women's education leaders. It also precipitated her involvement in the American Council on Education's Commission on the Education of Women, which had carried out most of the preparations for the fall gathering. In 1958, she joined the commission at the urging of Arthur Adams. But enlisting her was no easy task, as Adams recalled a few years later in a speech honoring Bunting. He remembered that "she questioned me closely as to whether or not this was a group which would make special pleas for women as women in a sort of neo-feminist fashion."[103] Bunting agreed to participate only after Adams had satisfactorily convinced her of the group's more moderate tone.

The Commission on the Education of Women, which had been established in 1953, served primarily as a national research agency and clearinghouse for information about women's education and educated women. It relied heavily on recent manpower studies regarding the workforce potential of older women and married women workers as it began investigating women's work and education patterns. That the absolute number of women entering colleges and universities increased steadily throughout the 1950s seemed encouraging. But their failure to pursue and complete higher degrees in the same percentages as men led the commission to suspect that women were not reaching their full potential. Instead of faulting them for a lack of motivation or determination, however, the commission investigated the widespread social attitudes and practices contributing to this problem.

The first major outcome of these explorations was the commission's 1955 publication, *How Fare American Women?*, which identified a discrepancy between women's education and societal expectations. Amid the Cold War demand for female talent, women's growing enrollments were accompanied by a sense of uncertainty about the purpose of their schooling, resulting in what the commission termed "an unrest about American women."[104] "Apparently," the commission noted, "we have not yet decided in this country whether women in their functions are to become first-class or second-class human beings. Is it any wonder then, that the education of women, wavering between the primary and secondary roles and some vague ideas of compromise, presents a confused and confusing picture?"[105]

By the time that Polly Bunting joined the commission in 1958, she had already encountered on her own much evidence to corroborate these phenomena. Her keen observations and active participation allowed Bunting to distinguish herself quickly, and within a year, she had been named chair. Bunting's involvement with this organization afforded her an additional avenue for investigating women's intellectual motivation and the utilization of female talent. It also focused her attention on understanding women's educational trajectories, how they differed from those of men, and what specific initiatives, such as continuing education and part-time study, might help sustain their intellectual momentum. Finally, it solidified her reputation as a leader in the field of women's education.

Bunting's membership on the Commission on the Education of Women coincided with another national appointment that would prove even more influential in her own intellectual development. In December 1957, not long after the second Soviet Sputnik, Bunting received an invitation to serve on the National Science Foundation's Divisional Committee for Scientific Personnel and Education. As the federal government geared up to allocate millions of dollars for expanding science and engineering education, the nine-member divisional committee found itself responsible for devising policies to ensure the maximum production of highly trained scientists, engineers, science teachers, and scientific workers. It carried out this task through various means, such as establishing summer programs for high school students, expanding the foundation's fellowship offerings, and compiling data on the country's scientific manpower supply.[106]

Bunting, who gravitated toward this kind of work, read over the available manpower reports with much interest. In doing so, she came across a study done for the President's Committee on Scientists and Engineers by Donald Bridgman, who had broken his data down by gender. What Bridgman's study revealed was that in the top 10 percent of high school graduates, women made up at least 90 percent of those not continuing to college.[107] Bunting remembers being surprised that this number was so high. But she remembers being even more surprised that her colleagues appeared unfazed. According to Bunting, "nobody on the Advisory Committee or the National Science Foundation staff proposed to do anything about this loss of talent. Nobody seemed to think it important." "They even seemed to wish to conceal the facts," she added, "as if they didn't want the country to know that almost all the bright males were continuing beyond high school."[108] Bunting was too baffled by this incident to respond right away. Instead, she mulled it over, replaying it in her mind. "The truth," she finally realized, "is that nobody values what women can do in the sciences, and therefore it doesn't seem of any importance in terms of scientific manpower if they don't go beyond high school." "If America knew that all the bright boys were going to college, no one would think there was a problem in the schools," she explained. But the same did not hold true for smart women, who "are not expected to do anything important later."[109]

Bunting relied on her own observations and conversations to make sense of this "waste" of female talent. Gradually, she began to formulate her theory about what she would later call "the climate of unexpectation" surrounding women's talents and training. Supported by a number of "hidden dissuaders," this phenomenon served to discourage women from academic success and limit their educational opportunities. Bunting suggested, for example, that the "climate of unexpectation" helped account for "why education didn't bother setting up part-time programs for married women, and why so few women bothered to go on in the sciences."[110] Although Bunting did not publicly use this phrase for several more years, the idea was brewing and was undoubtedly clarified through her involvement with both the National Science Foundation and the Commission on the Education of Women.

Back at Douglass, Bunting combined these interests and ideas in what would become one of the first educational programs designed for "mature" women: a mathematics retraining program for female college graduates. The program, which targeted housewives and other women who had "dropped out" of the paid labor force, reflected Bunting's overarching interest in encouraging women intellectually while accommodating their domestic duties. But in her conversations with the officials at the Ford Foundation, which agreed to sponsor the program in 1959, she emphasized instead their mutual interest in "utilizing" female brainpower.[111]

The initial phase of the program involved distributing a questionnaire to college-educated women residing within commuting distance of Douglass. The survey posed three questions: (1) Have you had two or more years of college mathematics?; (2) Would you be interested in taking a refresher course?; and (3) Would you be interested in obtaining full- or part-time work requiring mathematical training within the next four or five years? More than 600 women answered yes to all three questions. But when some of them failed to return the follow-up questionnaire, despite their reported interest, the project's staff contacted them to see what had happened. As

Bunting explained, "A surprising number of them had just gone ahead and found courses or even jobs of the kind we had suggested." "They didn't need a job or some program, just a prod," she continued. "But they did need to be brought together some, to have a place where they could go to get encouragement, and a little guidance. . . . They did need *that* sort of assistance very much."[112] Their responses, and the mathematics retraining program more generally, illuminated the importance of guidance, schooling, and work that allowed for the realities of women's lives. Bunting's program not only "tap[ped] a large reservoir of skill," as it had initially promised to do, but also tapped a desire among college-educated women for broader academic and occupational opportunities.[113]

Bunting realized, moreover, that the undervaluation of women's intellectual contributions was not limited to the sciences. Rather, it ran rampant in all areas of education and society. After five years at Douglass, Bunting assumed the presidency of Radcliffe College, where she embarked on another ambitious endeavor: the creation of the Radcliffe Institute for Independent Study. She envisioned the institute as a vehicle through which to counter the prevailing anti-intellectualism that restricted women's life choices, stunted their growth, and fostered "sheer frustration." The institute would serve as a haven for what Bunting called "intellectually displaced women" by providing them with stipends, workspace, and, above all, time to pursue academic projects of individual interest. Open primarily to women who had already earned advanced graduate degrees, the institute targeted two distinct audiences. The "associate scholars" component, which comprised the nucleus of the institute, aimed to support "gifted but not necessarily widely recognized women" whose careers had been interrupted by family responsibilities. While "associate scholar" awards were limited to women in the Boston area, the "resident fellows" component was open to women worldwide and sought to encourage the continued productivity of women who had already distinguished themselves in their fields.[114]

Clearly, the institute represented an attempt to provide a space where women's intellectual contributions would be valued and where the "climate of unexpectation" would fail to flourish. Likewise, the institute reflected Bunting's concern that American women were not reaching their personal potential and that something had to be done about it. But Bunting also justified the institute in terms of a wider societal need for "trained brainpower."[115] "The purpose of the institute," she explained, "is to assist able and educated women who wish to participate more effectively in the intellectual and social advances of our times. Too often in the past their talents have been ignored. This is a waste that can no longer be tolerated. . . . By opening up possibilities for achievement at the top, Radcliffe hopes to make a significant change in the climate affecting women's education and thus 'tap the vast reservoir of unused talent that lies hidden in the wasting educations of intellectually idle women.'"[116]

Bunting's announcement of the institute in November 1960 was well publicized and well received. Telephone calls and letters poured in from women all over the country. Educators expressed interest in starting similar programs at their institutions. The *New York Times* featured the program on its front page.[117] An editorial in *Newsday* predicted that Radcliffe's plan cannot "help but serve the best interests of the country."[118] And the *Harvard Crimson* proclaimed, "If the Institute for Independent Study is a success, it does not seem overly optimistic to prophesy that Radcliffe will have the honor of initiating a nationwide effort to salvage potentially effective women from intellectual stagnation and to use their talents for the benefit of all."[119]

By emphasizing women's dual roles, the Radcliffe Institute struck all the right notes in an era that clamored for womanpower while prizing American domesticity. Although it was not limited to women in science, it certainly benefited them and especially those who struggled to combine domestic and intellectual pursuits. The institute also expanded Bunting's national reputation. In May 1961, she was named the "Woman of the Year" in the field of education by *Who's Who of American Women*.[120] The following fall, she graced the cover of *Time*, which included a feature article on her. Shortly thereafter, she was appointed to the newly formed President's Commission on the Status of Women, which also drew on diffuse national security goals and manpower needs.

The President's Commission on the Status of Women

In December 1961, John F. Kennedy created the President's Commission on the Status of Women (PCSW) in response to pressure from several women's groups and his newly appointed director of the Women's Bureau and assistant secretary of labor, Esther Peterson. The executive order establishing the PCSW, which had been drafted by Peterson and Secretary of Labor Arthur Goldberg, announced that "it is in the national interest to promote the economy, security, and national defense through the most efficient and effective utilization and skills of all persons."[121]

Peterson and Kennedy had a long history and a shared interest in working-class issues. The Utah native and Brigham Young University alumna was introduced to the labor movement in 1929, when she enrolled as a graduate student at Columbia University's Teachers College. After earning her master's degree the following year, she taught at several schools for workers, including the innovative Bryn Mawr Summer School for Women Workers in Industry, and helped teachers to unionize in Massachusetts. She joined the Amalgamated Clothing Workers Union in 1939 and spent much of the following decade working as a labor lobbyist. It was in this capacity that she initially came into contact with Kennedy, who was then a young representative from Massachusetts. At the end of the 1940s, Peterson went abroad to Sweden and Belgium, where she became active in the international union movement. Upon returning to the United States in 1957, however, she refocused her attention on domestic politics and became a legislative representative in the Industrial Union Department of the AFL-CIO. She also resumed her relationship with Kennedy and strongly supported his bid for the presidency. Although a family illness forced her to turn down a full-time staff position with his campaign, she worked closely with Kennedy's advisors to ensure that he adequately addressed the concerns of labor. She was handsomely rewarded for her efforts when she became the highest-ranking woman in Kennedy's administration.[122]

Peterson was among the relatively few women who the newly elected president named to high-level posts. Despite the fact that women had helped Kennedy narrowly defeat Richard Nixon, he rewarded none of them with cabinet positions. Only Peterson and three others received Senate-confirmed appointments, while another dozen were named to minor or temporary posts. Disgruntled party women wasted little time in voicing their displeasure. The head of the National Woman's Party, Emma Guffey Miller, told Kennedy that "it is a grievous disappointment to the women leaders and ardent workers that so few women have been named to worthwhile positions. . . . As a woman of long political experience, I feel the situation has become serious and I hope whoever is responsible for it may be made to realize that the result may well be disastrous." The well-known journalist Doris Fleeson was even more succinct in her sneering when she wrote in her *New York Post* column, "At this stage, it appears that for women the New Frontiers are the old frontiers."[123]

Recognizing that his administration needed to express support for women in some way, Kennedy agreed to the creation of a commission on women. The idea, however, was hardly his own. For decades, various organizations had proposed federal task forces to examine opportunities for women. In 1948, the American Association of University Women asked

President Truman to form a committee for recommending ways to integrate women into the country's preparedness program. After being denied, the group tried again amid the Korean conflict but to no avail. A similar recommendation was included in the National Manpower Council's report on *Womanpower* that had been released in the spring of 1957. Although nothing came of it, the subject soon resurfaced after Kennedy's election. On Inauguration Day, the New York Business and Professional Women's Club wrote to Kennedy requesting that he create a panel to discuss the utilization of "mature" women. When the president sent along the suggestion to Peterson, she replied that a similar plan was already being considered. A coalition of pro-labor women with ties to Peterson had advocated for such a group as a means for sidestepping the contentious Equal Rights Amendment that was increasingly gaining support. Organized labor had long opposed the blanket legislation that would wipe out protective laws designed to prohibit the exploitation of women workers. Peterson shared this view and preferred instead "specific bills for specific ills."[124] Kennedy, who was similarly wary of the legislation, agreed that the creation of a commission would enable him not only to demonstrate interest in women's issues but also to avoid taking a stand on the Equal Rights Amendment. When publicly justifying this undertaking, however, Kennedy and his staff skillfully invoked Cold War concerns.[125]

Although Peterson had moved away from what historian Kathleen Laughlin calls "the womanpower focus" of her predecessor, Alice Leopold, it is evident that she did not dispense with it entirely. She did not sever Leopold's relationships with professional women's groups even as she worked to restore the bureau's traditional working-class base. Nor did she abandon Leopold's job placement initiatives, as they remained important to economic growth and the prospect of full employment. And while she seemed less interested in data collection than advocacy, she routinely invoked manpower statistics and the rhetoric that accompanied them, as is evident in the executive order creating the PCSW that she helped draft.[126]

Peterson's use of manpower rhetoric can also be seen in her addresses at meetings of professional women's groups and vocational conferences. In a speech that she gave in July 1961 to the National Federation of Business and Professional Women's Clubs, she remarked on the "unrealized potential of our modern American women" and criticized social conventions that deprived the country of women's capacities for scientific research. She also advocated flexibility in employment for professional women "whose talents are in such short supply" and explained that part-time work assignments would enable Americans "to make better use of the skills we should certainly need in our economy."[127] Similar themes surfaced throughout other speeches, including her keynote address at the Connecticut Valley Conference on the Employment Problems of Women, where she highlighted the country's need for women in scientific fields. The U.S. Department of Labor's press release covering the event provided the simple caption, "Womanpower—A Great Resource of Progress."[128]

Manpower concerns similarly informed the work of the PCSW, whose objective was to review the status of American women and make recommendations on how "to further enable women to develop their skills and to participate more fully in our Nation's domestic and international commitments."[129] The commission itself was chaired by Eleanor Roosevelt and consisted of twenty-six members. Among the eleven who came from the federal government were four members of Congress (two Republicans and two Democrats); the secretaries of the Departments of Commerce, Labor, Agriculture, and Health, Education, and Welfare; the attorney general; the chair of the Civil Service Commission; and Peterson, who also served as the commission's executive vice chairperson. The National Councils of Jewish Women, Catholic Women, and Negro Women sent delegates, as did the National Federation of Business and Professional Women's Clubs, the National Council of the Churches of Christ, the AFL-CIO, and the International Union of Electrical, Radio, and Machine Workers. Representing the world of higher education were Polly Bunting of Radcliffe College and Henry David, the president of the New School for Social Research. Significantly, David had also been the executive director of the National Manpower Council when it published *Womanpower*.[130]

The PCSW held its first meeting in February 1962 to discuss its principal task of preparing a report for the president. To carry out this assignment, the commission organized seven committees around key topics to be covered. These included civil and political rights, federal employment, private employment, protective labor legislation, social insurance and taxes, home and community, and education. Each committee was chaired by a member of the larger commission, and most included at least one additional PCSW member. The committees also consisted of external experts in each field, which enabled the commission to broaden support for its work among women's organizations.[131]

Even before the commission announced this plan, however, Sigma Delta Epsilon had expressed its support for the PCSW's aims. In January 1962, Ernestine Thurman, who was then the president-elect of the fraternity, wrote to President Kennedy, Esther Peterson, and Eleanor Roosevelt with a note of congratulations on the establishment of the commission. Thurman also offered Sigma Delta Epsilon's assistance and to share the fraternity's files. The following month, Katherine Ellickson, the executive secretary of the commission, contacted Sigma Delta Epsilon on behalf of Roosevelt and expressed hope that the fraternity would send a representative to an upcoming informational meeting of commission members and the heads of national women's organizations. Ellickson noted that she had been in touch with the fraternity's secretary, Betty McLaughlin, who was based in Washington, D.C. Because of the short notice, however, Sigma Delta Epsilon was unable to participate but designated Thurman and McLaughlin as delegates to any future meetings called by the commission.[132]

Meta Ellis, who had chaired the fraternity's Committee to Encourage Women to Enter Science, believed that Sigma Delta Epsilon should help the PCSW gather information about the status of female scientists. She corresponded frequently with Esther Peterson and, in June 1962, approached the fraternity's executive board with the suggestion that Sigma Delta Epsilon members write candid reports about the conditions faced by women in science. Ellis proposed that members discuss their personal experiences with pay and advancement opportunities at their respective places of employment. "Many of us would long to tell the story," she explained, "and yet we don't dare."[133] Instead of taking action, however, executive board members expressed concern that Ellis was acting in an official capacity without their permission. The officers then reminded Ellis that the fraternity had already offered its services to the commission and had named Thurman and McLaughlin as its formal representatives. In the end, collaboration between Sigma Delta Epsilon and the PCSW seems to have been limited and was not even acknowledged in the commission's final report, much to the chagrin of the fraternity's leaders.[134]

On the same day that she approached Sigma Delta Epsilon, Ellis made a similar request of the Society of Women Engineers. Although Ellis was not a member of the society at the time, she had recently applied to become one and would be accepted in July 1962.[135] She found that many of SWE's activities closely resembled the kind of outreach efforts that she had coordinated through Sigma Delta Epsilon. In the wake of the Soviet Sputniks, SWE had continued its vocational guidance activities, expanding its agenda to include continuing education and assisting married women in balancing domestic and professional responsibilities. The national society even agreed in 1958 to cooperate with the National Federation of Business and Professional

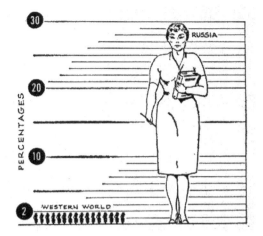

Society of Women Engineers promotional material comparing the percentage of women engineers in the Soviet Union and the percentage in Western nations, 1963. Courtesy of Society of Women Engineers National Records, Walter P. Reuther Library, Wayne State University.

Women's Clubs and other professional organizations in a study of intermittency in women's employment and how to help women between the ages of 35 and 55 reenter the labor force. Meanwhile, local sections addressed women's groups on such topics as the rewards of combining engineering employment and domestic life. Another example of SWE's broadened interests can be seen in the decision to modify the society's formal objectives, as outlined in its bylaws, to include "assist[ing] women engineers in readying themselves for a return to active work after temporary retirement to raise families."[136]

SWE members also advocated continuing education and reentry programs, as well as vocational guidance and general encouragement, through its ongoing collaboration with the federal government. In March 1960, the society was contacted by William G. Torpey of the recently reorganized Office of Civil and Defense Mobilization requesting SWE's participation in a series of nationwide "how to do it conferences" on the efficient utilization of scientific personnel. The society eagerly agreed and arranged to send former SWE president Beatrice Hicks and two other representatives to the upcoming one at the University of Arkansas. Although the conference was relatively small, it included some of the top educators, industrialists, and engineers in the state and allowed for much discussion and interaction. Hicks reported favorably on her experience, explaining that "I feel we had an excellent opportunity to tell them of the importance of educating more women in the engineering field and that they will in turn carry on work in their state toward implementing the specific moves necessary to promote this."[137]

SWE also agreed to help Torpey organize a "utilization" conference at the University of Pittsburgh in April 1962. Cosponsored by the university and SWE, the "Women in Professional Engineering" conference was held under the auspices of the Executive Office of the President of the United States. In line with SWE's interests and goals, most program speakers highlighted the shortage of scientific manpower and emphasized the need to encourage, recruit, and retain female engineers. Even Donald Feight, a manager in the industrial relations department of United States Steel Corporation who admitted up front that "I don't like women too well," concluded his address by acknowledging the importance of educating more female engineers in light of expanding opportunities in the space industry, research, and consulting work.[138]

SWE stressed similar manpower concerns in its interaction with industry, whose support it increasingly cultivated. One new initiative was the creation of "corporate memberships," which allowed firms to help fund SWE's scientific womanpower programs. In 1961, SWE proudly announced that two defense contractors, Bell Laboratories and General Electric, had become SWE's first corporate members.[139] Another example of SWE's collaboration with industry can be seen in the First International Women's Space Symposium that it cosponsored, along with twenty-seven other organizations, in February 1962 in Los Angeles. Underwritten by industrial firms, the conference drew over 100 high school girls and their teachers. The event featured addresses by SWE members, such as Beatrice Hicks, as well as representatives from NASA and the United States Air Force. The recent Soviet feat was a prominent theme, as was the idea that expanding women's representation in science would help the United States get ahead in the space race. But SWE and the other sponsoring organizations were careful to distinguish American women from their Soviet counterparts. Thus, while they arranged for the conference luncheon to include a speech by Jerrie Cobb, the first woman to pass the astronaut flight test, they also squeezed in a presentation by Edith Head, the costume director for Paramount Studios, who discussed women's space fashions. Head shared sketches of styles based on technical requirements, which included a shoulder bag designed to hold oxygen and power packs, a walking stick with radio equipment, and a reversible cape for extreme weather. She also designed a gray pressurized suit with bright red accessories, explaining that women should look attractive in space.[140] Like so many of SWE's efforts, this event sought to convey an urgent need for scientifically trained women while at the same time providing some reassurance that they could maintain their femininity.[141]

It was SWE's broader desire to expand education and employment opportunities for women that most interested Meta Ellis and sparked her suggestion that the society collaborate with the PCSW. The SWE executive board, however, vehemently disagreed with her proposal to have members submit reports exposing the discrimination that they faced in their careers. Vice President Aileen Cavanagh felt that Ellis's plan would "reduce ourselves to a bunch of anonymous tattle-tales."[142] SWE president Patricia Brown agreed with Cavanagh and suggested instead "documenting the diametrically opposed viewpoint—that of those women who have attained equal status."[143] Other board members concurred and decided that any communication with the PCSW should emphasize the positive side of engineering as a field for women. In explaining the board's decision to Ellis, Brown wrote, "Please don't think we are putting our heads in the sand; we recognize that there are many who are discriminated against. But we feel we would do more harm than good by an organized effort to report the viewpoints of women engineers who have not attained equal status." In other words, "We find it impossible to justify our dedication to encouraging young women to consider engineering as a career—which is our primary purpose—while at the same time conducting a Society-wide survey of discriminatory practices. In this case, we feel that it is best to 'let somebody else do it.'"[144] While some SWE members expressed annoyance that the society was not represented on the PCSW and believed that SWE had much to contribute to the commission, the society's steadfast refusal to document discrimination hindered closer collaboration between the two groups.

Much more involved with the PCSW was Polly Bunting, who was not only a member of the commission but also the chair of its Committee on Education.[145] The fifteen-member group included educators, policymakers, and representatives of women's organizations. Most, like Bunting, were particularly interested in college-educated women and their lives after graduation. Esther Raushenbush and Virginia Senders, for example, had pioneered continuing education programs at Sarah Lawrence College and the University of Minnesota, respectively. They found that many of their concerns regarding the education and employment trajectories of American women informed their work with the PCSW committee.[146]

At the committee's first meeting in May 1962, Bunting engaged members in a discussion of their views on the subject of women's education and what directions the committee should take. Bunting set the tone for much of the group's activities when she said the key issue was no longer making available to women what men had but rather looking at the needs of women that might be different.[147] The group then discussed a number of precirculated questions probing how and why women's social roles affected their educational experiences. Touching on the womanpower theme, members also helped identify "what social needs exist in our country which can be met by the skills of women properly trained and educated."[148] Although feminine fields such as nursing, social work, teaching, and library science received the most attention, the group raised familiar concerns about the waste of female intellect at all levels.

Threaded throughout the group's discussion was the importance of vocational guidance. One member, Agnes Meyer, expressed alarm that "the high school boys that were bright were taking English, mathematics, physics, and so on, but the girls who were as bright or even brighter were letting themselves off with home economics and tap dancing, or what not."[149] She especially faulted counselors for discouraging women from entering fields that seemed unfeminine. Several other members directed attention to the need for adequate guidance for "mature" women through continuing education. Additional concerns included women's homemaking roles, their responsibilities in their communities, and what one member termed "the problem of suburbia." The committee agreed to solicit background papers on as many of these topics as possible to assist it in its work.[150]

The committee's final report to the PCSW, which it submitted in March 1963, drew heavily on these themes. Vocational guidance enjoyed a prominent place in the committee's recommendations, as did continuing education. Flexibility in scheduling, the provision of financial aid, funding for day care, and even family planning (disguised as "education for family responsibility") were also included.[151] So was "vocational training adapted to the nation's growing requirement for skilled and highly educated manpower," reflecting the needs of the diffuse national security state.[152] But in its recommendations for expanding women's participation at all levels of education, the group also reaffirmed the importance of women's roles as wives and mothers. As the committee explained in its final report, "Widening the choices for women to contribute to the world beyond the doorstep does not imply neglect of their education for responsibilities in the home."[153] As Bunting had signaled at the committee's first meeting, she was less interested in challenging traditional gender roles than devising educational opportunities that fit the contours of women's lives. Her committee's recommendations, then, sought to accommodate rather than undermine American women's domestic duties in the Cold War world.

The PCSW's final report, *American Women*, which was delivered to President Kennedy in October 1963, similarly balanced the commission's interest in improving the condition of women with Cold War concerns. In its discussion of employment, the commission documented discrimination in hiring and promotion practices and called for an executive order in support of equal opportunity. It also advocated the increased use of part-time work assignments and the expansion of child care facilities. Additionally, the commission promoted protective labor legislation and the enactment of laws to ensure equal pay for comparable work. Many of these initiatives, the PCSW reasoned, would assist the country's manpower needs by promoting the utilization of women workers.[154] But at the same time that it urged greater opportunities for women, the commission left traditional gender roles largely intact. Predictably, the PCSW chose not to endorse the Equal Rights Amendment, due to the majority opinion that "constitutional changes need not now be sought."[155] While this decision stemmed mainly from the group's desire to uphold protective labor legislation and to seek protections under the Fourteenth Amendment instead, it also reflected some members' concern with the ERA's potential impact on family life.[156] The persistence of gender roles can be seen in other discussions as well, such as the recommendation by the Committee on Civil and Political Rights that husbands should continue to bear the primary responsibility for family support in light of women's childbearing and homemaking duties. Meanwhile, the Committee on Home and Community said that it was "regrettable" when economic necessity forced women with young children to work outside of the home.[157] More generally, the commission reaffirmed "the fundamental responsibility of mothers and homemakers and society's stake in strong family life."[158]

In the context of the Cold War, the PCSW carefully avoided berating women's roles within the home and family. Commission members, along with the other technocratic feminists discussed in this chapter, rarely questioned the responsibilities of mothers and wives. At the same time, however, they refused to limit women to those roles, and they criticized the forces that did. Their overarching message that much of the United States' womanpower was wasted resonated widely in the aftermath of the Sputnik scare. The international crisis not only bolstered their claims but also enlarged their base. Throughout the late 1950s and early 1960s, a growing number of technocratic feminists sought to expand educational and professional opportunities for women in both science and society. Carrying on the efforts of earlier reformers, they worked to provide personal encouragement to young women, improve vocational guidance, and change public perceptions regarding science as a field for women. Gradually, they extended their focus to assisting older women and married women with children in balancing scientific careers with family responsibilities. By calling attention to the complexities of women's lives, they also illuminated the frustrations that many faced. Ultimately, they raised questions as well as expectations that would soon take center stage with the second wave of American feminism.

CHAPTER FOUR

Science and the Second Wave

In October 1964, the Association of Women Students of the Massachusetts Institute of Technology sponsored a two-day symposium on American women in science and engineering. While "[a] conference at MIT on science and engineering is hardly a novelty," quipped the institute's president, Julius Stratton, "a symposium about women, on a campus . . . thought to be a man's preserve, may well have appeared . . . as something remarkable."[1] This observation was confirmed by the nearly 900 participants, whose attendance well surpassed the expectations of the planning committee. Initially conceived as a local gathering to discuss the career problems of MIT "coeds," the symposium drew 260 student delegates from 140 colleges, as well as 600 college deans, guidance counselors, scientists, high school students, and members of the Cambridge community. As the guest list expanded, so did the organizers' objectives. According to conference chair and MIT senior Carol Van Aken, what began as a "modest informational effort" quickly became a major investigation of scientific careers for women.[2]

The goals of the symposium, as outlined by Van Aken, were threefold. First, organizers aimed to acquaint female students with the myths and realities surrounding scientific work for women in the hope of encouraging them in these fields. Second, they sought to reveal to employers and educators some of the concerns harbored by female students and to stimulate shared solutions. Finally, organizers wished "to attract the favorable attention of industry, other educational institutions, and the public at large . . . to the desirability of decreasing the present barriers that now prevent maximum utilization of the abilities of qualified women."[3]

This interest in expanding opportunities for women in science by drawing on broader manpower concerns was well-worn territory for many program speakers, such as Polly Bunting and Lillian Gilbreth, who continued to be active in professional circles at the age of eighty-six. Other panelists, such as Mina Rees, who had worked at the Office of Scientific Research and Development during World War II and at the Office of Naval Research in the immediate postwar period, echoed this language as well. In her current position as dean of graduate studies at the City University of New York, Rees expressed a desire to encourage female mathematicians "particularly in view of the shortage" and mentioned how, to this end, she had made financial aid for child care available to her female students.[4] Columbia University physicist Chien-Shiung Wu adopted a similar approach in her remarks urging the acceptance of female scientists more generally. The Chinese-born wife and mother had completed her Ph.D. at Berkeley in 1940 before joining the Manhattan Project at Columbia in 1944. After the war, she stayed on at Columbia as part of a three-person research team that in 1956 shattered the principle of parity conservation. The two men on the team won the Nobel Prize for this achievement, while Wu was passed over. At the MIT symposium, she called for recognition of women's scientific abilities and pointed out the irony that "in a time when we cry for the lack of manpower in science and technology, we find that women's enrollment in science remains low and women employed in the field of science are still few." Wu, who was a contemporary of Virginia Gildersleeve, evidently shared her disdain for the "terrible waste of potential talent" arising from the marginalization and mistreatment of female scientists.[5]

Although many speakers highlighted "manpower" issues, some embraced more explicitly feminist language, thus signaling an important shift. The clearest example of this development was a presentation by sociologist Alice S. Rossi, who gave a meticulously documented paper on the barriers to women's scientific participation. While Rossi's extensive research on sex roles and occupational choice provided most of her evidence, her broader interest in these subjects came from personal experience. After completing her Ph.D. at Columbia in 1957, she combined raising three young children with a series of lectureships and research associate positions at the University of Chicago, where her husband taught sociology and directed the National Opinion Research Center. Although her nonfaculty status did not bother her initially, her outlook changed in the early 1960s when a male faculty member deliberately exploited her situation. Because university regulations prohibited research associates from submitting grant proposals in their own names, Rossi enlisted his support in applying to the National Science Foundation for funding. After the grant was awarded, he tried to keep the money for himself and fired her from the project. Outraged, she embarked on several large-scale investigations of sex roles and inequality and quickly became an authority on the topic. One of her earliest and best-known essays was her "Equality between the Sexes: An Immodest Proposal" that was published in the spring 1964 issue of *Daedalus*. Rossi's "proposal," which called for the obliteration of narrowly defined sex roles,

Attendees at the MIT Symposium on American Women in Science and
Engineering, 1964. Courtesy of MIT Museum.

more-involved parenting from fathers, the expansion of child care facilities, and the replacement of suburban homes with apartment buildings
in close proximity to both parents' work, caused quite a stir. Not only was
she charged with being a "monster," an "unfit mother," and an "unnatural
woman," but her husband even received an anonymous condolence card
for the "loss" of his wife.[6]

At the MIT symposium held that following fall, Rossi elaborated on
the themes contained in her provocative proposal. Focusing this time on
women and science, she lambasted male privilege and the notion "that
woman's role should be selfless, dedicated to being man's helpmeet, and
any work or career on the part of women should fill in the gaps of time and
energy left over from their primary obligations as wives and mothers."[7] She
also remarked on what she regarded as widespread agreement on the need
to encourage women in scientific fields and extricated the various factors
contributing to this push. Although she acknowledged a "national interest
in manpower utilization," she maintained that other reasons, such as the
pursuit of "individual personal satisfaction" and "a radical transformation
of the relations between the sexes," were equally important.[8]

Rossi's comment reflects the growing tension between technocratic
feminism and bolder claims to women's equality. As the 1960s and 1970s

wore on, blatant critiques such as Rossi's gradually edged out older, more conservative appeals. This development was made possible, in large part, by the recent emergence of second-wave feminism and broad-based support for women's rights. Discontent with the war in Vietnam, critiques of militarized science, and shifts in federal R&D priorities contributed further to this change. The activities of established women's societies as well as newly formed groups reflect these various phenomena, as many adopted openly feminist arguments in place of national security manpower concerns. At the same time, however, both old and new groups carried forward earlier feminist efforts to expand women's participation in scientific fields. Important continuities can be viewed not only in their identification of cultural barriers, advocacy of vocational guidance, and interest in balancing women's multiple roles but also in their periodic embrace of technocratic feminism.

Social Unrest Spreads

The early 1960s saw an upsurge of interest in women's issues and a renewed commitment to feminist activism. Despite its shortcomings, the President's Commission on the Status of Women had brought together hundreds of reformers and documented the inequities faced by women workers. It also spurred the creation of state commissions on the status of women, which would sprout up in every state but one by 1967.[9] The plight of white middle-class women received additional attention in Betty Friedan's *The Feminine Mystique* when it appeared with a splash in February 1963. Friedan's survey of her Smith College classmates revealed that many suffered from a malaise that she termed "the problem that has no name." An instant bestseller, Friedan's exposé of white suburbia struck a chord with countless women who identified themselves in its pages and were mobilized to action.[10]

Feminist concerns also made their way into the law, although with mixed results. Championed by the Women's Bureau and strongly supported by the United Auto Workers and other labor unions, the Equal Pay Act was passed by Congress in 1963. Within the first ten years of the act's enforcement, 171,000 employees were awarded $84 million in back pay alone. Although the original bill proposed equal pay for comparable work, the final version only mandated equal pay for the same work. This concession was a blow to those women employed in feminized sectors of the economy, where they seldom held the same jobs as men. The fact that the law did not include women in professional or administrative fields until it was amended in 1972 also restricted its reach.[11]

Another important legislative measure was the monumental Civil Rights Act of 1964. A key feature of the legislation, Title VII, prohibited discrimination in employment on the basis of not only race, color, religion, and national origin but also sex. Additionally, the act created a new agency, the Equal Employment Opportunity Commission, or EEOC, which was responsible for investigating relevant complaints. The commission was soon inundated with grievances from women across the country. Few, however, were taken seriously or found their complaints resolved satisfactorily. Early EEOC directors expressed little interest in sex-based discrimination, and most approached the subject with either boredom or hostility. The idea of enforcing the sex provision was also lampooned in the media. When the question of whether Playboy clubs would have to hire men was raised at the White House Conference on Equal Opportunity held in August 1965, the press quickly dubbed Title VII the "Bunny Law" and subjected it to much ridicule. The seriousness of the act was also called into question when the commission ruled that sex-segregated employment ads were legal. That Title VII did not apply initially to educational institutions further limited its effectiveness.[12]

The lack of serious attention to outlawing sex-based discrimination became a source of frustration for a growing number of women, including Betty Friedan, who had begun writing a new book on the subject. When her contacts in Washington invited her to attend the third national conference of state commissions on the status of women in June 1966, she took the opportunity to sound out participants. She held a small meeting in her hotel room, where twenty-eight women gathered to address problems with the EEOC and decided to offer a resolution at the conference the next day. When conference officials rejected this idea, the group hastily reconvened at lunch and decided to form the National Organization for Women, or NOW.[13]

In October 1966, NOW held its inaugural conference. The event drew to Washington, D.C., roughly two dozen professional women, including Alice Rossi, as well as a handful of sympathetic men. There, the group adopted its statement of purpose, which made clear its intent "to take action to bring women into full participation in the mainstream of American society now, exercising all the privileges and responsibilities thereof in truly equal partnership with men."[14] To that end, NOW called for equality not only in employment but also in education, policymaking positions, media representations, and domestic life. Membership in NOW grew quickly, from roughly 1,000 members in fourteen chapters in 1967 to approximately 40,000 members in 700 chapters in 1974, making it the largest feminist group in the United States.[15] Throughout the late 1960s and 1970s, NOW threw its energies into such activities as lobbying for the Equal Rights Amendment, working to repeal restrictive abortion statutes, advocating for child care centers, and filing class action lawsuits on behalf of women workers.[16]

Some NOW members, however, were concerned that the organization's broad agenda, stance on abortion, and militant tone would scare away potential supporters. Consequently, they left NOW to form the Women's Equity Action League (WEAL) in 1968. Although WEAL identified as a feminist organization and employed explicitly feminist language, it focused more narrowly on sex-based discrimination in education, employment, and tax law.[17]

While members of WEAL viewed NOW as too radical, many students and young women with ties to the Left, civil rights, and other social movements viewed NOW as not radical enough. Gradually, they gathered in their local communities and, by the end of 1967, had formed women's liberation groups in several cities across the country. In consciousness-raising, or rap, sessions, members drew on their personal experiences to identify broader patterns of sexism and to brainstorm solutions to shared problems. In doing so, they developed what they called "sexual politics" or "personal politics" to challenge male domination in both their private lives and the public world. Their organizing experience and campus activism informed their view of sexism as inextricably linked to American capitalism, imperialism, and racism. While some radical women would lend their support to the struggle for the ERA or the campaign for reproductive rights, most set their sights on changes that were even more sweeping.[18]

In the summer of 1970, feminists of various ages, backgrounds, and ideologies temporarily set aside their differences and came together for the first mass demonstration of second-wave feminism, the Women's Strike for Equality. Called by NOW, the strike commemorated the fiftieth anniversary of the woman suffrage amendment and mobilized tens of thousands of feminists across the country. Women marched, picketed, and protested in droves. In Boston, feminists distributed contraceptive foam on the commons and whistled at construction workers. Feminists in Rochester, New York, smashed teacups to protest women's underrepresentation in government. Others gathered in Dayton, Ohio, to hear welfare women and hospital union workers. In the District of Columbia, women staged a teach-in at the *Washington Post*. These demonstrations made clear to both antagonists and potential converts that feminism was a viable, influential, and broad-based movement.[19]

This upsurge of feminist activism took place amid the broader tumult of the 1960s and early 1970s. Frustration with the slow pace of change accelerated the struggle for African American civil rights. The assassination of Martin Luther King Jr. in April 1968 devastated hopes for a non-violent movement leading to a truly integrated society. In wake of King's death came some of the worst race riots in American history, an increased emphasis on black militancy, and the intensification of white backlash.[20] Meanwhile, student activists sought to challenge the status quo, both on campus and beyond. The fall of 1964 saw the beginning of the Free Speech Movement at Berkeley, when students protested the administration's efforts to restrict their political activities. Many had become disillusioned with the impersonal nature of the "mega-versity," which even distributed computerized punch cards to keep track of them. President Clark Kerr's description of the school as being part of "the knowledge industry" was accurate, given its status as the seventh largest university defense contractor. But it was also a source of irritation for many students, who viewed the corporatization of the university as divorced from their pursuit of wisdom and personal growth.[21] Similar discontents plagued college campuses nationwide. In 1968, just weeks after King's assassination, Columbia students protested the university's involvement in defense research and its plans to build a gymnasium in the predominantly black neighborhood of Morningside Park. The resulting occupation of school buildings, which lasted more than a week and ended with the arrest of hundreds of students, became one of the largest and longest student rebellions ever to take place at a major university, and the first at an Ivy League school.[22]

Much of the students' frustrations stemmed from the United States' involvement in the war in Vietnam. Initially, U.S. interest in influencing the outcome of Vietnam's civil war raised few eyebrows, as it seemed largely consistent with broader American efforts to contain communism. But as American military commitments increased and death tolls rose, so did discontent with American foreign policy and national security prerogatives. President Lyndon Johnson's behind-the-scenes decisions to commit additional troops there and to "Americanize" the conflict—despite his public claims that he had no intention of doing so—elicited charges of deception and a sense that he had tricked the nation into fighting a full-scale war with no end in sight.[23]

Rather than depend on the government or mass media for information about the war, professors, instructors, and students came together in March 1965 for a "teach-in" at the University of Michigan. Several thousand students and faculty participated in the event, which encouraged them to question authority and act in accordance with their beliefs. By the end of the year, similar demonstrations had taken place at some 120 colleges and universities. Antiwar protests erupted off campus as well. The largest one to date was held in April on the grounds of the Washington Monument. Organized by Students for a Democratic Society, the event drew more than 15,000 participants and established the growing antiwar movement as a force to be reckoned with. By 1968, antiwar protests were what historian David Farber describes as "the most organized and active component of a fervent student movement that involved millions of young people."[24]

The mass participation of young people in these protests was made possible, in part, by demographic changes. Students attending college during the mid to late 1960s were products of the post–World War II "baby boom" and swelled enrollments accordingly. Between 1950 and 1968, college enrollments jumped from roughly 2 million to approximately 7 million.[25] National security manpower initiatives, which had helped finance the education of hundreds of thousands of students, also facilitated the rise in college enrollments. By the mid-1960s, roughly 600,000 undergraduates had received federal loans through the National Defense Education Act, while 8,500 graduate students had claimed scholarships.[26] For much of the decade, graduate students and faculty continued to benefit from funding provided by such federal agencies as the National Science Foundation, the Department of Defense, the Atomic Energy Commission, and the National Institutes of Health. As the war in Vietnam escalated and the antiwar movement gained momentum, however, some turned against the very defense matrix of which they had become a part.

The antiwar movement brought to the fore a critique of what President Dwight Eisenhower most memorably termed the "military-industrial complex" in his 1961 farewell address. Eisenhower used the phrase to signal the close collaboration of military and corporate interests in determining national policy goals as well as their creeping and unwarranted influence.[27] In the context of the Vietnam War, students, scientists, and the public alike grew increasingly suspicious of the web of power relations and immense national security apparatus that Eisenhower had cautioned against. In 1967, Senator J. William Fulbright, a vocal opponent of the war in Vietnam, expanded the formulation to include higher education when he denounced the "military-industrial-academic complex."[28] Of particular concern to Fulbright and a growing number of observers was the fear that institutions of higher education had been reduced to mere appendages of the government and war machine.

The reliance of both universities and science on military monies seemed to offer evidence of complicity. While many scientists remained silent on the subject, some grew increasingly critical of the militarization of American science that had been under way for more than two decades. In March 1969, forty-eight faculty members at MIT signed a statement urging their colleagues to shift their research away from military technology and toward subjects aimed at solving environmental and social problems. Their protest was part of a larger "research strike" that they had called to raise awareness of the uses and abuses of science. Although most MIT students and faculty spent the day in their classrooms and laboratories as usual, and a few even organized a "work-in" as a counterprotest, the event attracted much attention and fueled debate over the relationship between science and the state. The press lauded the organizers for their efforts, and sympathizers at more than two dozen institutions of higher education announced similar plans.[29]

The concerns raised by the strike, along with antiwar sentiment more generally, affected national science priorities as well. Environmental, energy, and health research gradually commanded a larger fraction of federal research and development expenditures, whereas the share claimed by defense-related research declined steadily. This shift was due, in part, to the impact of the 1969 Mansfield Amendment, introduced by Senator Mike Mansfield (D-Montana), who was eager to decrease the military's influence on academic life. The provision, which was attached to a military authorization bill, prohibited the Department of Defense from financing research that was not directly tied to a specific military purpose. Although the amendment was dropped the following year, its effects and the concerns that had inspired it were longer lasting. Consequently, Department of Defense allocations to universities for basic research dropped steadily and by 1975 had reached 45 percent of what they had been just eight years earlier.[30]

Underlying these developments was a shift in national security prerogatives. When Richard Nixon assumed the presidency in 1969, he unleashed his "secret plan" for ending America's involvement in the Vietnam War by gradually withdrawing American troops and building up South Vietnam's military strength. Despite his staunch anti-Communist credentials, Nixon was also a realist who recognized that the war could not be won and that international stability was preferable to constant conflict. His goal was not to curb American influence or national security commitments but rather to prune them of what historian Michael Sherry calls "their most dangerous, costly, or politically onerous elements."[31] What this meant, according to Sherry, was that "the Cold War would still be waged, but with more focus on key allies and less on peripheral issues beyond the reach of American power," that "the weapons race would continue, but with arms agreements to make it more palatable, predictable, and amenable to American technological superiority," and that "the power would remain to uphold American economic might, but modified by rising competitors."[32] Consequently, the economic dimensions of national security became increasingly important and a key determinant of America's place and stake in the world. These goals also informed Nixon's efforts to open trade relations with China and pursue détente with the Soviet Union.[33]

With the resulting thaw in the Cold War, one group of observers remarked in 1971, "The military and political competition remains a constant spur to technical progress but is now a long-distance race and not a sprint."[34] Federal research and development expenditures, which had exploded by nearly 425 percent between 1953 and 1967, declined accordingly and continued the slowdown that had begun during the Vietnam conflict. When measured in constant dollars, this development was particularly dramatic: by the mid-1970s, the federal R&D budget had fallen by 20 percent when compared with 1967.[35]

As budgets contracted, so did anxieties about scientific shortages which were now replaced by new fears of a scientific surplus. Cold War manpower initiatives, it seemed, had produced an oversupply of Ph.D.s and a glut on the market. In 1969–70, the number of scientists and engineers on the federal payroll dropped slightly for the first time since the National Science Foundation began keeping count in 1954.[36] By the spring of 1970, the job situation had grown so severe that the American Institute of Physics announced a state of emergency. At scientific conferences across the country, leading manpower experts announced that the "talent hunt" was clearly over and would likely remain that way for two decades.[37]

Ironically, these concerns began circulating just as other developments promised to make possible the greater "utilization" of women. In 1967, under pressure from NOW, President Lyndon Johnson amended Executive Order 11246 to include sex. The revised document, Executive Order 11375, required that federal contractors not only refrain from discrimination in employment but also take "affirmative action" to ensure compliance.[38] Five years later, Title IX of the Education Amendments Act of 1972 was passed, prohibiting sex-based discrimination in schools receiving federal assistance. While best known for its impact on women's sports, Title IX more broadly paved the way for women to enter academic institutions and programs that had previously been off-limits. By the end of the decade, their overall collegiate enrollment would finally catch up with men's. The year 1972 also saw the Equal Rights Amendment pass Congress and begin what many assumed would be a quick ratification process.[39]

In this changed climate, technocratic feminism no longer held the same allure. Tethering feminist causes to an increasingly unpopular national security state seemed neither necessary nor desirable. Nor did most contemporary manpower assessments, which now warned of surpluses instead of shortages, support such an approach. The emergence of second-wave feminism, as well as new legal mechanisms for eliminating sex-based discrimination in education and employment, emboldened reformers who had previously shied away from anything resembling militancy. They were joined by new recruits to the feminist movement, who swelled the ranks of established women's organizations and helped redefine their image. New organizations for women in science also proliferated, drawing in older technocratic feminists, middle-aged professional women who had recently found their feminist calling, as well as students who had come of age amid the tumultuous 1960s and early 1970s.

The result was a curious blend of old and new initiatives. Even as second-wave activists worked to reap the benefits of recent legislation, lobby on behalf of feminist issues, and forge alliances with one another, they carried forward many of the same critiques already under way. Of particular concern were the persistent cultural attitudes and social conventions limiting women's participation in scientific fields. Second-wave activists also proposed many familiar solutions such as sponsoring career days, helping women balance professional and domestic life, and working to recast scientific careers as suitable ones for women. Furthermore, they occasionally resorted to technocratic feminism when it seemed advantageous to do so.

It is quite likely that these feminists had taken a page out of earlier activists' book. In the spring of 1970, Sigma Delta Epsilon member Margaret Stone observed that, at the most recent American Association for the Advancement of Science meeting, copies of the proceedings of the 1964 women and science symposium at MIT "were going as fast as though [they] were fresh off the press." The edited volume, entitled *Women and the Scientific Professions*, Stone acknowledged, "did not make the best seller list like Betty Friedan's *The Feminine Mystique*, but is far more valuable to women in science."[40] Although Alice Rossi's paper was the centerpiece of the collection, the addresses by older women such as Polly Bunting, Mina Rees, and Chien-Shiung Wu also resonated. Their identification of differential sex role socialization, education and work patterns that failed to accommodate the realities of women's lives, and various forms of discouragement remained both timely and pertinent. In the context of renewed feminist activism, however, "womanpower" had acquired a new meaning.

Established Societies Adopt a New Emphasis

Among the guests in attendance at the 1964 MIT symposium was Yvonne Clark, one of the few African American members of the Society of Women Engineers and the one who had been refused lodging at the 1957 SWE national conference in Houston. Although minority women remained a small fraction of both female scientists and women's scientific societies, the MIT organizers made a special effort to recruit women of color, contacting both government agencies and university administrators for help in identifying interested individuals. Clark was one of three black women representing Tennessee A&I State University, where she taught engineering at the time.[41]

Just months before the symposium took place, *Ebony* ran an article on Clark, who was described as a "35-year-old teacher-housewife."[42] She was lauded for her ability to combine her various interests in engineering, government consulting work, and domestic duties without a hint of difficulty. While she did admit that some male engineers seemed to resent having female colleagues, she was careful to note that this initial resistance "usually wears off."[43] Clark's downplaying of obstacles was typical of SWE's efforts to encourage women to enter the profession. A more candid picture of Clark emerged a few years later, however. In July 1973, *Mechanical Engineering* featured Clark in an article on women in the field. There, Clark discussed various challenges that she had faced in her life. Growing up in Kentucky, she attended an all-black high school. Because she was female, however, she was not allowed to take mechanical drawing. Reflecting on this experience, she said, "All of the myths about women not having heads for figures and being emotional scatterbrains are just that—myths. Women engineers do a good job, just as good as men. We're qualified and competent. It's not a man's field, and there's no reason we shouldn't be equal."[44] She also described her experience on the job market after graduating from Howard University as the first woman in the school's history to earn a B.S. in mechanical engineering. She quickly found that a female engineer "has to be twice as good to get hired, and being black just compounds the problem."[45]

Clark's frank tone was echoed by other SWE members featured in the same *Mechanical Engineering* spread. Eileen Duignan-Woods, a 1970 graduate of the Illinois Institute of Technology in Chicago, had spent more than a decade taking night classes and working her way through school. She first joined SWE in 1958 and was active in other organizations as well, such as the Equal Opportunity Committee of the American Society of Mechanical Engineers.[46] These experiences likely heightened her awareness of sex-based discrimination, which she discussed in her interview with *Mechanical Engineering*. She recalled being refused job interviews on account of her sex and admitted to being "somewhat bitter" about the situation. She also pointed to persistent prejudice against female engineers and observed that "it's nonsense to say that opportunities for women are 'unlimited' just because some brilliant young woman, loaded down with honors, gets a few good job offers upon graduation."[47] Duignan-Woods's comments made obvious that while women could succeed in engineering, more proactive measures were needed in order to ensure equality with men.

The willingness of both Duignan-Woods and Clark to discuss the status of women engineers by using the language of rights rather than of national security reflected a broader change taking place within SWE as a whole. Influenced by the women's movement, SWE increasingly embraced an explicitly feminist approach. Some sections assisted the state commissions on the status of women that had popped up across the country. One member, Jeanne Brodie, served on the one in Ohio, where she also chaired its Research Committee on Employment Practices.[48] Other sections began collaborating with feminist groups in their areas. Around 1968, SWE's Chicago section initiated contact with the local chapter of NOW in hopes of getting assistance with its Professional Guidance and Education program. This took place in the wake of an incident where one of its members was kicked out of a professional meeting held at the men's-only Chicago Engineers Club. The SWE group was delighted by the support that it received from NOW, and four of its members immediately joined. They recalled that through their involvement with NOW, "We learned about women's problems, women's rights (mostly lack of them) that we hadn't even realized. . . . We (in SWE) began to look at each other differently." In other words, "We had had our 'consciousness raised.'"[49]

SWE's new direction can also be seen in its open support for the Equal Rights Amendment, which had long been a source of contention in the organization. During the late 1950s and early 1960s, several individual members had urged the society to support the legislation, but with little success. The conservative climate of the early Cold War era as well as concerns about the society's tax-exempt status had prohibited any group action. In 1973, however, SWE decided that the society's tax status was not, in fact, at stake and went on record endorsing the amendment. In June of that year, SWE's national council of section representatives passed a resolution expressing its support for the ERA and urging state representatives to ratify it. Remarking on this move, SWE president Naomi McAfee (1972–74) explained that the society "has begun to stop being afraid to take a stand on those things in which it believes."[50]

This action helped bring SWE to the attention of feminist leaders, such as the feisty congresswoman Bella Abzug, who invited the society to participate in the 1977 National Women's Conference in Houston. SWE president Arminta Harness (1976–78) remarked that she was initially surprised by the invitation to serve as a delegate-at-large "because the Society of Women Engineers has not exactly been in the forefront of the women's movement." But she was also pleased by the recognition that it conferred.[51] The event, which was subsidized by Congress, was highly publicized and nationally televised. To build excitement, it was preceded by a fifty-one-day torch relay beginning in Seneca Falls, home of the first women's rights convention in 1848, and ending at the conference site. With much fanfare, the torch was finally passed to the three first ladies, Rosalynn Carter, Betty Ford, and Lady Bird Johnson, who presided over the opening ceremonies. The conference itself drew 2,000 delegates and more than 15,000 spectators from nearly every age, race, ethnic group, and walk of life. Doctors and welfare mothers, lawyers and farmers, housewives and nuns were all in attendance.[52] The National Plan of Action adopted by delegates was equally broad and consisted of twenty-six planks. Harness reported to SWE that she had supported the resolutions on business, credit, education, employment, and the Equal Rights Amendment but did not vote on what she called the "controversial issues" of reproductive freedom and sexual orientation "because those issues are not within the scope of our Society's policies."[53]

SWE's long-standing policy of avoiding confrontation was a sore spot for many members. This became particularly apparent in the ensuing debate over whether to hold conventions in states that had not ratified the ERA. Following the lead of other women's organizations, SWE's national council passed a resolution in 1977 declaring that the society would not hold conventions in nonratified states. By that point, however, SWE had already made plans for its 1978 convention in Atlanta. Because Georgia had not ratified the amendment, members were now torn over whether they should cancel their arrangements and risk alienating the Atlanta section or honor their previous agreement.[54] Former SWE president Aileen Cavanagh (1963–64) and member of SWE's Boston section expressed particular concern over the future participation of southern members. She argued that, in the wake of SWE's previous decision to boycott states where public assembly laws had prohibited integrated meetings, "the southern section formation went into dormancy, and southern members lost a valuable incentive to participate nationally in SWE." She also claimed that members living in nonratified states were precisely the ones most in need of the society's support.[55]

In a move that angered many members, SWE decided that the resolution would go into effect after the 1978 convention had taken place so that the group could meet in Atlanta as planned. Although she had gone along with the decision, former president Naomi McAfee later had second thoughts and came to believe that the society had compromised its stand on the ERA. When she was asked to give the closing address at the Atlanta convention, McAfee used the opportunity to share her displeasure with what she called the "conservative mindset of SWE" and criticized her fellow members for forgetting that "principles take precedence over commitments and equality is the most necessary of all principles."[56] She also lamented the relative lack of attention to the subject during the conference at large. Reflecting on the past several days' events, she remarked that while the group "discussed ecology, debated energy, defended the environment, and developed our egos," members only casually addressed "the most important E," meaning equality. With time running out for the ERA, she found this oversight "incomprehensible" and urged immediate action to help ensure ratification.[57] McAfee's speech had a polarizing effect on the audience. She later remembered that about half of the group stood up and cheered while the other half remained seated at their tables.[58] In the days and weeks that followed, however, a number of sections took up McAfee's call to arms and began their own boycott campaigns.[59]

SWE's embrace of feminist issues was also influenced by the society's changing demographics. Throughout the 1960s and 1970s, student participation jumped from 6 percent in 1960 to nearly 44 percent in 1975.[60] By the end of the 1970s, student sections had been formed at more than 170 colleges, universities, and technical institutes, where women were enrolling in increasing numbers. Between 1970 and 1980, the number of bachelor's degrees awarded to women in engineering increased from 350 to roughly 6,000. Women's overall proportion of degrees similarly expanded from approximately 1 percent to 10 percent during that same period.[61] Despite these changes, female students realized that engineering remained a male-dominated field and turned to SWE for support. Initially, student sections had been autonomous, and they had relatively little contact with the national organization. But as their numbers grew, so did their desire to play a larger role in SWE's governance. As a result, SWE amended its bylaws in 1976 to allow for voting student members on the national council of section representatives.[62] Students also organized the national student conference that immediately preceded SWE's annual convention, such as the June 1976 gathering held in Denver. Recruitment materials for both events, which overlapped by one day, reveal much about the changing tenor of the organization. The national SWE announced that the annual convention would commemorate the launching of Colorado's Viking Explorer spacecraft and would feature addresses on nuclear energy and as well as a tour of the U.S. National Oceanic and Atmospheric Laboratories in Boulder. By contrast, the student conference advertised rap sessions and, in a reference to campus culture, urged participants to "GET HIGH in Denver at the SWE National Student Conference and HANGOVER for the SWE Convention."[63]

Not surprisingly, the influx of students into SWE created generational rifts within the organization. Irene Peden, a class of 1947 University of Colorado graduate and one of SWE's early members, tackled these concerns directly in an address to a career guidance conference cosponsored by SWE and the Engineering Foundation in August 1973. Peden acknowledged that "there is a current tendency on the part of college women to say that . . . women of my generation are poor role models for women students, insofar as direct combat with sexism is concerned. We are not sufficiently outspoken, it is said, and not militant enough in our feminism."[64] Peden admitted that she and other early members of SWE had learned early in their careers "to be terribly tactful, even charming, on the job, and to avoid confrontations that would wound the male egos of peers and superiors. That was professional survival." She did not, however, find it fair to be dismissed entirely. "Although we typically did not have our consciousness raised very early in life," she insisted, "many of us have moved our points of reference considerably in recent years." Perhaps most important, in Peden's view, was that SWE's overall aim had always been to assist women and girls in their education and career paths. "One thing that hasn't changed is our desire to help you."[65]

Indeed, most of the initiatives that SWE carried out during the late 1960s and 1970s were what Naomi McAfee referred to as "continuations of older programs."[66] Concerned by the persistent stereotypes and cultural conventions that discouraged women's participation in engineering, both the national organization and student sections carried out a wide range of vocational guidance activities. As SWE members had done throughout the 1950s and early 1960s, the "second wave" of SWE held career days in local schools, wrote guidance literature, and sponsored career conferences. They also ran continuing education programs for women seeking to reenter the field as well as workshops on balancing the demands of family life and career. Increasingly, SWE sought to encourage even larger populations of girls and young women. In 1972, the society worked to reach preschool girls by collaborating with the *Mister Rogers* show in the development of an episode. The program featured one of SWE's young members talking to a four-year-old about a career in engineering. Similar initiatives included publishing a coloring book and partnering with the Girl Scouts of America.[67]

SWE's interest in challenging gender stereotypes, expanding options for young women, and helping female engineers succeed in their careers was shared by many in the broader women's movement. Some of the older members of the society were pleased with what they viewed as the movement's validation of their hard work. But others were concerned that SWE's earlier efforts were being obscured by newer women's groups. In 1977, long-time SWE member Aileen Cavanagh noted that before there was antidiscrimination legislation, "we worked within the profession to gain our place there. Unlike NOW and the Lib movement, we were engineering our own environment long before there was general consensus the environment needed any change." In other words, she explained, "SWE is not a splinter that sprung up from the women's movement of recent times, but part of the main trunk."[68] Arminta Harness voiced similar concerns in her December 1977 "President's Letter" which appeared in the *SWE Newsletter*. The society, which was approaching 10,000 members, was what Harness called "a moderate feminist organization." "For 27 years," she wrote, "we have quietly and steadfastly made our way within the technical community." Consequently, "all of us have been a little dismayed that our Society is not better known, and equally dismayed when someone assumes that we are one of the many new organizations spawned by the women's movement."[69]

The lack of recognition described by Harness and Cavanagh also plagued other established women's organizations, such as Sigma Delta Epsilon. In 1969, the women's scientific fraternity hosted its annual All Women in Science Luncheon at the American Association for the Advancement of Science meeting, as it had for decades. That year, however, the event was disrupted by twelve female graduate and postdoctoral students, depicted by the press as "wearing miniskirts and bell-bottomed pants," who stormed the gathering to protest women's inequality in science.[70] The leader of the demonstration, Rita Arditti of Harvard Medical School, read a prepared statement on behalf of the group declaring that "sexual oppression is both pervasive and institutionalized; within the scientific community it takes many forms."[71] She then railed against sex-stereotyping in education and employment, discriminatory promotion practices, sexual harassment, and the difficulties faced by women juggling family and career commitments. Arditti concluded by presenting a list of eight demands, which included ensuring compliance with equal pay laws and affirmative action programs, improving vocational guidance in high schools and colleges, and providing flexible work schedules and child care for working parents.[72]

In an attempt to quell the demonstration, Sigma Delta Epsilon president Marie Berg invited the protestors to discuss their concerns with members of her organization later that evening in the fraternity's hospitality suite. While some Sigma Delta Epsilon members expressed displeasure with the protestors' confrontational tactics and suggested different approaches for demanding women's equality in science, they were most upset that the protestors were "obviously unaware that we represented the one organization concerned most with this problem."[73] They told the protestors that they shared their interests and had even worked on behalf of some of them for many years. The fraternity had, for example, provided grants to female scientists with small children and worked with junior high and high school students to encourage them in science. "Nothing earth-shaking," Sigma Delta Epsilon member Margaret Stone admitted, "but a persistent endeavor."[74]

This incident forced many in the fraternity to reconsider the organization's broader purpose and image. Earlier that year, Sigma Delta Epsilon had revised its constitution to include in its objectives some of its outreach efforts. But many members remained concerned that the organization seemed outdated. In 1970 the president of the Beta Chapter, Grace Jacobs, observed that "in these days of new awareness of the woman in the world, of science going to the moon and of decreasing budgets, of more graduate students and fewer jobs, the united power of Sigma Delta Epsilon could be a force for great advancement or another fizzle."[75] Marie Berg also noted that honor societies themselves had come under attack lately by student activists and that some young women had even turned down invitations to join the fraternity on the grounds that it was exclusive and undemocratic.[76] Bernice Austrheim, president of Chicago's Chi Chapter, observed similar developments and wrote in her annual report that "there is a current

phenomena [*sic*] on our campus and other campuses of students not joining organizations that they consider to be old establishment. . . . The last
thing that would be desirable would be to have an old ladies club."[77] One
solution that members devised was changing the organization's name. In
1971, after much debate, the group amended its name to read Sigma Delta
Epsilon–Graduate Women in Science (SDE-GWIS). By clearly identifying itself as a professional women's organization, as opposed to a social sorority
or esoteric society, SDE-GWIS hoped to find a new audience and potential
membership base amid the growing women's movement.[78]

As second-wave feminism gained momentum, the fraternity also began
identifying with explicitly feminist concerns. This shift can be viewed, in
part, in the activities of local chapters. In 1969–70, Minnesota's Xi Chapter
sent statements to legislators about birth control, abortion, and tax exemp-
tions for children. Other groups held consciousness-raising sessions "to
explore feelings and less than desirable situations and in general to see if
there are situations where members can help each other."[79] Purdue University's Pi Chapter agreed to look into allegations of discrimination at its
home institution, where unfair hiring practices were suspected. The Tau
Chapter of Southern California similarly resolved to participate locally in
efforts to ensure that female scientists received equal pay and promotion
opportunities.[80] The University of Wisconsin's Beta Chapter led a campaign
to combat the discrimination faced by women in other professional organizations. Philadelphia's Rho Chapter even created its own Status of Women
Committee. Meanwhile, the Alpha Chapter at Cornell ran a program titled
"Equality of Opportunity for Women," which featured workshops and lectures. In addition to these activities, individual fraternity members joined
such organizations as NOW and WEAL. Omicron Chapter member Betty
McLaughlin, who had chaired the American Council on Women in Science in the late 1950s, began working for the Commission on the Status
of Women in Virginia. Meta Ellis, now Heller, who had recently relocated
to Seattle, served on the one that her governor convened in Washington
State.[81]

The national fraternity increasingly immersed itself in feminist politics
as well. During the late 1960s, it reprinted articles by feminist scholars,
such as Alice Rossi, in its newsletter.[82] At the same time, it reached out
to feminist organizations in a dual effort to demonstrate solidarity with
their causes and to generate support for its own efforts. In 1971, SDE-GWIS
teamed up with NOW to protest sexist representations of female scientists in
the *Chemical and Engineering News*. It also passed a resolution announcing

support for WEAL and offering to help the group in any way that it could. Additionally, SDE-GWIS held informational sessions on affirmative action at national science conferences and worked to secure the involvement of more women on federal advisory boards and review panels for funding agencies.[83]

The national organization's interest in feminist issues received additional attention at the "Women in Science" symposium that it sponsored at the 1970 annual meeting of the American Association for the Advancement of Science. The day-long event, which was covered by newspapers across the country, featured autobiographical presentations by female scientists as well as panel discussions about the status of women in scientific fields. Although the total number of female scientists and engineers had more than doubled in the past decade, from 13,551 in 1960 to 29,293 in 1970, they remained less than 10 percent of the overall science and engineering population. Women had made slight gains in the "hard" sciences like physics but continued to be concentrated in chemistry, psychology, and biological fields. They also remained underpaid and underemployed.[84]

In promoting the symposium, the organizers promised "a range of opinions . . . from 'conservative' to 'radical.'"[85] To this end, they included on the program not only established professionals such as Mina Rees, who had recently been elected as the first female president of the American Association for the Advancement of Science, but also outspoken activists and recent Ph.D.s, such as the psychologist Naomi Weisstein. Weisstein first became aware of sexism in academia as a graduate student at Harvard. At a luncheon held for new graduate students, she later recalled, the department chair leaned back in his seat, lit his pipe, and remarked that women did not belong in graduate school. Following his lead, the male graduate students then leaned back in their chairs, lit their own pipes, and expressed their hearty agreement. This incident was the first of many slights. Later, when she went to conduct her dissertation research, Weisstein was told that she could not use the equipment because she might break it (the fact that the male graduate students broke it every week seemed not to matter). After collecting her data at Yale instead, Weisstein returned to Harvard and was awarded her Ph.D. in 1964. But despite having graduated first in her class, she found herself unemployable. She accepted a National Science Foundation postdoctoral fellowship at the University of Chicago, where her husband, the radical historian Jesse Lemisch, was employed. Antinepotism rules, however, prevented her from joining the faculty as she had hoped. These and other formative experiences led her to help establish the Chicago Women's Liberation Union and fueled her academic work. Her article "Woman as Nigger, or How Psychology Constructs the Female," which was published in *Psychology Today* in 1969, quickly made the rounds in feminist circles and likely brought her to the attention of the "Women in Science" symposium organizers.[86]

Although the program speakers represented a variety of disciplines, age groups, and backgrounds, nearly all of them honed in on the persistent discrimination faced by female scientists. Ruth Hubbard talked about her experiences at Harvard, where she had spent the past two decades. After earning her Ph.D. in biology from Radcliffe in 1950, Hubbard joined Harvard as a research fellow before being promoted to research associate and lecturer. There, she continued her work on the biochemistry and photochemistry of vision in vertebrates and invertebrates. In 1967, she, along with her husband, George Wald (a Harvard biologist and outspoken opponent of the war in Vietnam), won the Paul Karrer Medal for their research in this area. Like Wald, Hubbard found herself radicalized by the social movements of the day. Although during her early career, she later explained, she carried out experiments and wrote papers in the accepted tradition without asking herself how she fit into the culture, the Vietnam War and the women's movement led her to look more closely at these assumptions.[87] At the 1970 "Women in Science" symposium, Hubbard lamented that there were few jobs available for women in science and noted that she had felt particularly discriminated against when looking for a teaching position. She also suggested that this "hyperconsciousness of 'little discriminations'" showed how women scientists very much saw themselves as trapped by limited options.[88]

Hubbard's concerns were shared by other panelists, including Christina Vander Wende, a professor of pharmacology at Rutgers University. Vander Wende had earned her Ph.D. in physiology and biochemistry in 1959 from Rutgers, when Polly Bunting was still in charge of its women's college. At the 1970 symposium, Vander Wende discussed her experiences after graduate school and said that she "definitely feels discrimination on a personal level."[89] Arie Lewin, an associate professor of behavioral science and management at New York University and the only man on the program, drew on his recent research findings to help quantify the experiences of Vander Wende and others. Confirming what most participants already knew or at least suspected, he reported that women were less likely to receive research grants from the National Science Foundation or the National Institutes of Health and that department chairs gave preference to male applicants. Lois

K. Miller, a graduate student at the University of Wisconsin, reminded the audience that many women encountered discrimination even earlier in their careers and long before they applied for grants. Miller explained that her first run-in with discrimination was in high school when she decided to become a biochemist.[90] Jean Simmons, the chair of the program and current president of Sigma Delta Epsilon, as it was still called at the time, elaborated on the points raised by Miller and connected them to the fraternity's ongoing activities.[91]

Throughout the late 1960s and 1970s, Sigma Delta Epsilon and later SDE-GWIS remained dedicated to the vocational guidance programs that the fraternity had initiated in the aftermath of the Soviet Sputniks but now framed them as efforts to combat sexism in schools and society. To that end, the organization continued to provide individual encouragement to high school students by inviting them to meetings, honoring them with special prizes at school science fairs, awarding scholarships, and leading them (and their mothers) on field trips to local laboratories.[92] The fraternity also continued helping female graduates balance the demands of work and family life. The Alpha Chapter, for example, expanded its Professional Skills Roster program to hundreds of women in nonscientific fields. The project was deemed so successful that the national organization tried to replicate it.[93] Similar projects were soon carried out by other women's scientific societies, which quickly sprouted across the country. Despite their differences, these new feminist organizations had a surprising amount in common with older groups.

New Women's Scientific Societies

The 1970s witnessed the proliferation of feminist organizations in science. They drew their membership from established professionals, recent graduates, and current students, many of whom had benefited from Cold War manpower initiatives such as the National Defense Education Act and National Science Foundation fellowships. Few, however, identified themselves as part of the national security state. Nor did they feel much need to, given the momentum of the women's movement, the real opportunities made available by Title IX, and the promise of antidiscrimination legislation. Increasingly, female scientists of all ages banded together in an effort to remedy the injustices that they and other women faced in their educational, occupational, and personal lives. While they varied in their radicalism, most embraced gradations of feminism.

Many of the "second-wave" science societies were formed when female scientists began organizing within their professional associations. By the end of the 1970s, women's committees and caucuses could be found in at least a dozen organizations, including the American Association for the Advancement of Science, the American Geological Institute, the American Society of Biological Chemists, the Institute for Electrical and Electronic Engineers, and the Endocrine Society.[94] One of the earliest was the Committee on the Status of Women Microbiologists, which was established within the American Society for Microbiology in 1970. Among its early members and chairs was Mary Louise Robbins, the former Sigma Delta Epsilon president who in 1958 had established the Committee to Encourage Women to Enter Science and headed up the National Council on the Participation of Women in Science.[95] The committee also included Jessie Price, one of the fraternity's relatively few African American members. (Price would serve as SDE-GWIS president from 1974 to 1975 as well as chair of the microbiologists committee from 1978 to 1979.)[96] Much like SDE-GWIS, the Committee on the Status of Women Microbiologists concerned itself with increasing women's representation in the field and remedying the discrimination that they faced at all levels of education and employment.[97]

In February 1972, female members of the Biophysical Society came together to form the Caucus of Women Biophysicists and the Committee on Professional Opportunities for Women. The effort was spearheaded by Rita Guttman, who had earned her Ph.D. from Columbia University in 1939 and spent most of her career teaching at the City University of New York's Brooklyn College. For thirty-four years, Guttman strung together a succession of teaching appointments and professorships there before finally being named full professor in 1970. "Time after time," she later recalled, "I was passed over for promotion. . . . Applicants who had not even been on the department's list for promotion when I was first proposed were passed over me at each rank."[98] Many of her male colleagues were either indifferent or oblivious to the situation. In the fall of 1971, she attended a department meeting where one of them even complained that women were overrepresented in the department when compared with the number of women in science overall. When he proposed that some of the female faculty be fired, Guttman suggested that a better solution would be to form a committee to understand why there were so few women in science in the first place. "But this suggestion," she explained, "like so many of my suggestions, was, of course, ignored."[99]

Frustrated, Guttman phoned her friend, Julia Apter, an ophthalmologist-turned-biophysicist, in Chicago to see if she knew of any feminist meetings being planned for the upcoming annual conference of biophysicists in Toronto. Apter said that she did not, so the two women decided to arrange one themselves. In Toronto, they gathered the female scientists in attendance to form a women's caucus as well as a standing committee on professional opportunities for women. According to Guttman, who chaired the two groups, "when we needed official standing, we few women acted as the committee; when we needed more daring, broader brushstrokes, we wore the hat of the caucus."[100] The core members of both the caucus and committee faced several challenges, including their paltry numbers, the fact that they were spread across the country, and their lack of funds. But through their organizing and strategic planning, they were able not only to support each other on an individual level but also to expand women's representation on the Biophysical Society's governing council. Although women constituted only 4 percent of the society's membership, they soon made up 40 percent of the council at large.[101]

Another early committee was the American Physical Society's Committee on the Status of Women in Physics, which was founded by Vera Kistiakowsky in 1971. The MIT physicist's long-standing interest in science and technology had been influenced by her family. Her father, George Kistiakowsky, was a physical chemist and Harvard professor who had worked on the Manhattan Project during World War II and later served as President Eisenhower's science advisor. In 1944, at the age of fifteen, she graduated from high school and enrolled at Mount Holyoke College. After earning her bachelor's degree in 1948, she began graduate work at the University of California at Berkeley and earned her Ph.D. in 1952. She worked for a year in the San Francisco Bay area before returning to Berkeley's Lawrence Radiation Laboratory to undertake postgraduate study in nuclear physics with the assistance of an American Association of University Women fellowship. From there, she went to Columbia University, where she worked with and enjoyed the mentorship of Chien-Shiung Wu. In 1959 Kistiakowsky relocated again, this time to the Boston area, to become an assistant professor at Brandeis University. She taught at Brandeis until 1963, when she joined MIT's laboratory for nuclear science as a staff member. In 1969 Kistiakowsky became a senior research scientist in the physics department and in 1972 would become the first female full professor of physics at MIT.[102]

Like many women of her generation, Kistiakowsky credited her interest in feminism to reading *The Feminine Mystique* and other feminist writings.

Although she did not read Friedan's book until the late 1960s, she found that its message hit close to home. Faced with societal pressures, she had married in 1951 and had two children while at Brandeis. She later admitted that the biggest obstacle she faced in her career was her own "internalization of the traditional view of the responsibilities of a mother."[103] While child care and household help allowed her to continue working full time, she was keenly aware that her career suffered in ways that her husband's did not. In 1965 she separated from her husband, and she finalized their divorce in 1970. During their separation, she became increasingly involved with feminist issues and joined organizations such as NOW. She also began studying the particular problems of female scientists.[104] She found, however, that other feminists occasionally charged her with being "too much from the establishment," as was the case at a 1972 women's education conference held at Mount Holyoke. On this point, she acknowledged that her career in a capital-intensive field required substantial government support and "establishment connections." "In this sense," she conceded, "I'm very much a member of the establishment." At the same time, she believed that her interest in women's equality set her apart. She assured the audience that "the establishment does not consider me a member of the establishment in my concern for these matters."[105]

What Kistiakowsky referred to as her "mixed credentials" played an important role in the development of the Committee on the Status of Women in Physics.[106] The group grew out of a panel on women in science held at the American Physical Society's annual meeting in January 1971. During the discussion, a male physicist claimed that there were no truly successful women in physics and that the only reason Marie Curie had won the Nobel Prize was because of her husband. Furious, Kistiakowsky, who was in the audience, resolved to take action. She drafted a petition urging the American Physical Society to create a committee on the problems faced by female physicists and gathered the signatures of fifteen women in the field. In April, the society's president approved the request and appointed Kistiakowsky to chair the new group.[107] One of the first things that Kistiakowsky did was raise operating funds. She promptly contacted the president of MIT, Jerome Wiesner, who helped her to procure a grant of $10,000 from the Alfred P. Sloan Foundation. She later remembered that "the American Physical Society nearly keeled over in a dead faint, because [ours] was the first committee that had ever come in with money of its own."[108] The Sloan Foundation grant allowed the committee to carry out an ambitious agenda: in just one year, it had produced an extensive report as well as a roster containing the names of more than 1,200 female physicists. Subsequent activities included writing a booklet on careers for women in physics, publishing a directory of female graduate students, hosting symposia on such subjects as affirmative action and career guidance, and testifying before Congress on legislation affecting women scientists.[109]

In addition to working within the American Physical Society, Kistiakowsky helped create the independent, Boston-based Women in Science and Engineering (WISE) group in 1971. She was assisted in this effort by two friends, Elizabeth Urey Baranger and Vera Pless, who served as co-organizers. Like Kistiakowsky, Baranger was an MIT physicist and the daughter of a prominent scientist. Her father, Harold Urey, won the Nobel Prize in chemistry in 1934 and was a key figure in the development of the atomic bomb and the Manhattan Project. She later recalled how her childhood home was frequently filled with prominent scientists, such as Maria Goeppert-Mayer, "who made me feel that there were women physicists out there doing this kind of work, and that it was not a strange thing for a woman to do."[110] Shortly after earning her Ph.D. in physics from Cornell University in 1954, Baranger joined the faculty at the University of Pittsburgh. She taught there until her husband was hired by MIT in 1969 and she moved with him and their children to Massachusetts. At this time, she also began working as a research physicist at the institute, where she met Kistiakowsky and Vera Pless.[111]

Although Pless would not be formally affiliated with MIT until 1972, when she took a job as a research associate in the electrical engineering department, her husband was a member of the institute's physics department. She had married him in 1952, just as she was completing her master's degree in mathematics at the University of Chicago. Initially, she had no intention of pursuing a career and was content to wait for him to finish the Ph.D. program in which he was then enrolled. But she quickly became restless and decided to pursue her own Ph.D. in algebra at Northwestern University. Because her husband accepted the job at MIT before she could finish her degree, she had to complete her graduate work *in absentia* and finally earned her doctorate in 1957. Two weeks after her dissertation defense, she gave birth to the first of the couple's three children, and she spent much of the next four years teaching part-time. Frustrated by the academic job market, she eventually accepted a position at the Air Force Cambridge Research Laboratory in 1963, where she remained until the Mansfield Amendment and dwindling defense allocations eliminated funding for many of the lab's projects.[112]

In 1971, Pless worked with Baranger and Kistiakowsky to organize a workshop on women in science for the eastern Massachusetts division of NOW's "Women in Academia" symposium. For many of the female scientists present, the session had a transformative effect. By meeting one another and discussing their shared problems, participants realized that their concerns were quite common to women in the field and that they were not alone. Kistiakowsky later recalled that the organizers "were struck by the enthusiastic response of the audience, who thought this was a great idea to get women scientists together, and one really should keep on doing it."[113] Consequently, Kistiakowsky, Pless, and Baranger decided to start a local group so that they could continue meeting, and thus, WISE was born.

Throughout the 1970s, WISE functioned as an informal organization of women scientists, engineers, and graduate students in the Boston area. It aimed "to improve the status of women scientists and engineers, and to educate and interest young women and girls throughout the school system in careers in science."[114] Meeting roughly once a month, the group held potluck dinners at members' homes or gathered at local restaurants, where they planned activities and discussed their progress. Meetings also frequently featured invited speakers, such as Bernice Sandler, who had spearheaded the landmark class action lawsuit against the University of Maryland in 1970, and Lilli Hornig, the chemist and president of the Higher Education Resource Service at Brown University. (Hornig, who had worked at Los Alamos during World War II, was the wife of President Johnson's science advisor, Donald Hornig.) One of the group's first projects was to assemble a roster of local women scientists, which it made available to area employers. Within several years, the roster contained 200 names, about half of which were on WISE's mailing list. Another major undertaking was the publication of *Goals for Women in Science* in 1972. The sixty-two-page booklet consisted mainly of recommendations for improving the education and employment of women in the field. These included the enforcement of antidiscrimination legislation, the provision of financial aid, the expansion of part-time work and study programs for mothers and wives, the elimination of sex-stereotyping in vocational guidance, and the general encouragement of girls and women with an interest in scientific careers. The publication was distributed to schools across the country, and a shortened version appeared in the MIT alumni magazine, *Technology Review*. Additionally, WISE planned special programs that took place in conjunction with national science conferences held in Boston. These opportunities allowed WISE to widen its reach while at the same time introducing local industry and education officials to broader conversations about women in science.[115]

Some WISE members, such as Vera Pless, were also involved in a local organization of female mathematicians that had been meeting since 1969. Organized by Wellesley College professor Alice Schafer, this informal group served as a precursor to the Association for Women in Mathematics that would be established two years later. Schafer conceived of these early gatherings as opportunities for women to enjoy encouragement and support, something that was sorely lacking in her own educational and occupational experiences. When she was applying to colleges in the early 1930s, a teacher had refused to write a letter of recommendation for her when she told him that she wanted to major in math. According to Schafer, he said plainly, "I won't write for you because girls can't do mathematics."[116] Undeterred, she attended the University of Richmond's Westhampton College and earned her bachelor's degree in mathematics in 1936. She then taught at the high school level for three years before enrolling in graduate school at the University of Chicago. Although she won a scholarship there, she felt that the faculty did not take the research potential of women seriously. At departmental functions, the female students were frequently tasked with preparing tea and washing dishes while the male students mingled with faculty and discussed new findings in the field. After earning her Ph.D. in 1942, Schafer held teaching positions at eight different colleges and universities before joining the faculty at Wellesley in 1962. While she enjoyed being in the classroom, she also felt that her career was limited to teaching from the start. Frustration with these experiences fueled her desire to assist other women, such as the female graduate students and recent Ph.D.s who comprised the bulk of the Boston-area group that she helped organize.[117]

Within two years, Schafer's organization had become an integral part of the independent Association for Women in Mathematics (AWM), which was established at a meeting of the American Mathematical Society in Atlantic City in January 1971. The driving force behind the national organization was American University professor Mary Gray. Significantly younger than the leaders of most women's scientific societies, Gray was born in 1939 and attended Hastings College in Nebraska during the 1950s, where she majored in mathematics and physics. After graduating *summa cum laude* in 1959, she spent a year in Germany as a Fulbright fellow before beginning graduate school at the University of Kansas. She later admitted that she chose to study mathematics because the government made it affordable for her to do so. With assistance from the National Science Foundation and the

National Defense Education Act, Gray earned her master's degree in 1962 and her Ph.D. in 1964. She taught for one year at the University of California at Berkeley and then went on to teach at California State University in Haywood. Shortly thereafter, she and her husband relocated to the Washington, D.C., area so that he could teach at the University of Maryland, while she joined American University.[118]

For much of her life, Gray was acutely aware of discrimination against women and minorities. In her first graduate school class, she was made to feel unwelcome when the instructor asked her, "What are you doing here? Why don't you stay home and take care of the kids?"[119] During the 1960s, she was also active in a number of social protests, such as the one that she organized when the local grocery store refused to hire American Indian students as baggers. She and other graduate students at Kansas filled up carts with expensive frozen food and abandoned them in the checkout lanes. After several days, the store capitulated and dropped its ban on hiring. While teaching in California, she also supported the struggles of local farmworkers.[120] Gray drew on these and similar experiences when protesting the condition of women in mathematics through the newly formed AWM. In one of her first acts as president, Gray tried to attend a meeting of the all-male executive council of the American Mathematical Society but was told to leave. When she responded that there was no provision in the by-laws requiring her to do so, she was informed that there was a "gentleman's agreement." Gray replied by saying "Well, obviously I'm no gentleman," and attended the meeting anyway. From then on the council meetings were open to all members.[121]

The AWM reflected Gray's impatience with the sexist practices of the major professional associations and the field more generally. Throughout the 1970s, the AWM staged consciousness-raising sessions at mathematics conventions, exposed unfair hiring and promotion practices, and sought solutions for balancing mathematical work and study with marriage and motherhood. It also protested objectionable images of girls and women in the media, guidance literature, and textbooks, such as problem sets that featured women calculating recipes and men calculating time travel to the moon. In conjunction with the mathematical conferences, it sponsored panels on such subjects as the history of women in the field and the current status of "black women in mathematics," which was held in January 1978. Of the twelve African American women in the United States holding Ph.D.s in mathematics, six of them participated in this session. More generally, the association championed such causes as the Equal Rights Amendment and affirmative action. Not only did it provide expert testimony before Congress, but it also advised women seeking to file lawsuits against their places of employment for noncompliance with federal guidelines. Gray, who was succeeded as president by Alice Schafer in 1973, even returned to school and earned a law degree in 1979 in order to advocate more effectively.[122]

Another prominent national organization was the Association for Women in Science (AWIS), which was established in April 1971 "to promote equal opportunities for women to enter the professions and to achieve their career goals."[123] The group grew out of a series of champagne mixers that had been held since 1967 at the annual Federation of American Societies for Experimental Biology meetings. These early gatherings had been arranged largely by Virginia Upton of West Haven V.A. Hospital. Upton, who had earned her Ph.D. in physiology from Yale in 1964, learned quickly after graduation that "there are two academic worlds, one for men and one for us, the latter most often involving untenured positions and lower pay."[124] She saw a need to bring female scientists together and, in July 1966, started inquiring whether such an idea was feasible. After deciding that it was, she used funding from laboratory supply houses to arrange the first annual reception, slated for the following spring. Although the mixers were largely social, they provided a way for female scientists to come into contact with one another and to discuss their shared problems. At the urging of Stanford Medical School's Judith Pool, the 1970 gathering included a program of speakers who addressed such subjects as job discrimination, unequal pay, and professional isolation. Out of this session developed plans for a formal organization that was finally created at the April 1971 meetings in Chicago.[125]

The founding meeting included roughly thirty young women and established professionals, such as Pool, who had earned her Ph.D. in physiology from the University of Chicago in 1946. Pool and Neena Schwartz, who was then at the University of Illinois College of Medicine in Chicago, were elected as copresidents of the newly formed group. Other charter members who took on leadership roles were biochemist Anne Briscoe of Harlem Hospital Center and Columbia University's College of Physicians and Surgeons, who volunteered to put out the association's newsletter, and the African American physiologist Eleanor Franklin of Howard University, who agreed to draw up the constitution. Meanwhile, Fann Harding of the National Institutes of Health took on responsibility for creating a registry of women scientists. Much like the rosters compiled by other women's organizations, the AWIS project aimed to help employers and government agencies identify women who could be used to fill job openings and advisory posts (and prevent them from claiming that there were no qualified women available).[126]

Another early activity undertaken by AWIS was to increase women's representation on the National Institutes of Health (NIH) technical panels and study sections that evaluated grant applications. AWIS members were particularly concerned that women's applications were not funded as frequently as men's. Upon investigation, AWIS learned that female scientists comprised an average of 2 percent of members of review panels and that some sections, including the one on breast cancer, had no women at all. Convinced that the NIH had violated the law by virtually excluding women from its advisory positions, the group resolved to sue the federal Department of Health, Education, and Welfare, which oversaw the NIH. In March 1972, AWIS became the lead plaintiff in the class action suit filed against the department's secretary, Elliot Richardson. Other plaintiffs in *AWIS et al. v. Richardson* included the Association for Women in Mathematics, the Caucus of Women Biophysicists, NOW, WEAL, and Naomi Weisstein. Although the case dragged on inconclusively for years, NIH officials quickly froze further appointments until the women had an opportunity to suggest names for open positions. Within months of their doing so, the number of women on selection panels jumped to 20 percent. Another important moment in the case came in August 1972, when the judge denied the defense's motion to dismiss and motion for summary judgment, thereby establishing AWIS's right to sue the federal government because of discrimination.[127]

The lawsuit, which was reported widely in the press, attracted many new recruits to AWIS. Although most of AWIS's early members were in the life sciences, due to the association's start at the Federation of American Societies for Experimental Biology meetings, an increasing number came from other scientific fields, such as physics and engineering. By August 1972, AWIS claimed nearly 1,000 members, and by September of the following year, that number had grown to 1,400.[128] In 1975, AWIS was also accepted as an affiliate of the American Association for the Advancement of Science, thus increasing its visibility further.[129]

Enforcement of antidiscrimination legislation quickly became one of AWIS's main activities, and in 1973 the association established the Affirmative Goals and Actions Committee. With the help of institutional representatives, the committee helped monitor affirmative action compliance in dozens of colleges, universities, and industrial laboratories. It also tracked fair employment practices in government agencies and informed them, along with their congressional representatives, of any infractions. Additionally, the committee assisted individual women in navigating legal channels. As committee chair Helene Guttman explained, "The role of AWIS is to watch and counsel (and hand-hold when necessary)."[130] By the spring of 1976, AWIS reported that it had responded to approximately fifty appeals for help from female scientists and students who had experienced sex-based discrimination. Although in most cases AWIS acted in a behind-the-scenes advisory capacity or as an unofficial mediator, it also filed lawsuits as *amicus curiae*.[131]

Not all of AWIS's activities, however, were litigious. Keeping with the tradition of earlier activists, AWIS also devoted considerable energy to combating negative portrayals of female scientists, providing young women with role models, hosting forums to discuss the social and cultural challenges faced by women in the field, and sustaining female scientists in their education and employment. Much of this work was carried out at the local level by more than a dozen chapters across the country. The Oregon chapter, for example, organized numerous student outreach activities, such as visiting junior and senior high school classes, holding career days, leading laboratory tours for female students, and running an undergraduate honors seminar at Oregon State University where women scientists were brought in as guest speakers. Meanwhile, other chapters sponsored panel discussions on balancing career and family commitments, held grant-writing workshops, and worked with school counselors to plan career information sessions for young women.[132] Another important mechanism for achieving these goals was the national organization's AWIS Educational Foundation, which was established in 1974 with personal funds from then president Estelle Ramey. The foundation enabled AWIS to accept tax-free contributions from interested donors as well as to provide scholarships for women science students, organize vocational guidance programs, sponsor conferences, and issue publications. The foundation awarded its first scholarships in April 1975 to three doctoral students and AWIS members.[133]

Ramey and other members of AWIS also drew on their professional expertise to protest demeaning representations of women in both science and society. Ramey, who was an endocrinology specialist and professor at Georgetown University School of Medicine, had earned her Ph.D. in physiology from the University of Chicago in 1950. She was described by the press as a "subdued liberationist" who had quietly pursued her research until 1970, when she burst onto the national scene. In what became known as "the Battle of the Raging Hormones," Ramey took on Hubert Humphrey's former physician and political advisor, Edgar Berman, after he told a Democratic National Committee task force that women were unfit to hold high office because of monthly hormonal imbalances. In an effort to prove his point, he inquired hypothetically about what would have happened if the country had had a menopausal female president during the Bay of Pigs invasion. Both in person and in the press, Ramey debated Berman and challenged the basis of his scientific knowledge. According to Ramey, during the incident in question, the president actually had a hormonal imbalance: not only was John F. Kennedy afflicted with Addison's disease, but the medications prescribed for it could also result in dramatic mood swings. Ramey quickly became a sought-out speaker on women's rights who was known for her zingers and was even nicknamed "the Mort Sahl of Women's Lib," in reference to a popular comedian.[134]

As president-elect of AWIS in 1972, Ramey waged a campaign against the textbook company Williams and Wilkins for using pornographic illustrations of women in its medical texts. In contrast to the few images of men that it included, which Ramey referred to as "discreetly posed and virtuously clothed," the images of women resembled *Playboy* pinups. In an open letter to AWIS members that was subsequently reprinted by *Time* and *Newsweek*, Ramey lambasted the use of "coy undulating nymphs to illustrate anatomical landmarks such as the left big toe."[135] Ramey also found fault with such unfounded claims as, "The 'little bit' of difference in a woman's built-in biology urges her to ensnare a man. Such is the curse of estrogen."[136] Ramey, as well as individual AWIS members, flooded Williams and Wilkins with threats to boycott all of its textbooks. Shortly thereafter, the president of the company met with Ramey and agreed to take the book off of the market until revisions could be made.[137]

While Ramey was pleased with this outcome, she also realized that the struggle for women's equality was far from over. She believed that women needed to continue finding ways to enhance their economic and political clout and expressed support for the creation of new groups in pursuit of that aim. This was the theme of Ramey's November 1972 keynote address at the organizational conference of the Federation of Organizations for Professional Women (FOPW). Held in Arlington, Virginia, at Marymount College, the gathering had been largely arranged by AWIS's Fann Harding, who, along with Virginia Upton, chaired an AWIS committee tasked with exploring the possibility of forming a coalition of women's groups. In the summer and early fall of 1972, Harding, who was also a member of Sigma Delta Epsilon–Graduate Women in Science, floated the idea at several small gatherings of professional women in the Washington, D.C., area. Their enthusiasm for an umbrella organization resulted in the November 1972 meeting where FOPW was formed.[138]

The event drew together forty-six participants from forty organizations. Representatives from nearly every major women's scientific society were in attendance, including Naomi McAfee (Society of Women Engineers), Elizabeth Baranger (American Physical Society's committee on women), Mary Louise Robbins (American Society for Microbiology's Committee on the Status of Women Microbiologists), Mary Gray (Association for Women in Mathematics), Jean Simmons, Margaret Stone, Ariel Hollinshead (Sigma Delta Epsilon–Graduate Women in Science), and Marie Cassidy (Caucus of Women Biophysicists). Other activist organizations, such as the American Association of University Women, WEAL, and NOW, also sent delegates. According to Harding, their decision to form a broad-based coalition "marks and reflects a maturing women's movement."[139]

Within two years, the FOPW and its affiliate organizations represented more than one million women. Most of the federation's work, however, was carried out by its committees. In January 1973, the federation's Legislative Committee sponsored a one-day seminar on the status of women. Held at the headquarters of the National Woman's Party, the group urged the prompt ratification of the Equal Rights Amendment, the expansion of federal programs designed to assist women, and increased attention to the concerns of racial minorities. Meanwhile, the Committee on Careers focused on occupational opportunities for female professionals. Within months of the federation's founding, the committee had already embarked on a career guidance and counseling survey. Concurrently, the federation's Research Committee planned studies on such topics as the effect of continuing education on the employment of women returning to the paid work force and the influence of role models in encouraging women to enter and remain in male-dominated fields.[140]

Most significant, FOPW was instrumental in creating a network of influential women in Washington, D.C. Beginning in 1975, the FOPW held an annual cocktail party to fete the contributions of women in Congress and to provide opportunities for networking. Several years later, in 1978, it published *Washington Women: A Directory of Women and Women's Organizations in the National Capital*, which provided contact information for women's organizations, congressional representatives, and other high-ranking women in the federal government. At the end of the decade, the federation also created an Equal Rights Amendment task force and provided a hotline counseling service to women's caucuses working to persuade scientific and professional societies to endorse the ERA. These contacts would prove particularly important to women's advocates seeking to influence public policy and secure federal support for their goals.[141]

The Persistence of Technocratic Feminism

While women's scientific societies did not rely heavily on technocratic feminism during the 1960s and 1970s, preferring instead arguments based on rights and explicit claims to equality, they did invoke national security prerogatives and scientific manpower concerns occasionally. Of these groups, the Society of Women Engineers remained most obviously connected to the defense matrix. SWE presidents Naomi McAfee and Arminta Harness, for example, both had strong military ties. McAfee worked for Westinghouse Electric Corporation's Defense and Electronic Systems Center in Baltimore, while Harness, a retired Air Force officer, was in charge of planning for Westinghouse Hanford Company's nuclear development laboratory. Defense contractors were also well represented among SWE's corporate membership, which quickly expanded as firms sought to demonstrate compliance with fair hiring practices. Between the late 1960s and 1976, the number of corporate members increased from five to more than fifty and included such newcomers as Lockheed Missiles and Space Company, Grumman Aerospace Corporation, and Raytheon. Energy companies, such as Shell Oil and Gulf Research and Development Company, were also well represented in light of new national anxieties stemming from the recent energy crisis. The Atomic Energy Commission and its successor agency, the Energy Research and Development Administration, advertised widely in the *SWE Newsletter* and took out full-page ads touting "Brain Power. Our most important energy resource."[142]

The close association between SWE and national security prerogatives, however, occasionally made the society feel like an outcast among other women's organizations. In December 1977, Arminta Harness reported on a recent State Department meeting of nongovernmental women's leaders that she had attended. While she described the gathering as a "fascinating experience," she was also disturbed by what she called "the expression of peace-at-any-price, anti-defense, and anti-technology sentiments by a large number of organization spokeswomen." She disagreed with their calls to cut defense budgets but also realized that "the credibility of the scientific and engineering community is distressingly low—particularly among women."[143]

During the early 1970s, other women's scientific societies also invoked national security prerogatives in some way, although to a lesser extent and not as deliberately. In these cases, they usually concerned themselves with the economic, rather than military, aspects of national security. They frequently highlighted contemporary manpower concerns and the new legal ramifications of failing to use female intellect fully. The most widespread example can be seen in the ubiquitous registry and roster projects that many groups undertook in recognition of the need to "utilize" women more effectively. In letters to potential sponsors, AWIS explained that its registry project was devised to help the association meet its two basic goals: "providing American institutions with access to this largely untapped supply of talent and to provide the women with access to some of the highly responsible and decision-making positions which need them."[144] Women's scientific societies frequently made use of existing manpower data while compiling their rosters and sought to collaborate with scientific agencies. There was even talk of AWIS taking over the National Science Foundation's National Register of Scientific and Technical Personnel, which had originally been created during World War II as the National Roster of Scientific and Specialized Personnel.[145]

One particularly sought-out source of expertise was the Scientific Manpower Commission, which was affiliated with the American Association for the Advancement of Science. Founded in 1953, the commission functioned as a nonprofit corporation concerned with the recruitment, training, and utilization of scientific personnel. Its executive director, Betty Vetter, had joined the commission in 1963 and tirelessly compiled statistics on the education, employment, and status of women in scientific fields. Most of her findings revealed that women were grossly "underutilized" and their talents "wasted." Vetter had much interaction with women's scientific societies, participated in their forums, and spoke at their meetings. Many groups also reprinted her comments in their publications in order to justify and generate support for their own efforts.[146]

Another source of support for scientific womanpower was the National Science Foundation, whose ongoing interest in identifying scientific talent continued to benefit feminist organizations and individual members. In 1974 the FOPW requested and received $32,000 to finance its project on women's participation in scientific fields.[147] Other organizations and individuals received funding through the foundation's new Women in Science Program, which had been established in 1975 to help "tap the underutilized scientific resource which women represent."[148] In its first year, the program awarded nearly $1 million in grants for science career workshops and science career facilitation projects. Two WISE members were represented among the winners in the inaugural competition. Miriam Schweber of Simmons College received funding to hold a workshop for college women about education and employment opportunities in scientific fields. Meanwhile, Rita Blumstein used her award to organize a reentry program in polymer science at the University of Lowell (now the University of Massachusetts at Lowell).[149] By 1979, the Women in Science initiative had expanded to include the Visiting Women Scientists Project, which selected 30 women (out of 600 volunteers) to visit 120 high schools and colleges across the country. Participants carried out many of the same activities as earlier activists: they visited small classes, made presentations to large groups, and met on an individual basis with interested students, teachers, and counselors.[150] The Women in Science Program was advertised widely in the newsletters of professional women's groups and was assisted by individual members. At the 1978 Women in Science Careers Workshop held at Hood College, for example, Estelle Ramey gave the keynote address.[151]

Ramey, as well as other second-wave activists, periodically invoked technocratic manpower concerns when they found it advantageous to do so. In July 1973, Ramey wrote to Anne Armstrong, a counsellor to President Nixon and founder of the White House Office of Women's Programs, seeking her assistance. Drawing on data from the Scientific Manpower Commission, Ramey expressed concern that the unemployment rate for women scientists seeking full-time work was two to four times higher than their male counterparts. According to Ramey, "This is obviously an insupportable waste of a major natural resource—trained women's brains."[152] Later that month, Ramey contacted Senator Warren Magnuson, who chaired a subcommittee of the Senate Appropriations Committee that dealt with labor, health, education, and welfare and was currently considering affirmative action policies. (Magnuson was the same individual who had, nearly three decades earlier, introduced the National Science Foundation bill modeled on Vannevar Bush's *Science, the Endless Frontier*.) In her correspondence with Magnuson, Ramey charged that "in a nation that cavalierly wastes its irreplaceable natural resources, there is no greater waste than the gross under utilization of the trained brains of American women."[153] That fall, Ramey also agreed to appear on a panel at the upcoming American Association for the Advancement of Science meeting, where she, along with manpower experts such as Dael Wolfle, would discuss "scientific manpower in the 70s."[154] Similarly, in a 1976 address on the admission and attrition of women in graduate school, Elizabeth Baranger argued that women's underrepresentation in scientific fields "means that a human resource of the nation is untapped and underutilized."[155]

The most explicit and expansive expression of technocratic feminism, however, can be seen in the activities surrounding the Women in Science and Technology Equal Opportunity Act, which was introduced by Senator Edward Kennedy (D-Massachusetts) and attached to the annual National Science Foundation authorization. Although the bill aimed to ensure "equal opportunity" for women in science, as the title suggested, it strategically invoked national security prerogatives and manpower concerns to shore up support for the legislation. No stranger to politics and an ardent supporter of women's rights, Kennedy, who chaired a special subcommittee on the National Science Foundation, believed that more attention to women in science was needed. In June 1975 he wrote to the director explaining that the foundation's decision "to limit its activities to a few experimental projects and problem assessments indicates to me a lack of concern over the fact that women have not had equal access to careers in science." "Of even greater concern," Kennedy added, "is the loss to the nation of the potential of their scientific and technical skills."[156] Kennedy then requested a work plan outlining how the foundation could better encourage women to pursue scientific careers.[157]

In response, the National Science Foundation asked Janet Welsh Brown to convene a group of "young" women scientists to solicit their input. Trained as a political scientist, Brown was the 1975–76 president of FOPW as well as the director of the American Association for the Advancement of Science's Office of Opportunities in Science, which had been created in 1972 to address the concerns of women and minorities. These positions, as well as her location in Washington, D.C., gave Brown access not only to formal channels of power but also to the sizable community of female scientists in the area. She found that her activist efforts relied heavily on both.[158]

Under the auspices of the American Association for the Advancement of Science and with funding from the National Science Foundation, Brown arranged a conference titled "The Participation of Women in Scientific Research." The four-day event finally took place in October 1977, after considerable delays in the National Science Foundation's approval process. The conference drew together sixty women who held Ph.D.s in an array of science and science-related fields, from anthropology to zoology. Jewel Plummer Cobb, a biologist and the first African American woman on the National Science Board, which oversaw the National Science Foundation, served as honorary chair (Brown had been instrumental in putting forward Cobb's name for the board position several years earlier). Unlike Cobb, however, who had completed her Ph.D. in 1950, most participants were in their late twenties and early thirties and had earned their doctorates within the past six years. They had been selected from three sources: nominations by women's science organizations, suggestions from science department chairs at major research universities, and lists of graduates from ten other universities that were chosen for geographical balance. According to the conference organizers, most "grew up in the Sputnik era, when science and technology were national priorities," and represented "a wide variety across the feminist/antifeminist spectrum."[159] The group listened to speakers from government, industry, and academia, read background papers, and shared their personal experiences. They also drafted policy recommendations for the National Science Foundation and met with Senator Kennedy to discuss plans for legislation addressing women in science.[160]

Many of the group's concerns made their way into Kennedy's Women in Science and Technology Equal Opportunity Act (S. 2550), as did the input of Vera Kistiakowsky, Brown's network of Washington women, and others with whom Kennedy and his staff had been in contact for the past several years. Some of the conference participants were also in attendance when Kennedy introduced the legislation in February 1978. Armed with charts based on materials from Betty Vetter, Kennedy outlined women's underrepresentation in science, their higher unemployment rates, their lower salaries, and the need for swift congressional action. His plan called for spending $250 million over ten years on improving science teaching in the seventh to twelfth grades, offering training programs for faculty and guidance counselors, sponsoring workshops for students and their parents regarding career opportunities in scientific fields, providing continuing education for college graduates, awarding fellowships and traineeships, and expanding community outreach initiatives. These measures, the bill promised, would "promote the full use of human resources in science and technology through a comprehensive program to maximize the potential contribution and advancement of women in scientific, professional, and technical careers." Additionally, they would secure "the Nation's preeminent position in science and technology" and "[exert] a strong multiplier effect on the gross national product."[161] At this time, however, neither Kennedy nor his slate of experts could make a strong enough case for the legislation. At the Senate hearings in April, only one person, the sociologist Lucy Sells, testified on behalf of women's issues, arguing that "math filters" hindered women's efforts to pursue scientific careers. Ultimately, the bill died in committee.[162]

Determined, Kennedy introduced a modified version of the legislation in the next congressional session. The revised bill (S. 568) drew heavily on a recent conference titled "Expanding the Role of Women in the Sciences," which had been cosponsored by the AWIS Educational Foundation and the New York Academy of Sciences in March 1978. Among the 500 attendees were Estelle Ramey and Neena Schwartz from AWIS, Janet Welsh Brown from FOPW, Vera Kistiakowsky from WISE, and Naomi McAfee from SWE (McAfee was also the president-elect of FOPW at the time). Although the conference contained some bright notes, such as reporting on the National Science Foundation's Women in Science Program, many of its findings were quite gloomy. According to Sheila Pfafflin, the president-elect of AWIS and one of the event organizers, "If this conference has one predominant message, it is how far we really are from achieving the goal of equal opportunity for women in science."[163] The sense of despair expressed by Pfafflin was heightened by the stalling of support for the Equal Rights Amendment and the quickly approaching deadline, which were addressed by several program speakers. The previous month, NOW had announced a state of emergency for the amendment and, along with other women's groups, fervently lobbied for an extension. Although Congress eventually granted one, the fate of the ERA hung in the balance.[164]

The emerging backlash against the gains of the women's movement signaled the growing power of the New Right and weariness with social change. The late 1970s also saw mounting concern with America's place in the world, especially in light of the recent reductions in research and development spending. Corporate, academic, and military leaders increasingly charged that cuts in Department of Defense allocations had made the United States militarily vulnerable, while others lamented that America had fallen behind its foreign competitors in technological innovation. By the end of the decade, the notion that American military and economic security required an enlarged investment in research and development became commonplace. This argument not only influenced the national science policy of President Jimmy Carter but also would come to dominate the administration of Ronald Reagan.[165]

It was in this context that a significant number of women's organizations threw their weight behind Kennedy's legislation, which included a range of bold initiatives (such as reimbursing legal expenses incurred from filing lawsuits against employers) but still retained the technocratic manpower concerns expressed in the original version. Thus, while recognizing that "women have long been denied equal educational and employment opportunities in scientific fields," the bill also claimed to promote broader national interests, economic security, and technological advancement.[166] In August 1979, Eleanor Smeal, the president of NOW, and Anne Briscoe, the president of the AWIS Educational Foundation, both testified before Congress on the bill's behalf. Briscoe expressed particular concern that, after a decade of antidiscrimination legislation, female scientists continued to experience unequal educational, employment, and advancement opportunities. "In terms of utilization of our human resources," Briscoe claimed, "we are still wasting nearly half of our potential scientific talent at a time when this country needs the most it can nurture."[167]

At the second set of hearings held in March 1980, a parade of feminists testified in support of the bill, including the president of the FOPW, Margaret Dunkle, who claimed that "our country cannot continue to be denied the scientific talents, creativity, and skills of women."[168] Betty Vetter presented recent statistics documenting the waste of female intellect, while Shirley Malcom (Brown's successor at the American Association for the Advancement of Science), the biologist W. Ann Reynolds of Ohio State University, and Mary Kostalos of Chatham College, who had run a reentry program for female chemists, lent their support as well. AWIS and Alice Schafer also submitted statements in favor of the legislation, while Jewel Plummer Cobb advocated strongly on its behalf.[169] Behind the scenes, AWIS president Sheila Pfafflin urged association members to endorse the bill and tell Senator Kennedy that "we agree with your position that this legislation addresses a situation which is of importance not only to the women affected, but also to the future scientific well-being of the country."[170]

In December 1980, the women in science bill passed Congress and was signed into law by President Carter. Most women's scientific societies were pleased with what they viewed as the expansion and institutionalization of their activist efforts. As AWIS's Anne Briscoe had explained in her congressional testimony, "Many of us are now doing on a small scale some of what S-568 would greatly expand: we are going to high schools and colleges and attempting to interest young girls in careers in the sciences."[171] In addition to career guidance, the new law supported continuing education, grants, and a visiting professorship program. The legislation also established within the National Science Foundation the Committee on Equal Opportunities in Science and Technology, as well as separate subcommittees on women and minorities. Conservative opposition, however, had resulted in drastic reductions to the proposed budget, as well as the elimination of some of the legislation's bolder initiatives, such as the provision of reimbursements for plaintiffs in antidiscrimination lawsuits. The future of the legislation was made even less clear by Carter's recent defeat to Ronald Reagan just a few weeks earlier. The change of administration meant that funding would not be forthcoming in 1981, as the Office of Management and Budget wanted "no new starts" in federal programs.[172] Nevertheless, feminist efforts to secure the bill's passage helped establish gender equity in the sciences as a public policy issue.

This achievement relied heavily on feminists' blending of calls for "equal opportunity" with a renewed emphasis on technocratic manpower concerns. For much of the 1960s and 1970s, as this chapter has demonstrated, both old and new proponents of feminism had largely steered away from national security goals and scientific manpower prerogatives. Amid scientific shortages, critiques of military science, and an unpopular war in Vietnam, technocratic arguments seemed less compelling. The growth of broad-based support for women's rights and a burgeoning women's movement, moreover, enabled feminists of all ages to embrace the language of equal rights. In doing so, they made notable gains in education and employment, where they benefited from recent antidiscrimination legislation. This shift in emphasis can also be seen in the activities of the women's scientific societies that proliferated during this period, bringing together generations of feminists. Older technocratic feminists now framed their ongoing outreach efforts as explicitly feminist ones, as did new recruits. Increasingly, however, as opposition to the women's rights movement mounted, so did feminists' willingness to draw on older manpower concerns to protect their gains. Few saw this approach as inconsistent but rather as a pragmatic strategy designed to maximize support for their goals. It was also one that reformers would extend in the decades ahead, as they continued to work on behalf of expanding and improving women's scientific participation.

Epilogue

In February 1982, the New England Chapter of AWIS hosted a wine and cheese reception to fete Edward Kennedy for his championing of the women in science legislation. The event, which was cosponsored by a number of women's organizations such as the Boston section of the Society of Women Engineers, was attended by approximately 300 women and men, including the senator himself. Several women's groups that had previously collaborated with Kennedy also sent representatives to participate in the ceremony. Nancy Russo of FOPW presented the senator with a framed poster from its "Woman Scholar Series." Vera Kistiakowsky, the current president of the national AWIS, gave Kennedy a pin emblazoned with the association's name.[1]

The ceremony also provided a platform for criticizing the most recent attacks on the legislation, which had resulted in another round of budget cuts. With the exception of the visiting professorships, none of the programs contained in the act that Kistiakowsky, the FOPW, and other feminists had helped Kennedy to prepare received congressional funding for the coming year. In his remarks to the audience, Kennedy railed against the Reagan administration for "wasting the talents of the nation's women" and neglecting "our greatest untapped natural resource."[2] The president of the New England chapter, Stephanie Bird, similarly charged, "It is not simply that we deserve equal rights and opportunities, rather it is to the advantage of all of us that such a valuable resource not be wasted."[3]

Although Kennedy and women's groups had previously invoked technocratic manpower concerns when advocating for the legislation, they did so here with even more vigor. The current social and political climate helps explain why. The so-called Reagan Revolution had resulted in significant setbacks for American women. The backlash against the gains of the women's movement curtailed public support for feminism and would result in the defeat of the Equal Rights Amendment that summer. At the same time, the Reagan administration worked to refortify the national security state by funneling monies into federal research and development. By 1986, federal R&D expenditures would account for roughly $57 billion, a 27 percent

Nancy Russo of the Federation of Organizations for Professional Women with Edward Kennedy at a reception in his honor, February 1982. Photograph by Lilian A. Kemp. Courtesy of Schlesinger Library, Radcliffe Institute for Advanced Study, Harvard University.

increase over the pre-downturn peak levels in 1967 (in constant dollars). Much of this growth was in the defense sector, which by the end of the decade would command 70 percent of the federal research and development budget and approximate spending proportions from the 1950s.[4] The Cold War, it seemed, was once again in full swing.

As budgets swelled, so did concern with ensuring an adequate supply of scientific "manpower." While fears of a scientific shortage turned out to be unjustified, the very prospect of such a crisis elicited significant attention from both the press and policymakers.[5] Just weeks before the Kennedy reception, the *Boston Globe* carried a story reporting on projected trends in the field of engineering. Lieutenant General James W. Stansberry, who was in charge of developing electronic weaponry for the Air Force, was quoted as saying, "The problem is: There are not enough engineers. . . . We are at the stage now of recognizing the problem and beating the drum about it."[6] Earl S. King, the chief recruiter for Westinghouse's Defense and Electronic Systems Center (where, incidentally, Naomi McAfee of the Society of Women Engineers worked), lamented the recent hiring difficulties he had faced that fall. Despite pouring nearly $30,000 into newspaper and radio advertisements, recruiter wages, and travel expenses, King only managed to hire two people due to the fierce competition for available personnel. Lynne Brown, an economist at the Federal Reserve Bank of Boston, predicted that "when the new defense spending is felt . . . the manpower problems will be worse than ever."[7]

The identification of female scientists as a valuable source of scientific manpower offered Kennedy and Bird a pragmatic and politically savvy defense of the women in science legislation. This strategy, as we have seen, had long aided reformers, especially in conservative times. During World War II, Virginia Gildersleeve persuaded Columbia's School of Engineering to admit female students by citing the wartime demand for "trained brains." Employing similar logic, she and Lillian Gilbreth collaborated with industry officials and government bureaucrats to establish short-term science and engineering training programs for women. Although many female scientists found themselves displaced or demoted when immediate manpower needs subsided, newly defined national security prerogatives resulted in a push for "perpetual preparedness." Amid the emerging Cold War, organizations such as the Society of Women Engineers and Sigma Delta Epsilon held career conferences, published vocational literature, and provided personal encouragement to female students in pursuit of this aim. Increasingly, they turned their attention to combating "feminine fallout" by assisting older women and married women in balancing scientific work and domestic life. Polly Bunting's mathematics retraining program at Douglass and her institute at Radcliffe similarly situated women's education and employment within a diffuse national security state.

These efforts were significant not only because they expanded opportunities for women in an era generally hostile to their interests but also because they paved the way for later reforms. With the resurgence of organized feminism in the 1960s and 1970s, technocratic feminists were joined by other activists who shared their desire to encourage and support female scientists. Although most second-wave activists distanced themselves from national security goals and embraced more explicitly feminist language, they extended many of the outreach efforts already under way. Popular activities included hosting career conferences, writing guidance literature, providing scholarships, and assisting women in balancing family life with scientific careers. They also, on occasion, invoked technocratic manpower concerns in defense of their efforts. This was especially the case as the antifeminist backlash gained momentum.

While technocratic feminism proved useful, however, it also constricted possibilities for change. The identification of women as an "untapped" source of scientific talent rendered impossible any serious critiques of their subsequent commodification and utilization. The pretext that womanpower was available (and exploitable) rested at the heart of this technocratic discourse and helps account for why otherwise implausible allies expressed any willingness to cultivate female intellect. Tethering women's scientific participation to the manpower needs of the nation also undermined feminist interest in equality. As a member of the War Manpower Commission's Women's Advisory Committee remarked in 1943, "Winning the war is the big thing, and the particular considerations of women in the winning of the war is the secondary thing."[8] Thus, through activists' own maneuvering, women's rights were relegated to second place.

Technocratic feminists' proclaimed interest in women's utilization, rather than women's liberation, also left little room for a radical restructuring of sexual relations or scientific life. Their advocacy of part-time work and study programs did help create opportunities for women that corresponded to their life patterns. But these activities did not pose any serious challenge to women's subordinate status in science or society. Most technocratic feminists, moreover, regarded scientific schooling and work as areas where properly counseled women could be readily inserted. Consequently, they repeatedly denied associations between masculinity and scientific success, insisting instead that "brains have no sex" and that bright girls need not fear the loss of their femininity. That science was a masculine enterprise seemed to be an unfortunate but ultimately reversible circumstance once more women entered the field.

During the 1970s, many second-wave feminists shared this view of science as an arena where women could succeed if given a fair chance. As a result, much of their work in the classroom and the courtroom was aimed at ensuring equitable access and advancement opportunities. As time wore on, it became evident that disparities in pay and promotion persisted, as did the isolation that many female scientists felt, despite women's increasing representation in both education and employment. Although women's share of Ph.D.s in science and engineering doubled during the 1970s, they remained concentrated in the biological and behavioral sciences where they had historically been most welcome.[9] Women did make notable gains in fields such as engineering, where the percentage of bachelor's degrees awarded to women reached a new high of nearly 15 percent in 1985. They remained, however, greatly outnumbered by men.[10] Meanwhile, in academia, the percentage of women scientists increased from 14 percent to 19 percent between 1974 and 1984, but of these, 25 percent were not on the tenure track, compared with just 9 percent of their male peers.[11] Across the board, women scientists remained more likely to be unemployed, underemployed, and underpaid.[12] Consequently, efforts aimed at simply including more women in science were increasingly questioned by some feminist scientists and theorists who espoused more radical critiques of science itself. By examining scientific methods, cultures, and values, these feminists articulated how assumptions about gender were inextricably tied to the practice of science and the production of knowledge. Some even viewed science as so irreparably masculine that they advocated replacing conventional practices with female-centered alternatives.[13]

As these viewpoints gained currency, women's scientific societies could not help but take notice. In the spring of 1982, AWIS printed in its newsletter an article by member Carol C. Halpern entitled "I Dream of a Feminist Science" and encouraged readers to ask themselves, "As women, should we go along with the system or try to change the system?"[14] Halpern's piece described her recent decision to leave her research lab, explaining that the scientific establishment only prized characteristics associated with men, namely, "a strong sense of competitiveness with the main focus on self with work carried out in a hierarchical structure—the laboratory."[15] Rather than continuing what she regarded as a fruitless struggle for acceptance, she advocated for the creation of a science more consistent with her own values and "evolving philosophy of life."[16] According to the newsletter editors, Halpern's article generated more correspondence than any topic had in years. One response that they reprinted came from Ruth Berman, who identified herself as "an 'older' woman scientist, with degrees from and experience working in Ivy League universities and major institutions."[17] Berman found that Halpern's piece hit particularly close to home and led her to question whether AWIS might reexamine its approach to assisting female scientists. She noted, "Most AWIS activities now seem to be predicated on the assumption that by just continuing to press for more jobs for women in science, women will gradually be infiltrated into the established male science hierarchy." "Is this idea credible any longer?" she inquired, and suggested that it was not.[18]

In light of these concerns, a growing number of feminist scientists and women's scientific societies debated whether they could or should seek more fundamental changes. In 1987, the Alpha Chapter of Sigma Delta Epsilon–Graduate Women in Science took up this question at a potluck dinner meeting that it arranged with the widely acclaimed feminist physicist-turned-philosopher and historian of science Evelyn Fox Keller, who drew on her recent writings on the subject to offer some insights.[19] This theme also received considerable attention at chapter meetings, national conferences, and in the pages of organizations' newsletters, as members increasingly questioned their own research practices and priorities.[20] Other approaches focused on creating what biologist and women's studies proponent Sue Rosser would later term a "female-friendly science." The concept, which was most widely popularized in Rosser's 1990 book of the same name, called on educators to recognize the presence of masculine perspectives in science and to demonstrate the relevance of scientific problems to women's lives and experiences.[21]

As women's scientific societies considered how they might better facilitate the success of female scientists, they most frequently returned to familiar approaches, such as providing personal encouragement and mentoring. Building on its earlier initiatives, Sigma Delta Epsilon–Graduate Women in Science introduced its Big Sisters program in 1985. By matching female students with professional women in their areas of interest, the program aimed to provide "the same advantages that men have traditionally enjoyed from the 'old boys' network."[22] Meanwhile, the Society of Women Engineers expanded its own Big Sister program with help from a $500,000 grant that the society received from NASA during the 1988–89 fiscal year.[23] A three-year grant from the Alfred P. Sloan Foundation similarly assisted AWIS to expand its "Mentoring Project." One of the major outcomes of the award was the publication of the guidebook, *A Hand Up*, which featured more than fifty short essays offering advice to female scientists at all stages of their careers.[24]

Federal agencies, universities, industries, and various organizations also embarked on a range of efforts to make science more "female friendly." Although the National Science Foundation's visiting professorships for women scientists aimed primarily to assist individual women carry out their research and to diversify existing faculties, the program additionally required that participants spend 30 percent of their time teaching and encouraging female students in some way. Throughout the 1980s and early 1990s, visiting professors engaged in such varied activities as establishing Society of Women Engineers chapters, forming mentor networks among graduate students, and teaching courses about women in science in conjunction with their host institutions' women's studies programs.[25] Around the same time, the Girl Scouts of America not only expanded its offerings of science-related merit badges but also benefited from the American Association for the Advancement of Science's new Girls and Science program which helped train troop leaders in educational techniques, beginning in 1989.[26] That same year, Douglass College announced the creation of a math and science dormitory for female students that was named after previous deans and scientists, Polly Bunting and Jewel Plummer Cobb. The Bunting-Cobb Residence Hall provided a home to 100 undergraduate students, as well as the 10 graduate students who lived there and served as mentors and tutors. Residents enjoyed access to an on-site computer lab, a science and engineering reference library, and a seminar program. The initiative proved so popular that the college had to start a waiting list.[27]

Despite the evolution of feminist approaches to science, there remained a strong interested in achieving a "critical mass." There also remained the occasional reliance on technocratic manpower concerns. In her preface to AWIS's mentoring guide, *A Hand Up*, the cardiologist and first female director of the National Institutes of Health, Bernadine Healy, credited the enrollment of women in science and medicine with staving off a "brainpower shortage" and "an erosion of the scientific talent base."[28] The announcement of the Bunting-Cobb Residence Hall that appeared in the *New York Times* claimed that the dormitory would help "address the national shortage of female scientists and engineers" and assist the United States in remaining competitive in science and technology.[29] In an opinion piece that was published in *The Scientist* in the fall of 1987, Betty Vetter, the director of the recently renamed Committee on Professionals in Science and Technology, was even more direct in her appeal to technocratic manpower concerns. Vetter surveyed recent trends in women's education and employment and bemoaned the continued underrepresentation of women in scientific fields. She warned "that women do not participate equally with men in science . . . should be a cause of concern for the nation." "If this trend continues," Vetter explained, "America's ability to maintain international technological competitiveness over the next two decades will be in jeopardy." Her overarching message was perhaps best expressed, however, in the article's succinct title: "Forget Affirmative Action. Think National Survival."[30]

The immediacy of Vetter's warning became less dire with the end of the Cold War and the demise of the Soviet Union. As policymakers reordered national security priorities, federal outlays for scientific research and development decreased, most notably in the defense sector.[31] Fears of a scientific shortage also diminished during the 1990s, despite early projections and escalating concerns regarding America's global competiveness. In 1990, the president of the American Association for the Advancement of Science, Richard C. Atkinson, had predicted that the demand for scientists would outstrip supply by nearly 400,000 persons by the year 2000. But as the decade progressed, economic indicators failed to provide evidence of a shortage. The number of American-born science and engineering graduates remained constant, while a growing dependence on foreign-born students and scientists resulted in an overall expansion of the scientific workforce. So significant was this shift that, by the end of decade, more than half of all science and engineering Ph.D.s in the United States under the age of 45 were foreign born.[32]

This trend was curtailed in the wake of the terrorist attacks that took place on September 11, 2001. As the United States tightened its immigration policies and visa restrictions, the number of first-time, full-time science and engineering graduate enrollments among international students declined by about 8 percent for men and 1 percent for women.[33] Renewed fears of scientific shortages were heightened by new national security commitments both at home and abroad. Amid the global "war on terror" and the quest for "homeland security," federal expenditures for scientific research and development once again increased. While an emphasis on global competiveness remained important, most of this spending took place in the defense sector. By 2006, federal spending for defense-related research and development had grown at an average annual rate of 7.4 percent, while nondefense R&D expenditures had climbed at an average rate of 4.5 percent each year.[34]

These developments shaped not only the contours of the national security state but also efforts to improve women's participation in science, as reformers once again turned to technocratic feminism. The most prominent example took place in the firestorm of controversy ignited by the 2005 "Summersgate" incident. In January of that year, Harvard University president Lawrence Summers addressed a room of roughly forty people who had gathered in Cambridge to attend the National Bureau of Economic Research's Conference on Diversifying the Science and Engineering Workforce. Many of those present at the closed invitational meeting had spent much of the past two decades researching women in science and were therefore shocked to hear Summers's provocative comments on the subject. According to Summers, women's representation in high-ranking positions lagged behind men's for three reasons: women's inability or unwillingness to put in the eighty-hour workweeks required for tenure and promotion; biological differences between women and men in determining ability and preferences for scientific work; and patterns of discrimination and socialization.[35] He viewed the last reason at the least important of the three, ranking it behind both "the high-powered job hypothesis" and "issues of intrinsic aptitude."[36]

Many feminist scholars and scientists in attendance, such as Sue Rosser and the engineering professor Denice Denton, who was the chancellor designate of the University of California, Santa Cruz, at the time, reported being deeply offended by Summers's remarks. MIT biologist and Harvard Ph.D. Nancy Hopkins found his comments so upsetting that she walked out halfway through the talk. Later that day, in an unrelated e-mail exchange with a *Boston Globe* reporter, Hopkins leaked details of the incident, which quickly became front page news and sparked an outpouring of both criticism and support for the Harvard president.[37] In the weeks and months that followed, hundreds of newspapers, websites, popular publications, and television programs covered an increasingly impassioned debate over the validity of Summers's claims and the implications of his actions. In the process, they refocused attention on the status of women in science and the perennial question of how far they still had to go before achieving equality with men.

Summers's remarks made obvious to many women in science that their struggle was far from over. In response, a small group of female scientists and engineers, including Denton and Rosser, petitioned Congress to help expand opportunities for women in scientific fields. They called for an in-depth examination of the cultural factors, economic components, and discriminatory practices affecting female scientists. They also advocated for proactive measures, such as the enactment of federal legislation, the provision of fellowships, and new mentoring opportunities, that would support the education and employment of women. It is significant that, in doing so, they relied heavily on national security prerogatives and scientific manpower concerns, warning of "the negative ramifications of having one-half of our nation's population removed from [these] fields." "Unless we act now, on a national level, to address the lack of women in math and science, our nation runs the risk not only of losing its technological prowess, but its national security as well."[38]

These familiar concerns and strategies quickly attracted broad-based support. The petition circulated widely and by May included the names of more than 5,000 female scientists and engineers. Some, such as Nancy Hopkins, had been present for Summers's now infamous address. Others came from women's scientific societies, such as the Society of Women Engineers, which was especially well represented. Hundreds of students affiliated with SWE chapters across the country endorsed the petition's goals.

So did some of the society's earliest members, such as Patricia Brown, who had compiled *Women in Engineering* in the 1950s and who had served as president in the early 1960s. Naomi McAfee, who had overseen the society during feminism's second wave and who had later assumed leadership positions in both AWIS and FOPW, lent her name as well. Also included was Fann Harding, who not only had helped establish FOPW in the early 1970s but also was active in AWIS and Sigma Delta Epsilon–Graduate Women in Science.[39]

The presence of these names, and the petition more generally, highlights the interconnectedness of feminist efforts to improve women's scientific participation. By recognizing these points of convergence, we can better see how the history of feminist interest in science is marked by far more continuity than has been previously understood. An insistence on the need to dismantle gender stereotypes and encourage women in the field is long-standing, as is the use of scientific manpower concerns. Consequently, the older women who had embarked on their activism in the early years of the Cold War likely viewed the petition as an extension of their previous work. At the same time, the precarious balancing of explicitly feminist issues with national security prerogatives must have struck some second-wave activists as similar to their own efforts in advancing the women in science legislation more than two decades earlier. That their work remained unfinished was also apparent, as noted by several of the petition's authors who, in a separate article, called for a campaign to "fulfill the promises of the Science and Technology Equal Opportunity Act" some twenty-five years later.[40]

Defying easy categorization, the search for scientific womanpower is a cumulative and ongoing one that bears important lessons for the present as well as the past. In part, technocratic feminism continues to shape discussions surrounding women in science, as can be seen amid the growing national preoccupation with cybersecurity, or the defense of computer systems from malicious attacks. The widespread use of computers by the military, government, schools, financial institutions, transportation centers, and personal homes (to name just a few) has made vulnerable nearly every aspect of American society. So important are these systems that President Barack Obama called cyberthreats to them "one of the most serious economic and national security challenges we face as a nation."[41] In 2012, U.S. Secretary of Defense Leon Panetta warned that a breach of the nation's computing systems would be akin to a "cyber-Pearl Harbor."[42] Other politicians and pundits have termed the struggle for cybersecurity the "New Cold War."[43] Consistent with these analogies, there has emerged in recent years an influx of federal funds to cyber-related fields as well as increased concern with "scientific womanpower." Since 2006, the National Science Foundation has funded workshops on "Cool Careers in Cybersecurity for Girls" in the hope of attracting middle-school students to computer science. In 2011, the Society of Women Engineers began offering a $10,000 Cybersecurity Scholarship that was funded by Applied Computer Security Associates, a nonprofit organization.[44] These various initiatives reflect the broader opinion that, as one *Huffington Post* contributor recently wrote, "to effectively fortify American cyberdefense . . . the U.S can't afford to neglect the talent and brain power of half its population."[45]

While technocratic concerns and national security imperatives have most obviously informed efforts to improve women's scientific participation, they can be found in other feminist struggles as well. The recent decision to include women in combat positions, for example, has been defended on various grounds, including the need to make better use of the nation's "brainpower" in modernized warfare.[46] In the debate over gay marriage, some supporters have argued that legalization would protect American competiveness and security by staving off the "brain drain" that they predict will occur as talented couples seek more hospitable places to live.[47] On a global scale, international organizations have worked to empower women and girls in developing countries by maximizing their "untapped potential." These efforts, which have assisted such varied groups as women coffee producers in East Africa to Cambodian silk entrepreneurs, purport to boost not only local economies but also regional stability and national security.[48] What these seemingly disparate examples reveal is a broader recognition of technocratic feminism as a viable tool for social change. This is not to say that technocratic feminism is the only, or even most effective, approach used by reformers in pursuit of their goals. Certainly, rights-based arguments have been levied quite successfully in defense of gay marriage, women's combat inclusion, and support for women-owned businesses. The same holds true for arguments made on behalf of recruiting women to cybersecurity and science more generally. Although explicit calls for equality have helped reframe the issues in ways that the conservative claims of technocratic feminism could not, they have also struck some reformers as less safe or less suitably strategic. The past and present appeal of technocratic feminism, then, is its promise of expediency and resonance with wide audiences even—if not especially—in the absence of broad-based support for women's rights.

Reclaiming the history of technocratic feminism and situating it within a long women's movement illustrates continuities in feminist activism across time and space. This history helps us to comprehend the range of possibilities faced by feminist reformers, as well as the problems that they encountered. Technocratic feminism has indeed proven useful in securing funding for feminist programs, forging alliances with unlikely allies, challenging gender stereotypes, and providing much needed encouragement to women and girls. It has been less successful, however, in tackling the deep-rootedness of women's subordination in both science and society. In many cases, the same manpower concerns that technocratic feminists appropriated tended to disadvantage women. Moreover, reformers' reliance on national security prerogatives necessarily, but unfortunately, limited their ability to launch meaningful critiques of them. That technocratic discourse has both advanced and subsumed feminist goals remains the central issue and unresolved dilemma at the heart of technocratic feminism.

Notes

Abbreviations

AAUW Archives	American Association of University Women Archives, 1881–1976, microfilm edition, American Association of University Women Archives, Washington, D.C.
BPW Records	Records of the National Federation of Business and Professional Women's Clubs, National Federation of Business and Professional Women's Clubs Archives, Washington, D.C.
Bunting Records	Mary Ingraham Bunting Records of the President of Radcliffe College, 1960–72, RG II, Series 4, Radcliffe College Archives, Schlesinger Library, Radcliffe Institute for Advanced Study, Harvard University, Cambridge, Massachusetts
CEW Records	American Council on Education, Commission on the Education of Women Records, 1953–61, B-22, Schlesinger Library, Radcliffe Institute for Advanced Study, Harvard University, Cambridge, Massachusetts
Columbia WWII Collection	Columbia University in World War II Collection, University Archives, Rare Book and Manuscript Library, Columbia University, New York, New York
Dean's Office/Departmental Correspondence	Dean's Office and Departmental Correspondence, 1904–60, Barnard College Archives, Barnard Library, Barnard College, New York, New York
Douglass College Dean Records	Records of the Dean of Douglass College (Group I), 1887–1973 (RG 19/A0/01), Special Collections and University Archives, Rutgers University, New Brunswick, New Jersey
Farley Papers	Jennie Farley Papers, #25-3-2710, Division of Rare and Manuscript Collections, Cornell University Library, Ithaca, New York
Ford Foundation Records	Ford Foundation Archive, Rockefeller Archive Center, Sleepy Hollow, New York

Gilbreth Papers	Frank and Lillian Gilbreth Papers, Karnes Archives and Special Collections, Purdue University Libraries, West Lafayette, Indiana
Gildersleeve Papers Columbia	Virginia Crocheron Gildersleeve Papers, 1898–1962, Rare Book and Manuscript Library, Columbia University, New York, New York
Gildersleeve Personal Papers	Personal Papers of Virginia Crocheron Gildersleeve, ca. 1910–63, Barnard College Archives, Barnard Library, Barnard College, New York, New York
Guttman Papers	Rita Guttman Papers, A/G985, Schlesinger Library, Radcliffe Institute for Advanced Study, Harvard University, Cambridge, Massachusetts
Harding Papers	Fann Harding Papers, MS 320, Special Collections Department, Iowa State University Library, Ames, Iowa
Iota Sigma Pi Records	Iota Sigma Pi Records, MS 321, Special Collections Department, Iowa State University Library, Ames, Iowa
IWPR Papers	Institute of Women's Professional Relations Papers, 1928–41, B-5, Schlesinger Library, Radcliffe Institute for Advanced Study, Harvard University, Cambridge, Massachusetts
Kistiakowsky Papers	Vera Kistiakowsky Papers, MC 485, Institute Archives and Special Collections, Massachusetts Institute of Technology, Cambridge, Massachusetts
Leopold Papers	Alice Koller Leopold Papers, 1953–56, A-30, Schlesinger Library, Radcliffe Institute for Advanced Study, Harvard University, Cambridge, Massachusetts
MIT Associate Dean for Student Affairs Records	Records of the Office of the Associate Dean for Student Affairs, AC 22, Institute Archives and Special Collections, Massachusetts Institute of Technology, Cambridge, Massachusetts
MIT Oral History	Massachusetts Institute of Technology, Oral History Program, oral history interviews on women in science and engineering, MC86, Institute Archives and Special Collections, Massachusetts Institute of Technology, Cambridge, Massachusetts
NSF Records	Record Group 307: Records of the National Science Foundation, National Archives and Records Administration, Archives II, College Park, Maryland

Office of Education Records   Record Group 12: Records of the Office of
                              Education, National Archives and Records
                              Administration, Archives II, College Park,
                              Maryland
         Patterson Papers   Jean Nickerson Patterson, Curtiss-Wright
                              Engineering Cadettes Records, RS 21/7/148,
                              Special Collections Department, Iowa State
                              University Library, Ames, Iowa
            PCSW Records   United States, President's Commission on the
                              Status of Women Records, 1961–63, B-26,
                              Schlesinger Library, Radcliffe Institute for
                              Advanced Study, Harvard University, Cambridge,
                              Massachusetts
          Peterson Papers   Esther Peterson Papers, 1884–1998, MC 450,
                              Schlesinger Library, Radcliffe Institute for
                              Advanced Study, Harvard University, Cambridge,
                              Massachusetts
      Raushenbush Papers   Esther Raushenbush Papers, 1945–79, 80-M243,
                              Schlesinger Library, Radcliffe Institute for
                              Advanced Study, Harvard University, Cambridge,
                              Massachusetts
          Reynard Papers   Elizabeth Reynard Papers, 1934–62, A-128,
                              Schlesinger Library, Radcliffe Institute for
                              Advanced Study, Harvard University, Cambridge,
                              Massachusetts
          Roscher Papers   Nina Matheny Roscher Papers, MS 578, Special
                              Collections Department, Iowa State University
                              Library, Ames, Iowa
       SDE–Alpha Records   Sigma Delta Epsilon, Alpha Chapter Records,
                              #37-4-835, Division of Rare and Manuscript
                              Collections, Cornell University Library, Ithaca,
                              New York
             SDE Records   Sigma Delta Epsilon Records, #3605, Division of
                              Rare and Manuscript Collections, Cornell
                              University Library, Ithaca, New York
           Shouse Papers   Catherine Filene Shouse Papers, 1878–1998,
                              MC448, Schlesinger Library, Radcliffe Institute for
                              Advanced Study, Harvard University, Cambridge,
                              Massachusetts
              SWE-Boston   Records of the Society of Women Engineers—
                              Boston Section, 2001-M17 and 2001-M58,
                              Schlesinger Library, Radcliffe Institute for
                              Advanced Study, Harvard University, Cambridge,
                              Massachusetts

Introduction

1. Summers, "Remarks at NBER Conference on Diversifying the Science and Engineering Workforce," http://www.president.harvard.edu/speeches/summers_2005/nber.php.

2. Denton et al. to Senators Ron Wyden and George Allen, http://www.mentornet.net/wyden-allen.

3. Rossiter, *Women Scientists in America*, vols. 1–3. For an earlier treatment in the European context, see Schiebinger, *The Mind Has No Sex?*

4. Schiebinger, *Has Feminism Changed Science?*, 68.

5. Although college women's enrollment increased throughout the post–World War II period, their percentage of the student population decreased, due largely to the influx of veterans using the GI Bill. This phenomenon, along with the overall expansion of research universities and research initiatives, rendered women what Linda Eisenmann terms "incidental students." See Eisenmann, *Higher Education for Women in Postwar America*, 6, 43–57.

6. Wheaton, "Challenging the 'Climate of Unexpectation,'" 99–101; Friedan, *The Feminine Mystique*, 13; Mary Ingraham Bunting, "Oral Memoir," interview by Jeannette Bailey Cheek, September–October 1978, transcript, 87–88, Schlesinger Library, Radcliffe Institute for Advanced Study, Harvard University, Cambridge,

Massachusetts. Similar critiques by historians can be found in Meyerowitz, "Beyond the Feminine Mystique," and Coontz, *A Strange Stirring*. For additional insights into Friedan's radical past, see Horowitz, *Betty Friedan and the Making of The Feminine Mystique*.

7. The idea of a "bridge" comes from Lynn, *Progressive Women in Conservative Times*, 3. The literature addressing women's activism in the mid-twentieth century is increasingly vast. Some excellent edited collections include Meyerowitz, *Not June Cleaver*, and Laughlin and Castledine, *Breaking the Wave*.

8. Gabin, *Feminism in the Labor Movement*; Hartmann, *The Other Feminists*; Deslippe, *"Rights Not Roses"*; Cobble, *The Other Women's Movement*.

9. Lynn, *Progressive Women in Conservative Times*; Alonso, "Mayhem and Moderation"; Zarnow, "The Legal Origin of 'The Personal Is Political.'"

10. Weigand, *Red Feminism*; Storrs, "Red Scare Politics and the Suppression of Popular Front Feminism."

11. D'Emilio, *Sexual Politics, Sexual Communities*; Bérubé, *Coming Out Under Fire*; Solinger, "Extreme Danger"; Gallo, *Different Daughters*.

12. Rupp and Taylor, *Survival in the Doldrums*; Harrison, *On Account of Sex*; Hartmann, "Women's Employment and the Domestic Ideal"; Meyerowitz, "Sex, Gender, and the Cold War Language of Reform"; Eisenmann, *Higher Education for Women in Postwar America*.

13. May, *Homeward Bound*, 14.

14. The classic account of Women Strike for Peace is Swerdlow, *Women Strike for Peace*. A more recent treatment can be found in Estrepa, "Taking the White Gloves Off."

15. McEnaney, *Civil Defense Begins at Home*, 5, 88–89.

16. Dudziak, *Cold War Civil Rights*; Borstelmann, *The Cold War and the Color Line*; Von Eschen, *Race against Empire*.

17. Meyerowitz, "Sex, Gender, and the Cold War Language of Reform," 114.

18. Ibid., 108–13.

19. Eisenmann, *Higher Education for Women in Postwar America*; Harrison, *On Account of Sex*; Hartmann, "Women's Employment and the Domestic Ideal."

20. Rossiter, *Women Scientists in America*, vols. 1–3; Schiebinger, *Has Feminism Changed Science?*; Bix, "Feminism Where Men Predominate"; Oldenziel, "Multiple-Entry Visas"; Mack, "What Difference Has Feminism Made to Engineering?"; Kohlstedt, "Sustaining Gains."

21. Cobble, *The Other Women's Movement*, 1.

22. Hewitt, *No Permanent Waves*; Laughlin and Castledine, *Breaking the Wave*.

23. Scholars calling for a "long women's movement" have done so following the footsteps of Jacquelyn Dowd Hall's similar recasting of the civil rights movement. See, for example, Laughlin, Gallagher, Cobble, Boris, Nadasen, Gilmore, and Zarnow, "Is It Time to Jump Ship?" Cobble discusses this idea most explicitly on 87–88. For Hall's original formulation, see Hall, "The Long Civil Rights Movement."

1. Virginia C. Gildersleeve, "We Need Trained Brains," *New York Times Magazine*, March 29, 1942, 18.

2. Gildersleeve, *Many a Good Crusade*, 265; Elizabeth Reynard, "How Trained Brains Are Used in the War Effort (Being the Thorts [*sic*] of E.R. Concerning Dean Gildersleeve's HOME WORK)," n.d., and "Educational Implications of This Use of Scientists," ca. 1942, both in folder 153, box 11, Reynard Papers. The Manhattan Project would not be designated as such until August 1942. See Groves, *Now It Can Be Told*, 17.

3. Gildersleeve, "We Need Trained Brains," 37.

4. For an overview of the historic relationship between science and war, see Roland, "Science and War."

5. Kevles, *The Physicists*, 290–91, 289; Baxter, *Scientists against Time*, 6, 36, 419–47; Rife, *Lise Meitner and the Dawn of the Nuclear Age*, 178–250.

6. Bush, *Pieces of the Action*, 32–33. The most comprehensive biography of Bush to date is Zachary, *Endless Frontier*.

7. Bush, *Pieces of the Action*, 31–32, 36–37; Vannevar Bush, "Science and National Defense," *Journal of Applied Physics* 12, no. 12 (December 1941): 823–25. For a more detailed overview of the NDRC, see Stewart, *Organizing Scientific Research for War*, 7–34.

8. Conant, *My Several Lives*, 236.

9. Dupree, *Science in the Federal Government*, 370; Kevles, *The Physicists*, 298. For an analysis of the importance of the research contract more generally, see Dupree, "The Great Instauration of 1940."

10. Pursell, "Science Agencies in World War II," 363–64; Kevles, *The Physicists*, 299–300; Dupree, *Science in the Federal Government*, 371–72.

11. Geiger, *Research and Relevant Knowledge*, 6; Dupree, *Science in the Federal Government*, 373; Baxter, *Scientists against Time*, 125; Kevles, *The Physicists*, 299–300.

12. This number represents 315 industrial laboratories and 150 academic institutions. Baxter, *Scientists against Time*, 125; Bush, *Endless Horizons*, 111; William L. Laurence, "Science Mobilizes a Test-Tube Army," *New York Times*, January 3, 1943, A32.

13. Hart, *Forged Consensus*, 125–26, 128; Cochrane, *The National Academy of Sciences*, 405. The most comprehensive account of the scientific contributions of women in the navy is Williams, *Improbable Warriors*. Over the course of the war, more than 100,000 women served in the WAVES, but the overwhelming majority were concentrated in clerical and hospital work. The same pattern held true for the other military services. See Hartmann, *The Home Front and Beyond*, 37.

14. Sherry, *In the Shadow of War*, 69, 73; Craven and Cate, *Army Air Forces in World War II*, 6:187; Hart, *Forged Consensus*, 121.

15. Bush, "Science and National Defense," 824; Baxter, *Scientists against Time*, 19.

16. The roster was originally developed as a joint project of the National Resources Planning Board and the Civil Service Commission. It was later transferred

to the War Manpower Commission in April 1942. Over the course of the war, the roster registered 690,000 men and women. Leonard Carmichael, "The National Roster of Scientific and Specialized Personnel," *Science* 92, no. 2381 (August 16, 1940): 135–37; Louis Starks, "'Brains' of Country Indexed in Defense," special to the *New York Times*, January 23, 1941, 1; "National Roster of Scientific and Specialized Personnel," *Journal of Applied Physics* 14, no. 8 (August 1943): 380–84; Baxter, *Scientists against Time*, 127.

17. Stewart, *Organizing Scientific Research for War*, 256; Baxter, *Scientists against Time*, 127; Cochrane, *The National Academy of Sciences*, 406. Cochrane explains that "although the OSRD contract with the Academy was terminated in September 1943 as the emergency subsided, the Office of Scientific Personnel, as an agency of the Academy, continued to operate throughout the war and after, recruiting trained men in critical fields for university laboratories and industry, working with Selective Service to prevent unwise drafting, assisting in the operations of the National Roster, and serving, through the Roster's facilities, the specialized needs of OSRD and other agencies."

18. Stewart, *Organizing Scientific Research for War*, 256.

19. Cardozier, *Colleges and Universities in World War II*, 165–79.

20. A brief history of the program and its goals, along with reproductions of the winning essays for 1942, can be found in Science Service, *Youth Looks at Science and War*. For additional information regarding the program, see Terzian, "'Adventures in Science,'" and Phares, *Seeking—and Finding—Science Talent*.

21. Roland, "Science and War," 264; Dupree, *Science in the Federal Government*, 372; Reingold, "Vannevar Bush's New Deal for Research," 315; Leslie, *The Cold War and American Science*, 2–8. The term "defense matrix" comes from Mullins, *The Defense Matrix*.

22. Gildersleeve, *Many a Good Crusade*, 18, 20–21, 25; Rosenberg, *Changing the Subject*, 121. Harry's untimely death at the age of twenty-one had a profound effect on the Gildersleeve family. The house, which used to bustle with visitors and activity, fell quiet and lonely, "with plenty of time for reading." Gildersleeve, *Many a Good Crusade*, 34.

23. Gildersleeve, *Many a Good Crusade*, 34–35, 39, 47, 49, 51–53, 58–59, 62–65; Rosenberg, *Changing the Subject*, 54, 121–22.

24. Associated Press, "Dean Gildersleeve of Barnard Dead," *New York Times*, July 9, 1965, 1, 29; V. C. Gildersleeve, "Whither the Graduate," *New York Times*, June 2, 1935, XX2; Gildersleeve, *Many a Good Crusade*, 99–104; Rosenberg, *Changing the Subject*, 124–29; Rosenberg, "Virginia Gildersleeve," http://www.columbia.edu/cu/alumni/Magazine/Summer2001/Gildersleeve.html. With regard to the opening of the medical school, Gildersleeve had offered to help raise $50,000 to cover the cost of new women's facilities, which she did with help of the American Medical Women's Association and "an old gentleman from Texas." See Rosenberg, *Changing the Subject*, 127–28.

25. Gildersleeve, *Many a Good Crusade*, 71; Rosenberg, *Changing the Subject*, 123; Associated Press, "Dean Gildersleeve of Barnard Dead," 29; "Suffrage League," *Barnard Bulletin* 13, no. 4 (October 21, 1908): 1. Gildersleeve herself also

worked on behalf of suffrage. She was a member, for example, of the New York State Woman Suffrage Party and the National College Women's Suffrage League. See "Suffragists to See President," *New York Times*, October 25, 1917, 18, and Harper, *History of Woman Suffrage*, 5:663–64.

26. Rosenberg, *Changing the Subject*, 123; Gildersleeve, *Many a Good Crusade*, 71.

27. At the time of Gildersleeve's appointment, the American Association of University Women was still the Association of Collegiate Alumnae and would remain so until 1921. Office of Public Relations, Barnard College, Biography of Virginia Crocheron Gildersleeve, September 1962, folder: Gildersleeve Biographies, box 1, Gildersleeve Personal Papers; "Virginia C. Gildersleeve," biographical sketch, December 1940, folder 27, reel 2, AAUW Archives; Gildersleeve, *Many a Good Crusade*, 126–31.

28. "Barnard Dean Finds Anti-Feminism on the Rise," *New York Times*, September 15, 1934, 17; Rosenberg, *Changing the Subject*, 121, 124.

29. Gildersleeve, *Many a Good Crusade*, 97–98.

30. Gildersleeve, "We Need Trained Brains," 18; "Notes After a Conference," minutes of a meeting of representatives from the Seven Sister colleges, sent to Virginia Gildersleeve, January 24, 1942, folder: "Miscellaneous re: Barnard," box 3, Gildersleeve Papers Columbia; Reynard, "How Trained Brains Are Used in the War Effort (Being the Thorts [*sic*] of E.R. Concerning Dean Gildersleeve's HOME WORK)," n.d., and "Educational Implications of This Use of Scientists," ca. 1942, both in folder 153, box 11, Reynard Papers. During the war, the OSRD issued Columbia University 73 contracts, totaling $23,521,412.63, thus making it the fourth largest OSRD contractor. Statistics are found in Baxter, *Scientists against Time*, 456.

31. The National Committee on Education and Defense was established in August 1940 by the American Council on Education and the National Education Association. The umbrella organization initially consisted of representatives from fifty-five national educational organizations, including the American Association of University Women, the National Association of Deans of Women, the American Association for Advancement of Science, and the Society for the Promotion of Engineering Education. Five more organizations were later added, bring the total to sixty. Zook, Foreword to *Organizing Higher Education*, iii–v; Meta Glass to Virginia C. Gildersleeve, September 5, 1941 (list of organizations printed on back of National Committee on Education and Defense stationery), folder 85, box 6, Dean's Office/Departmental Correspondence. The name of the women's committee is reported inconsistently. See, for example, "Subcommittee on Women in College and the National Defense," January 15, 1941, and "Committee on Women in College and National Defense," n.d., both in folder 85, box 6, Dean's Office/Departmental Correspondence. Later, it was reorganized as the Committee on College Women Students and the War.

32. Meta Glass assumed the presidency of Sweet Briar College in 1925 and remained in that position until her retirement in 1946. She served as the national president of the American Association of University Women from 1933 to 1937. "Dr. Meta Glass," biographical sketch, [1946], and "Meta Glass," fellowship

announcement, *Journal of the American Association of University Women* 56, no. 4 (May 1963), clipping, both in folder 29, reel 2, AAUW Archives.

33. "Sub-Committee on Women in College and Defense," September 3, 1941, 1, folder 85, box 4, Dean's Office/Departmental Correspondence. For more on McAfee, see Akers, "Horton, Mildred McAfee."

34. Cowan, "Lillian Moller Gilbreth"; Lancaster, *Making Time*, 30–31. It was not until college that Gilbreth changed her name to Lillian, which she viewed as more dignified. See Lancaster, *Making Time*, 54.

35. Des Jardins, *Lillian Gilbreth*, 12; Lillian Gilbreth quoted in Lancaster, *Making Time*, 41.

36. Lancaster, *Making Time*, 41, 45, 54–58; Des Jardins, *Lillian Gilbreth*, 12, 21–22; Cowan, "Lillian Moller Gilbreth," 271.

37. Cowan, "Lillian Moller Gilbreth," 271–72; Lancaster, *Making Time*, 125; James N. Landis, "Lillian Moller Gilbreth, 1878–1972," in National Academy of Engineering, *Memorial Tributes* (Washington, D.C.: National Academy of Engineering, 1979), 1:89–94.

38. Cowan, "Lillian Moller Gilbreth," 271–72; Lancaster, *Making Time*, 123–24; Des Jardins, *Lillian Gilbreth*, 103–5; Trescott, "Women in the Intellectual Development of Engineering," 157–59; Gilbreth and Carey, *Cheaper by the Dozen*. Under the Gilbreth family system, all members played some role. Older children woke and dressed younger ones. Chores were assigned based on age and ability: taller children dusted tabletops while shorter children dusted legs and lower shelves. Although she was included in her siblings' retelling of this experience in *Cheaper by the Dozen*, Mary, a twelfth child, had died of diphtheria in 1912.

39. Cowan, "Lillian Moller Gilbreth," 272; Des Jardins, *Lillian Moller Gilbreth*, 118–43; Lancaster, *Making Time*, 228; Witzel, *The Encyclopedia of the History of American Management*, 213–16.

40. Rossiter, *Women Scientists in America*, 1:252–54, 262, 315.

41. Lancaster, *Making Time*, 283–86, 292, 301, 309.

42. "Report of Conference of College and University Presidents and Representatives of National Defense Agencies of Government, July 30–31, 1941," *Higher Education and National Defense* 13 (August 13, 1941): 3; "Sub-Committee on Women in College and Defense," September 3, 1941, 1, folder 85, box 4, Dean's Office/Departmental Correspondence.

43. "Sub-Committee on Women in College and Defense," September 3, 1941, 1, folder 85, box 4, Dean's Office/Departmental Correspondence.

44. Gildersleeve, *Many a Good Crusade*, 259.

45. "Baltimore Conference," *Higher Education and National Defense*, no. 20 (January 19, 1942): 1; National Committee on Education and Defense and United States Office of Education, *Higher Education and the War: The Report of a National Conference of College and University Presidents, Held in Baltimore, Md., January 3–4, 1942* (Washington, D.C.: American Council on Education, 1942).

46. "Report of Discussion by Section on Women in College at the Baltimore Conference," January 3, 1942, 1–2, folder 85, box 4, Dean's Office/Departmental Correspondence.

47. National Committee on Education and Defense and United States Office of Education, *Higher Education and the War*, 153–58.

48. Institute of Women's Professional Relations, *War Demands for Trained Personnel*, v; Memorandum for the Dean from Occupation Bureau, March 23, 1942, folder 70, box 4, Dean's Office/Departmental Correspondence. Both Virginia Gildersleeve and Lillian Moller Gilbreth had long-standing relationships with the institute. Gilbreth, for example, was one of the original members of the institute's board of directors. "Institute of Women's Professional Relations," pamphlet, 1929, folder 1, box 1, IWPR Papers. Other evidence of Gilbreth's and Gildersleeve's early collaboration with the Institute can be found in the proceedings of the Institute's 1935 Career Conference, folder 12, box 2, IWPR Papers. For the founding of the institute, see Catherine Filene Dodd, "Preparing Women for Work," *New York Times*, December 30, 1928, 43.

49. Rossiter, *Women Scientists in America*, 1:263–64; Edwards, "Shouse, Catherine Filene"; Filene, *Careers for Women*, vi–vii, xiv, 410–43; Isabel Turlington, "Careers for College Girls," *Woman's Journal* 14, no. 3 (March 1929): 15, 43.

50. Andree Brooks, "A Pioneer Feminist Savors Grandmother Role," *New York Times*, May 10, 1981, CN1, 15.

51. Wasniewski, *Women in Congress*, 240–43; Foerstel, *Biographical Dictionary of Congressional Women*, 280–81; Brooks, "A Pioneer Feminist Savors Grandmother Role," CN1, 15; "Institute of Women's Professional Relations," pamphlet, 1929, folder 1, box 1, IWPR Papers. In 1934, the institute was relocated to Connecticut College, where Woodhouse accepted a position as professor of economics.

52. Kathleen M'Laughlin, "Sidelines Stressed for Girl Chemists," *New York Times*, April 16, 1939, 25; Ruth O'Brien quoted in ibid.

53. Genevieve Reynolds, "Professional Women Urge Wartime Program to Train College Students for War Effort," *Washington Post*, March 10, 1942, clipping, folder 262, box 14, Shouse Papers; "To Discuss War Demands: Women's Professional Relations Institute Calls Conference," *New York Times*, March 19, 1942, 27; Nona Baldwin, "Agencies Seeking Scientific Women," *New York Times*, March 15, 1942, 31; Nona Baldwin, "Asks Colleges Aid Women's War Jobs," *New York Times*, March 21, 1942, 12. After divorcing her first husband, Alvin, Catherine Filene Dodd married Jouett Shouse in 1931.

54. Baldwin, "Agencies Seeking Scientific Women"; Institute of Women's Professional Relations, *War Demands for Trained Personnel*, 6–9, 11–14, 21–22, 216 (George Bailey quoted on 7).

55. Institute of Women's Professional Relations, *War Demands for Trained Personnel*, 31–33; statistics regarding women's representation on the National Roster come from Rossiter, *Women Scientists in America*, 2:25. Perhaps because of its broader criteria, the 1938 edition of the misleadingly titled *American Men of Science* directory listed women as 7 percent of all scientists. See Rossiter, *Women Scientists in America*, 1:132–33, 136.

56. Institute of Women's Professional Relations, *War Demands for Trained Personnel*, 31–33, 42 (Kathryn McHale quoted on 42).

57. Ibid., 42.

58. "Kathryn M'Hale Resigns," *New York Times*, November 2, 1949, 31; Levine, *Degrees of Equality*, 21–22, 25–29.

59. "To Guide War Jobs of Trained Women," special to the *New York Times*, April 11, 1942, 8; Blaeuer, "History of the National Roster of Scientific and Specialized Personnel," 50–55.

60. "Professional Registration," *Women's Work and Education* 14, no. 4 (December 1943): 4–5.

61. Robert Leigh, "Suggested Program for Full Utilization of Specialized Womanpower," April 1942, and Committee on Women in College and Defense, meeting minutes, April 22, 1942, folder 85, and National Roster of Scientific and Specialized Personnel, meeting minutes, May 15, 1942, folder 70, all in box 4, Dean's Office/Departmental Correspondence; Margaret S. Morriss, "College Women Students and the War," *Educational Record* 24, no. 1 (January 1943): 37.

62. Morriss, "College Women Students and the War," 35, 42.

63. "New NS Guide Lists Openings," *Barnard Bulletin* 47, no. 41 (April 5, 1943): 4; Gildersleeve, "Report of the Dean of Barnard College for the Academic Year Ending June 30, 1942," 5–8, folder 17d–17dd, box 2, Dean's Office/Departmental Correspondence.

64. Gildersleeve, "Report of the Dean for the Academic Year Ending June 30, 1941," 14–15, folder 17dd, box 2, Dean's Office/Departmental Correspondence.

65. Gildersleeve, *Many a Good Crusade*, 104, 257.

66. Rosenberg, *Changing the Subject*, 167. It appears as though women had taken engineering classes before but were barred by the trustees at the request of the School of Engineering in an effort to ameliorate the social problems posed when men and women geologists were sent into the field. Rosenberg indicates that this decision was essentially upheld in 1911 when professors in the applied sciences persuaded the trustees to amend university statutes "to permit them to exclude women from earning a degree in the School of Mines, Engineering, and Chemistry" (ibid., 347 [n. 3]).

67. Gildersleeve, *Many a Good Crusade*, 104.

68. J. K. Finch to the Faculty of Engineering, October 6, 1942, and attached "Memorandum on the proposal to admit women to the undergraduate engineering course at Columbia," folder 13, box 2, Dean's Office/Departmental Correspondence.

69. Finch, "Memorandum on the proposal to admit women to the undergraduate engineering course at Columbia," 2, folder 13, box 2, Dean's Office/Departmental Correspondence.

70. Ibid., 1, 5–6.

71. "Women Engineers," December 7, 1942, folder 13, box 2, Dean's Office/Departmental Correspondence.

72. Virginia Gildersleeve to James K. Finch, November 4, 1942, and "Women Engineers," December 7, 1942 (quotation), folder 13, box 2, Dean's Office/Departmental Correspondence.

73. Rossiter, *Women Scientists in America*, 2:14.

74. "New 'Women Only' Courses Are Started at Ohio State," *New York Times*, June 14, 1942, D5; Benjamin Fine, "Liberal Arts Eclipsed by Vocational Courses,"

New York Times, January 24, 1943, E7; Dorothy W. Weeks, "Wilson Modifies Science Courses," *New York Times*, July 12, 1942, D5.

75. Williams, *Improbable Warriors*, 22–23.

76. Virginia C. Gildersleeve, "How Barnard Can Help Win the War," address to Barnard College, January 13, 1942, folder: Addresses, box 2, Gildersleeve Personal Papers.

77. Eva Hansl, "College Graduates and the War," notes for a talk to the graduate students of Catholic University, Thursday, May 6, 1943, folder: Occupations—Professional and Technical, 1943, box 202, entry 22, Women's Bureau Records.

78. Margaret Hickey, "What's Next for the College Trained Woman" (address, Careers Convocation, University of Cincinnati, February 15, 1945), Speeches and Broadcasts of Margaret A. Hickey, 1944–45, Records of the Women's Advisory Committee, WMC Records.

79. Fine, "Liberal Arts Eclipsed by Vocational Courses"; Solomon, *In the Company of Educated Women*, 188.

80. Baumgartner and Petersen, *Quair*, no page numbers.

81. "Freshman Questionnaire" results, 1943–46, Statistics, 1938–49, Douglass College Dean Records.

82. Cardozier, *Colleges and Universities in World War II*, 117; Turner, "Education of Women for Engineering in the United States," 122.

83. When the program was established in fall 1940, it was originally called Engineering Defense Training (EDT). During the fiscal year 1941–42, it was known as Engineering, Science, and Management Defense Training (ESMDT). It was then renamed Engineering, Science, and Management War Training and remained so until the program's end in 1945. The final report notes that, despite the change in names, "the entire program from 1940 through 1945 was essentially one continuous program." Armsby, *Engineering, Science, and Management War Training Final Report*, xi, 46–47.

84. The enrollment of African Americans, which was not broken down by sex, amounted to 1.4 percent. Ibid., viii–ix, 47; Rossiter, *Women Scientists in America*, 2:15; "Electrical Principles and Measurement," course announcement [1943?], folder 5, box 21, Columbia WWII Collection.

85. Turner, "Education of Women for Engineering in the United States," 72; Frances M. Tallmadge, "Engineering Training for Women," *Journal of Higher Education* 15, no. 7 (October 1944): 380.

86. Rex B. Beisel, "Chance Vought Scholarships in Aeronautical Engineering at New York University," n.d., folder 85, box 6, Dean's Office/Departmental Correspondence; "Dormitory Is Leased for N.Y.U. Students," *New York Times*, February 21, 1943, 31. The Chance Vought Scholars were named after the late naval aircraft designer Chance Vought. They were the first women to take courses at NYU's College of Engineering. Their degrees, however, were granted from their home institutions.

87. The eighth school, Northwestern, did not participate in the end. "Engineer Courses Draw Many Women," *New York Times*, January 14, 1943, 16; "Curtiss-Wright to Pay 800 Girls to Attend Engineering Colleges," *New York Times*, December 6, 1942, 1. See also McIntire, "Curtiss-Wright Cadettes," especially page 29.

88. McIntire, "Curtiss-Wright Cadettes," 58–59 (cadette quoted on 59).

89. Ibid.

90. Mary Glover, "With One Purpose—Victory!" *The Cadetter* (March 1943): 1, folder 4, box 1, Patterson Papers.

91. Armsby, *Engineering, Science, and Management War Training Final Report*, 47; McIntire, "Curtiss-Wright Cadettes," 33; C. T. Reid to Virginia C. Gildersleeve, December 30, 1942, folder 17d, box 2, Dean's Office/Departmental Correspondence.

92. Gladys F. Gove, Director, Vocational Service, National Federation of Business and Professional Women's Clubs, Inc., to George W. Case, October 30, 1942, folder: "Complaints—Students. Cunningham, Rosa E. (Drake University)," box 2, entry 221, Office of Education Records; "21,000 Women on Roster of Specialized Personnel," unspecified newspaper clipping, December 26, 1942, folder: "Occupations Professional and Technical," box 202, entry 22, Women's Bureau Records.

93. "College Women Students and the War," reprinted in George F. Zook, "The President's Annual Report," *Educational Record* 24, no. 3 (July 1943): 211–12.

94. "Stevens Offers Course for Women," *New York Times*, January 5, 1942, 14.

95. "Columbia Training Women Engineers," *New York Times*, September 12, 1942, clipping, folder 11, box 21, Columbia WWII Collection; Amy Spear, "The History and Organizational Structure of SWE," March 1992, 2, Series 11, SWE Records (unprocessed). See also Gildersleeve, *Many a Good Crusade*.

96. For an excellent analysis of sex segregation in industry during World War II, see Milkman, *Gender at Work*. More general examinations of persistent discrimination and the tenacity of gender stereotypes during the war include Rupp, *Mobilizing Women for War*; D'Ann Campbell, *Women at War with America*; Anderson, *Wartime Women*; and Honey, *Creating Rosie the Riveter*.

97. Warren Bruner quoted in McIntire, "Curtiss-Wright Cadettes," 20.

98. Emily Hannan, talk given at meeting of the Schenectady Business and Professional Women's Clubs, November 1941, sent to Frances V. Seepk, December 5, 1941, folder 712, reel 122, AAUW Archives.

99. Elsie Eaves, "Wanted: Women Engineers," *Independent Woman* (May 1942): 132.

100. Virginia Gildersleeve to Pearl Kazin, May 12, 1943, folder 17dd, box 7, Dean's Office/Departmental Correspondence; Lillian Moller Gilbreth, "You and Your Job," speech given at the New Jersey College for Women, [1940–41], Douglass College Dean Records.

101. Rossiter, *Women Scientists in America*, 2:16.

102. Moxon and Peabody, *Twenty-Five Years*, 24; Fredericka Belknap quoted in Esther W. Hawes, faculty of New Jersey College for Women meeting minutes, March 9, 1942, Douglass College Dean Records.

103. Gloria Brooks Reinish, interview by Lauren Katya, May 22, 2003, transcript, 14–15, box 3, SWE Pioneers.

104. Howes and Herzenberg, *Their Day in the Sun*, 80, 85; Rossiter, *Women Scientists in America*, 2:7. For more information on Mina Rees, see Williams, *Improbable Warriors*. Williams also argues that women who served in the military

"received even fewer guarantees than civilian women that they would be able to pursue their area of expertise and that they would be given an intellectually challenging assignment." See Williams, *Improbable Warriors*, 10.

105. Rossiter, *Women Scientists in America*, 2:4.

106. Baxter, *Scientists against Time*, 127.

107. Rossiter, *Women Scientists in America*, 2:6–7.

108. Livingston W. Houston quoted in "New R.P.I. Policy Will Admit Women," *New York Times*, September 13, 1942, 19; "Womanpower Available," *Women's Work and Education* 13, no. 3 (October 1942): 9.

109. Minutes of meeting on "Training of College Women for War-Time Employment," December 17, 1942, folder: Training—ESMDT, box 210, entry 22, Women's Bureau Records.

110. Minutes of meeting of Women's Advisory Committee, War Manpower Commission, January 13, 1943, p. 9, folder: Women's Advisory Committee—WMC Agenda, etc., box 7, entry 36, WMC Records.

111. Bertha M. Nienburg, "War Work for Women in May 1942," folder: Occupations Professional and Technical, 1942, box 202, entry 22, Women's Bureau Records.

112. Charles N. Mason to Mary H. Brille, January 8, 1947, folder 223: Correspondence 1947, box 686, Bulletin 223, Women's Bureau Records.

113. Lillian M. Gilbreth, "Women's Colleges as Reservoirs for Employment . . . At What Levels?" in "College Women and War Industry: Proceedings of the Conference of Representatives of War Industries and Women Colleges," *Journal of the American Association of University Women* 36, no. 3 (Spring 1943): 140–43. Gilbreth's concern with inefficiencies in the mobilization of women can also be seen in her 1946 review of *The History of the Boston Chemical Warfare Procurement District*, where she writes that this process was "involved, opportunistic, and far less efficient than it would have been if planning would have been done" (folder 10, box 27, Gilbreth Papers).

114. Minnie L. Maffett, untitled speech, [1942–44?], box 83, BPW Records.

115. Ibid.

116. Lillian M. Gilbreth, "Women in Engineering," *Mechanical Engineering* 64, no. 12 (December 1942): 856–57, 859.

117. Glover, "With One Purpose—Victory," *The Cadetter* (March 1943): 2, folder 4, box 1, Patterson Papers.

118. H. Marjorie Crawford, "Comments on Positions by National Secretary," *The Iotan* 4, no. 1 (March 1944): 9.

119. Eaves, "Wanted: Women Engineers," 133, 159.

120. Steele, *Careers for Girls in Science and Engineering*, 25.

121. Walter J. Murphy quoted in Institute of Women's Professional Relations, *War and Post-War Employment*, 110–11.

122. Margaret A. Hickey, "Trends in the Labor Market," radio address, January 26, 1944, box 1, Speeches and Broadcasts of Margaret Hickey, 1943–44, Records of the Women's Advisory Committee, WMC Records.

123. Chase Going Woodhouse quoted in Institute of Women's Professional Relations, *War and Post-War Demands for Trained Personnel*, i–iii.

124. Esther R. Bien to Dean of Women, March 19, 1943, and Virginia Gildersleeve to Esther Bien, March 23, 1943, folder 17d, box 7, Dean's Office/Departmental Correspondence.

125. Virginia C. Gildersleeve, "Educating Girls for the War and the Post-War World," draft, January 4, 1943, and Postscript, October 10, 1943, addresses 1943, box 2, Gildersleeve Personal Papers.

126. Columbia University, report on "Women in Scientific Fields" sent to Women's Bureau, 1946, folder 223: Correspondence 1946, box 686, Bulletin 223, Women's Bureau Records.

127. For an excellent analysis of the postwar period's impact on female scientists, see Rossiter, *Women Scientists in America*, 2:27–49.

128. Cardozier, *Colleges and Universities in World War II*, 224; Ross, *Preparing for Ulysses*, 91–124. For other studies of the GI Bill, see Olson, *The GI Bill, the Veterans, and the Colleges*, and Mosch, *The GI Bill*.

129. Hartmann, *The Home Front and Beyond*, 106.

130. Alice C. Lloyd, "Women in the Postwar College," *Journal of the American Association of University Women* 39, no. 3 (Spring 1946): 131.

131. Ibid.; Helen M. Hosp, "Doors Closing for Women Students," *Journal of the American Association of University Women* 39, no. 3 (Spring 1946): 167; Cornell University quoted in Hosp, "Doors Closing for Women Students," 167; Hartmann, *The Home Front and Beyond*, 106; Rossiter, *Women Scientists in America*, 2:31; Solomon, *In the Company of Educated Women*, 189.

132. Hosp, "Doors Closing for Women Students," 167; Solomon, *In the Company of Educated Women*, 189. While some women's schools eventually reinstituted their all-female policies, others permanently adopted coeducation.

133. Rossiter, *Women Scientists in America*, 2:32–33. Rossiter also points out that, despite a significant increase in the number of applicants, Radcliffe's female enrollment was not allowed to reach 400 again until 1957. Meanwhile, male graduate enrollment at Harvard soared from 1,088 in 1946 to 1,960 in 1947.

134. Ibid.

135. Phyllis Pollock Magat to author, New Jersey College for Women Questionnaire, no. 50, 8, in author's possession.

136. Geraldine Lynch Krueger, president of Columbium Chapter ISP (Columbia University), to Dr. Essie White Cohn, University of Denver, November 12, 1949, folder 6, box 18, Iota Sigma Pi Records.

137. Solomon, *In the Company of Educated Women*, 190.

138. Hartmann, *The Home Front and Beyond*, 106; Eisenmann, *Higher Education for Women in Postwar America*, 54.

139. Dorothy Lawrence Stephens to author, New Jersey College for Women Questionnaire, no. 122, 4, in author's possession.

140. Eisenmann, *Higher Education for Women in Postwar America*, 54–55.

141. Irene Peden, interview by Lauren Kata, March 2, 2002, transcript, 14, box 3, SWE Pioneers.

142. Ibid., 12.

143. Juliette M. Moran, interview by Laura Sweeney, December 20, 2001, transcript, 10, 12, 16, 22, and Juliette M. Moran, curriculum vitae, box 3, Women in Chemistry Oral History Project.

144. Arnold Dresdent to Mrs. Von Mises, October 20, 1947, quoted in Rossiter, *Women Scientists in America*, 2:35–36, 399 (n. 22).

145. Rossiter, *Women Scientists in America*, 2:35–36.

146. Women's Bureau, Report on Interview with M. H. Trytten, January 7, 1947, folder 223: Correspondence 1947, box 686, Bulletin 223, Women's Bureau Records.

147. Armsby, *Engineering, Science, and Management War Training*, 44–47; Rossiter, *Women Scientists in America*, 2:25.

Chapter Two

1. Eleanor F. Horsey and Donna Price, "Science Out of Petticoats," *Journal of the American Association of University Women* 40, no. 1 (Fall 1946): 13–16.

2. Bush, *Science, the Endless Frontier*, 1–3, 15, 18–19, 28, 129.

3. Horsey and Price, "Science Out of Petticoats," 13, 16.

4. The history of national security politics and the national security state is covered most fully in Yergin, *Shattered Peace*; Leffler, *A Preponderance of Power*; Hogan, *A Cross of Iron*; Stuart, *Creating the National Security State*; and Zelizer, *Arsenal of Democracy*.

5. Harry S. Truman to joint session of Congress, October 23, 1945, text reprinted in "President Truman's Proposals for Year's Training of American Youth," *New York Times*, October 24, 1945, 3.

6. Bush, *Endless Horizons*, 82–83.

7. Henry Stimson and James Forrestal to National Academy of Sciences, quoted in Bush, *Science, the Endless Frontier*, 12; also printed in "New Board of Scientists Is Appointed for the Development of Weapons of War," *New York Times*, February 12, 1945, 32.

8. David Sarnoff, "Science for Life or Death," *New York Times*, August 10, 1945, 6.

9. Dupree, *Science in the Federal Government*, 373.

10. Steelman, *Science and Public Policy*, 5:16, 70; Geiger, *Research and Relevant Knowledge*, 26–27; Rossiter, "Science and Public Policy since World War II," 276; Task Force on Science Policy, "A History of Science Policy in the United States, 1940–1985," 29–30. Extended analyses of the NIH include Donald Swain, "The Rise of a Research Empire: NIH, 1930–1950," *Science* 138 (1962): 1233–37; Strickland, *Politics, Science and Dread Disease*; and Fox, "The Politics of the NIH Extramural Program, 1937–1950."

11. Hewlett and Anderson, *A History of the United States Atomic Energy Commission*, vol. 1; Hewlett and Duncan, *A History of the United States Atomic Energy Commission*, vol. 2; Kevles, "K_1S_2: Korea, Science, and the State," 315; Sherry, *In the Shadow of War*, 137; Wang, *American Scientists in an Age of Anxiety*, 219–20; Geiger, *Research and Relevant Knowledge*, 22. For one contemporary account of the commission's interest in medicine, see Harry M. Davis, "The Atom Goes to Work for Medicine," *New York Times*, September 22, 1946, 15, 49, 50.

12. Public Law 588, 79th Cong., August 8, 1946, quoted in Schweber, "The Mutual Embrace of Science and the Military," 17; Kleinman, *Politics on the Endless Frontier*, 148. See also Allison, "U.S. Navy Research and Development since World War II," and Sapolsky, *Science and the Navy*.

13. Kleinman, *Politics on the Endless Frontier*, 148; Kevles, "K$_1$S$_2$: Korea, Science, and the State," 315; Steelman, *Science and Public Policy*, 2:56.

14. Kevles, *The Physicists*, 355, 363–64.

15. Steelman, *Science and Public Policy*, 2:3–5. Although most of the research funded by the Office of Naval Research was basic research, it also provided substantial support to the Naval Research Laboratory, where both basic and applied research were carried out. See Steelman, *Science and Public Policy*, 2:59.

16. Both the Joint Research and Development Board and the Research and Development Board were chaired by Vannevar Bush, who resigned in October 1948. Kleinman, *Politics on the Endless Frontier*, 149–50; York and Greb, "Military Research and Development," 192–93; Stuart, *Creating the National Security State*, 169–73; Hogan, *A Cross of Iron*, 229–34.

17. Geiger, *Research and Relevant Knowledge*, 19.

18. Bush, *Science, the Endless Frontier*, 26.

19. Kevles, "The National Science Foundation and the Debate over Postwar Research Policy, 1942–1945," 24; England, *A Patron for Pure Science*, 25.

20. Cochrane, *The National Academy of Sciences*, 463–64; Stuart, *Creating the National Security State*, 168; Harry S. Truman, "Authorization for Study," October 17, 1946, reprinted in Steelman, *Science and Public Policy*, 1:69. See also Blanpied, *Science and Public Policy*, http://www.aaas.org/spp/yearbook/chap29.htm.

21. Steelman, *Science and Public Policy*, 1:6–7; Stuart, *Creating the National Security State*, 168.

22. Steelman, *Science and Public Policy*, 1:3.

23. Harry S. Truman quoted in "Truman Signs Bill for Science Study," special to the *New York Times*, May 11, 1950, 24.

24. Public Law 507, 81st Cong., http://www.nsf.gov/about/history/legislation.pdf.

25. Ibid.; Cochrane, *The National Academy of Sciences*, 482; England, *A Patron for Pure Science*, 109; Kevles, "Principles and Politics in Federal R&D Policy, 1945–1990," xv; Office of the Federal Register, *The United States Government Manual 2011*. See also Rudolph, *Scientists in the Classroom*, 57–81.

26. Sherry, *In the Shadow of War*, 140; Wang, *American Science in an Age of Anxiety*, 38, 220; Galison, "Physics between War and Peace"; Rudolph, *Scientists in the Classroom*, 44; Kevles, *The Physicists*, 379–80 (HUAC quoted on 379); Kevles, "Principles and Politics in Federal R&D Policy, 1945–1990," xvi; Harold B. Hinton, "Atom Fellowships Are Cut Sharply," special to the *New York Times*, December 16, 1949, 19; "Oppenheimer, the 'Father of the Atomic Bomb' Was a Bafflingly Complex Man," *New York Times*, February 20, 1967, 32.

27. See, for example, Woods, *Black Struggle, Red Scare*. For a broader history of McCarthyism in the United States, see Schrecker, *Many Are the Crimes*.

28. Storrs, "Attacking the Washington 'Femmocracy,'" 118–52 (quotation on page 125); Hartmann, *The Home Front and Beyond*, 156; Storrs, "Red Scare Politics and the Suppression of Popular Front Feminism," 518–19.

29. Storrs, "Attacking the Washington 'Femmocracy,'" 126; Storrs, "Red Scare Politics and the Suppression of Popular Front Feminism," 519; Rung, *Servants of the State*, 153. Storrs also provides "fragmentary evidence" that women were disproportionately charged in federal employee loyalty cases. Although women comprised approximately 3 percent of high-level employees, they made up about 18 percent of high-level cases. Moreover, the agencies most frequently involved in such cases were also the ones where women enjoyed either "high status" or "recently improved status." See Storrs, "Attacking the Washington 'Femmocracy,'" 124.

30. Storrs, "Red Scare Politics and the Suppression of Popular Front Feminism," 520–21; Levine, *Degrees of Equality*, 81.

31. Quoted in Meyerowitz, "Sex, Gender, and the Cold War Language of Reform," 108.

32. Storrs, "Red Scare Politics and the Suppression of Popular Front Feminism," 521; Hartmann, *The Home Front and Beyond*, 156–57. See Walls, "Defending Their Liberties."

33. Rupp and Taylor, *Survival in the Doldrums*, 139.

34. See, for example, Horowitz, *Betty Friedan and the Making of* The Feminine Mystique.

35. Meyerowitz, "Sex, Gender, and the Cold War Language of Reform," 107; Hartmann, "Women's Employment and the Domestic Ideal."

36. Rossiter, *Women Scientists in America*, 1:102, 2:28; "Zapoleon, Marguerite Wykoff," in *The National Cyclopedia of American Biography*, vol. N-63 (Clifton, NJ: James T. White, 1984), 143; "Zapoleon, Marguerite Wykoff," obituary, November 6, 2003, http://articles.sun-sentinel.com/2003-11-06/news/0311061519_1_memorial-service-sun-city-center-fl/4; Zapoleon and Stolz, "Helen Bradford Thompson Woolley," 658.

37. "Zapoleon, Marguerite Wykoff"; Women's Bureau, *The Outlook for Women in Science*, ii, v–vii; Rossiter, *Women Scientists in America*, 1:28.

38. Women's Bureau, *The Outlook for Women in Science*, 1, 5.

39. Ibid., 1.

40. Ibid., 28–29.

41. Zapoleon estimated that only five African American women earned doctorates in physical or biological sciences between 1876 and 1943. While it seemed that a larger number of them had earned master's or bachelor's degrees in science, there were no statistics to confirm that number. Women's Bureau, *The Outlook for Women in Science*, 34, 54–62. See also Eisenmann, *Higher Education for Women in Postwar America*, 56–57, for additional statistics about the racial demographics of postwar college students.

42. Women's Bureau, *The Outlook for Women in Science*, 31.

43. Ibid.

44. Ibid., 33.

45. Ibid.

46. Ibid., 29–31.

47. Rossiter, *Women Scientists in America*, 2:75.

48. Ibid.

49. Women's Bureau, *The Outlook for Women in Science*, 30.

50. Mary L. Willard, "Look Ahead!," *Sigma Delta Epsilon News* 10, no. 2 (December 1944): 3–4, Early Sigma Delta Epsilon Newsletters folder, box 6, SDE Records.

51. Tryon, *Investment in Creative Scholarship*, 12, 30–31.

52. Ibid., 33.

53. See, for example, Morgan, *A History of Iota Sigma Pi,* and Wahlin, *87-Year History of SDE-GWIS*. Another account of the history of Sigma Delta Epsilon can be found in "Brief History of Sigma Delta Epsilon, Graduate Women's Scientific Fraternity," ca. 1958, folder 10, box 1, SDE–Alpha Records.

54. Turner, "Education of Women for Engineering in the United States, 1885–1952," 122. Turner offers slightly different statistics on page 188, where the total number of first professional degrees in engineering awarded to women from 1945–46 to 1949–50 totals only 528. What accounts for this discrepancy is not clear, although she did use different source bases. In both cases, however, the number of women earning first professional degrees in engineering was much higher after the Second World War than during it. See also Puaca, "Cold War Women." Portions are reproduced in this chapter with the permission of Palgrave Macmillan.

55. Eisenmann, *Higher Education for Women in Postwar America*, 4, 44–45,

55. Women's enrollment dropped temporarily in 1950 and 1951, but so did men's enrollment. In general, the overall upward trend persisted.

56. Ibid., 21–23.

57. United States Census, 1950, http://www.census.gov/prod/www/abs/decennial/1950.html; National Manpower Council, *Womanpower*, 283.

58. Kindya, *Four Decades*, 11; Amy Spear, "The History and Organizational Structure of SWE," March 1992, 2, Series 11, SWE Records (unprocessed); Bix, "Supporting Females in a Male Field"; Bix, "From 'Engineeresses' to 'Girl Engineers' to 'Good Engineers.'"

59. Drexel Society of Women Engineers, registration form for First Conference of Women Engineering Students, held April 2 and 3, 1949, Series 11, SWE Records (unprocessed).

60. Doris McNulty, "History of SWE" (notes for speech given at the Society of Women Engineers birthday celebration, [1960?]), Series 11, SWE Records (unprocessed); Phyllis Evans Miller, "History of the Society of Women Engineers," [1952], Series 11, SWE Records (unprocessed); "History of the Society of Women Engineers," [1950], Series 11, SWE Records (unprocessed); "Society of Women Engineers: Drexel Institute of Technology," program, folder: Pre-SWE Student Conference, Series 11, SWE Records (unprocessed); "Women Engineers Unite," *New York Times*, April 4, 1949, 21.

61. "Women Engineers Meet at Hotel Edison to Form a Society," *The Woman Engineer* 1, no. 1 (May 1949): 1; Mildred Paret quoted in Kindya, *Four Decades*, 11; "Women Engineers Organize," *New York Times*, March 8, 1948, 26; Mary

Stokes, "Detailed Reply to the 8 Items of Letter 12-5-51," Series 11, SWE Records (unprocessed).

62. Lillian Murad to Katharine Stinson, June 8, 1952, Series 11, SWE Records (unprocessed).

63. See, for example, Rosenberg, "American Atomic Strategy and the Hydrogen Bomb Decision."

64. Sherry, *In the Shadow of War*, 183.

65. Kevles, "Principles and Politics in Federal R&D Policy, 1945–1990," xvi.

66. Ibid., xvi; see also Kevles, "K_1S_2: Korea, Science, and the State," 320.

67. Benjamin Fine, "Education in Review: Colleges Plan to Cooperate with Government and among Themselves in an Emergency," *New York Times*, July 30, 1950, E9; "Engineers Get Set to Cope with Crisis," *New York Times*, September 16, 1950, 30.

68. Malcolm M. Wiley quoted in "Women Engineers Urged," *Christian Science Monitor*, October 27, 1950, clipping in Series 11, SWE Records (unprocessed).

69. Nina Hodgson, "Market for Science Majors Up, Demand Outruns the Supply," *Smith College Associated News*, October 31, 1950, 1, 6; Kindya, *Four Decades*, 47.

70. Eugene Rabinowitch, "Scientific Womanpower," *Bulletin of Atomic Scientists* 7, no. 2 (February 1951): 34.

71. Rossiter, *Women Scientists in America*, 2:51–52.

72. Ibid., 53.

73. Eric Pace, "Arthur S. Flemming, 91, Dies; Served in Eisenhower Cabinet," *New York Times*, September 9, 1996, B10; Flemming Is Named to Manpower Post," special to the *New York Times*, February 9, 1951, 9; Flemming, *Arthur Flemming*, 91–93, 100, 118. For information on Flemming's later career, especially with respect to programs related to aging, see Green, "A Historical Study of Arthur S. Flemming."

74. Flemming, "Some Personnel Needs of the Government War Agencies," 101, 104.

75. Arthur Flemming quoted in Glendy Culligan, "Rosie's Bright Kid Sister Comes On to Work Now," *Washington Post*, November 6, 1951, B5.

76. Pickren and McKeachie, "Dael Wolfle (1906–2002)."

77. For a comparison of the Bush and Wolfle reports, see Rossiter, *Women Scientists in America*, 2:54–55.

78. Dael Wolfle, *America's Resources of Specialized Talent*, 163–64, 167–69, 226–41 (quotation on 229).

79. Ibid., 239.

80. National Science Foundation, Interim Report, Encouraging Scientific Talent, sent to the Commission on the Education of Women, January 5, 1955, folder 100, box 7, CEW Records. Original drafts of Karzon's and Blizard's reports can be found in folder 100, box 7, CEW Records.

81. Cole, *Encouraging Scientific Talent*, 77.

82. Ibid., 77, 87, 184–85.

83. Ibid., 132.

84. Karzon, "Appendix A."

85. Rossiter, *Women Scientists in America*, 2:57–58.

86. National Manpower Council, *A Report on the National Manpower Council*, 7. See also Hartmann, "Women's Employment and the Domestic Ideal."

87. National Manpower Council, *A Report on the National Manpower Council*, 11, 13–17.

88. Rosenberg, *Changing the Subject*, 211–13 (Eli Ginzberg quoted on 213).

89. National Manpower Council, *Womanpower*, vii–xxviii (National Manpower Council quoted on vii).

90. National Manpower Council, Information Memorandum No. 114, "Report on Dissemination of Womanpower," June 13, 1957, folder 81, reel 145, AAUW Archives.

91. National Manpower Council, *Womanpower*, 9.

92. Ibid., 7–39; Rosenberg, *Changing the Subject*, 213–14; Rossiter, *Women Scientists in America*, 2:59.

93. National Manpower Council, *Womanpower*, 254.

94. Ibid., 217–18, 283–84 (National Manpower Council quoted on 283).

95. Ibid., 218, 256, 283–84.

96. Doris McNulty, "History of SWE" (notes for speech given at the Society of Women Engineers birthday celebration, [1960?]), folder: SWE Histories, 1950–92, and Society of Women Engineers, guest list for Second Annual Convention, held May 27 and 28, 1950, folder: SWE organization meeting, both in Series 11, SWE Records (unprocessed).

97. Dot Merrill to Arlene Davis, Marie Pulaski, and Ada Richardson, January 14, 1953, folder: 3.30.16, Section Affiliations Committee, 1952–53, Series 8: Committees (Sections, Statistics, Student Activities), SWE Records (unprocessed).

98. Elsie Eaves, "The Society of Women Engineers, USA, at 25," May 1976, 1, folder: SWE Histories, 1950–92, Series 11, SWE Records (unprocessed); Miriam Gerla to Mary Stokes, January 3, 1952, folder: SWE-history, Series 11, SWE Records (unprocessed); Kindya, *Four Decades*, 9–10; BK Krenzer, "Our Greatest Achievement," *U.S. Woman Engineer* (January/February 1989): 5–7; Arminta J. Harness, "SWE's Golden Era: A 'Do It Ourselves' Spirit," *U.S. Woman Engineer* (January/February 1989): 9–10.

99. Evelyn Fowler, interview by Lauren Kata, May 15, 2003, transcript, 1–8, box 1, SWE Pioneers; Troy Eller, SWE archivist, to author, March 27, 2012.

100. Anna Longobardo, interview by Lauren Kata, May 22, 2003, transcript, 6–8, box 2, SWE Pioneers.

101. Society of Women Engineers, Certificate of Incorporation, February 13, 1952, folder 4, box 1, SWE Records (unprocessed).

102. Gerla to Stokes, January 3, 1952, Series 11, SWE Records (unprocessed); "Emblem Committee," *Journal of the Society of Women Engineers* 2, no. 1 (September 1951): 9; "Convention Notes," *The Woman Engineer* (Summer 1950): 1; Phyllis Evans and Phyllis Diamond, notes from Society of Women Engineers Council Meeting, May 27, 1950, box 1, SWE Records (unprocessed). The emblem had actually been designed and used by the Philadelphia group but was adopted as the national emblem at Camp Green.

103. "Hicks, Beatrice A(lice)," in *Current Biography Yearbook*, edited by Marjorie Dent Candel (New York: H. W. Wilson, 1957), 255–57; Bix, "Hicks, Beatrice Alice"; "Beatrice Hicks, Society's First President, Dies," SWE *Newsletter* (November/December 1979): 5.

104. Evans and Diamond, notes from Society of Women Engineers Council Meeting, May 27, 1950, box 1, SWE Records (unprocessed); "Second Annual Convention of the Society of Women Engineers," *The Woman Engineer* 1, no. 6 (May 1950): 2.

105. Rossiter, *Women Scientists in America*, 2:338–39; Kindya, *Four Decades*, 12–13; Emma C. Barth, minutes of meeting of SWE Board of Directors, September 6, 1952, Chicago, Illinois, folder 18, box 1, SWE Records (unprocessed).

106. Beatrice Hicks quoted in "Spotlight," *The Woman Engineer* (Summer 1950): 1.

107. Kevles, "Principles and Politics in Federal R&D Policy, 1945–1990," xviii.

108. Katharine Stinson, "President's Message," *Journal of the Society of Women Engineers* 4, no. 1 (September 1953): 2.

109. "Convention Committee," *Journal of the Society of Women Engineers* 1, no. 1 (Spring 1951): 9; "Convention Notes: The Effect of the Current Emergency on Women in Engineering," *Journal of the Society of Women Engineers* 1, no. 1 (Spring 1951): 9.

110. Kay Broughton, notes from SWE business meeting, March 10, 1951, folder: Membership Meeting, 1951–94, Series 2: Subseries 2e, Membership Meeting Minutes, SWE Records (unprocessed).

111. "Women Engineers See Field Widening," *New York Times*, March 11, 1951, 47; no title, *Journal of the Society of Women Engineers* 1, no. 1 (Spring 1951): 13; "Convention Notes: Welcoming Address," *Journal of the Society of Women Engineers* 1, no. 1 (Spring 1951): 10.

112. Phyllis Evans Miller to "Shareholder," December 6, 1951, folder 6.50.3 Misc Corres; Eaves, Elsie, 1942, 1946, 51–57, Series 4, SWE HQ SWE Records (unprocessed).

113. Beatrice A. Hicks, "Women as Engineers: Development of Potential Source of Engineering Talent Is Advocated," *New York Times*, September 19, 1951, 30.

114. B. A. Hicks to H. Marion [*sic*] Trytten, August 24, 1951, folder: President Beatrice Hicks; report FY51; box: Officers Series, President; President-Elect; Vice President; 1st, 2nd Vice President; Series 3: Officer Files; SWE Records (unprocessed); Cochrane, *The National Academy of Sciences*, 406.

115. B. A. Hicks to Arthur S. Flemming, August 24, 1951, folder: President Beatrice Hicks; report FY51; box: Officers Series, President; President-Elect; Vice President; 1st, 2nd Vice President; Series 3: Officer Files; SWE Records (unprocessed).

116. George R. Hickman to Kay E. Broughton, printed in "Employment Opportunity," *Journal of the Society of Women Engineers* 2, no. 1 (September 1951): 13.

117. Ibid.; Kindya, *Four Decades*, 51.

118. "National Scientific Register," *Journal of the Society of Women Engineers* 2, no. 2 (January 1952): 13; Kindya, *Four Decades*, 51.

119. Harold G. Bowen to Beatrice Hicks, October 19, 1951, folder: SWE Correspondence 1950/51, Series 8: Committees (Newsletters, Sections, Students, Misc), SWE Records (unprocessed).

120. Ibid.; "Conference on Manpower Shortage," *Journal of the Society of Women Engineers* 2, no. 2 (January 1952): 12; Beatrice Hicks quoted in "Conference on Manpower Shortage," 12.

121. Patricia Brown quoted in Lois Cress, "Women Engineers: We Need More," *Sunday Denver Post*, June 16, 1963, 5; Bix, "From 'Engineeresses' to 'Girl Engineers' to 'Good Engineers,'" 27–32.

122. Engineers' Council for Professional Development, *Engineering as a Career*, 18.

123. Beatrice A. Hicks to Engineers' Council for Professional Development, July 6, 1951, folder: SWE Correspondence 1950/51, Series 8: Committees (Newsletters, Sections, Students, Misc), SWE Records (unprocessed).

124. Ibid.

125. Engineers' Council for Professional Development, *Engineering*, 27; Hicks to Willis F. Thompson, December 4, 1951, folder: SWE Correspondence 1950/51, Series 8: Committees (Newsletters, Sections, Students, Misc), SWE Records (unprocessed).

126. Engineers' Council for Professional Development, *Engineering*, 3, 4, 22.

127. Lillian Murad to "Colleague," June 17, 1953, folder: 3.30.17 Statistics, 1953–59, Series 8: Committees, Sections, Statistics, Student Activities, SWE Records (unprocessed); Women's Bureau, *Employment Opportunities for Women in Professional Engineering*.

128. Kessler-Harris, *Out to Work*, 306; Laughlin, *Women's Work and Public Policy*, 41–45.

129. The median age of employed respondents was 29.3 years old, while the median age of women classified as engineers in the 1950 census, where only one-third of female engineers were listed as single, was 31. Women's Bureau, *Employment Opportunities for Women in Professional Engineering*, 18–21.

130. Society of Women Engineers, in cooperation with U.S. Department of Labor and Women's Bureau, "Survey of Women Engineers, 1955," folder 14, box 1, Leopold Papers.

131. See, for example, National Manpower Council, *Womanpower*, 10, 21; Rosen, *The World Split Open*, 20. See also "Special Reports: Table 8-Marital Status of the Experienced Civilian Labor Force, by Detailed Occupation and Sex, for the United States: 1950," 1B-93, United States Census, 1950, http://www.census.gov/prod/www/abs/decennial/1950.html. The 1950 census actually suggests that female engineers were more likely to be married than most female professionals. In 1950, 54 percent of female engineers reported being married, whereas 32 percent reported being single. In contrast, 44 percent of female teachers reported being married, with the same percentage reporting being single.

132. Dwight D. Eisenhower quoted in Women's Bureau, *Employment Opportunities for Women in Professional Engineering*, cover page.

133. Women's Bureau, *Employment Opportunities for Women in Professional Engineering*, 1.

134. Arthur S. Flemming quoted in Stinson, "Some Facts about Engineering as a Career for Women," 22; see also Arthur S. Flemming quoted in McDowell, "Educating Women for Engineering," 7.

135. Hicks, "Our Untapped Source of Engineering Talent," 4, 6.

136. Spreadsheet documenting distribution of *Women in Engineering*, 1956, folder: PG&E 1956, Series 8: Committees (Admissions, Bylaws 1954, PG&E, 1956, TV and Film), SWE Records (unprocessed).

137. These letters are located in folder: PG&E, 1956, Series 8: Committees (Admissions, Bylaws 1954, PG&E, 1956, TV and Film), SWE Records (unprocessed).

138. Vida Grace Hildyard to Brown, October 30, 1955, folder: PG&E, 1956, Series 8: Committees (Admissions, Bylaws 1954, PG&E, 1956, TV and Film), SWE Records (unprocessed).

139. Gerla, "President's Report," *SWE Newsletter* 3, no. 6 (February 1957): 3.

140. Beatrice Hicks, "Annual Report of the President of the Society of Women Engineers, July 1, 1950, to July 1, 1951," *Journal of the Society of Women Engineers* 2, no. 1 (September 1951): 7.

141. Mildred M. Hickman to Hicks, March 31, 1953, folder: 6.50.3 Misc Corres; Hicks, Beatrice, 1951–53, Series 4 SWE HQ, SWE Records (unprocessed); Emma C. Barth, "Report of the Board of Directors to the Membership of the Society of Women Engineers Covering the Period from March 1952 to March 1953" (report delivered at Annual Convention, March 29, 1953), 2, folder: Membership; Minutes, 1950s, Series 2, SWE Records (unprocessed); Lois G. McDowell, "Professional Guidance and Education," *Journal of the Society of Women Engineers* 4, no. 1 (September 1953): 3; Catherine W. Eiden, "Replies to Questions Asked in U.S. Treasury Dept. Letter of June 16, 1959," 4, no folder, Series 3, SWE Records (unprocessed).

142. Eiden, "Replies to Questions Asked in U.S. Treasury Dept. Letter of June 16, 1959," 4, no folder, Series 3, SWE Records (unprocessed).

143. E. Elise Hosten, "Annual Report of the Professional Guidance and Educational Committee for Year 1952–1953: Detroit Section Society of Women Engineers," 1, folder 2-1, box 2, SWE-Detroit.

144. "Activities of the Sections: Pittsburgh Section," *Journal of the Society of Women Engineers* 2, no. 4 (June 1952): 10; McDowell, "Professional Guidance and Education," 2–5.

145. Houston Section SWE, "Report," February 1956, folder 3.99 Misc; Professional Guidance and Education Reports, 1954–61, Series 8: Committees (Newsletter, Sections, Students, Misc), SWE Records (unprocessed).

146. Marilyn B. Harmon, "Report of the Professional Guidance and Education Committee of the Los Angeles Chapter of the SWE, 1955–1956," folder: 3.99 Misc; Professional Guidance and Education Reports, 1954–61, Series 8: Committees (Newsletter, Sections, Students, Misc), SWE Records (unprocessed).

147. Aileen Cavanagh, "Society of Women Engineers—Minutes. Membership Meeting," June 6 and 7, 1959, St. Louis, Missouri, folder: 3.06 Treasurer, 1958–59, Series 3: Officer Files, SWE Records (unprocessed).

148. Maxine V. Janczarek, "Detroit Section PG&E Committee, 1956," folder: 3.99 Misc; Professional Guidance and Education Reports, 1954–61, Series 8: Committees (Newsletter, Sections, Students, Misc), SWE Records (unprocessed).

149. Margaret Eller, interview by Lauren Kata, June 11, 2003, transcript, 29, box 1, SWE Pioneers.

150. Lydia Pickup to SWE Members at Large, [1960], folder: 3.30.5 Career Guidance; Professional Guidance and Education, 1956–59, Series 8: Committees (Career Guidance), SWE Records (unprocessed).

151. Gerla, "Taking Stock of SWE," February 27, 1957, folder: Speeches re: SWE, Series 11: SWE History, SWE Records (unprocessed).

152. Virginia Tucker to Gerla, December 5, 1957, Series 3, SWE Records (unprocessed).

153. Margaret A. Kearney to Beatrice A. Hicks, December 10, 1952, folder: Board of Directors, Misc., 1953/54, Series 8: Committees (Newsletters, Sections, Students, Misc), SWE Records (unprocessed).

154. Betty J. Yost, Statistics Committee Chairman, to All Board Members with attached statistics, February 5, 1959, no folder, Series 8: Committees (Admissions, Bylaws 1959, PG&E 1956, TV and Film), SWE Records (unprocessed); Minutes, Society of Women Engineers Board of Directors Meeting, Philadelphia, Pennsylvania, February 1952, folder 14, box 1, SWE Records (unprocessed); Kindya, *Four Decades*, 16.

155. William F. Ballhaus, "The Challenge of Our Untapped Resources" (paper presented at the National Conference on Women in Engineering, October 15, 1963), Series 12: Women in Engineering, SWE Records (unprocessed).

156. Rossiter, *Women Scientists in America*, 2:95–98, 149–50, 258.

157. Ibid., 75–77.

158. Patricia Brown, interview by Lauren Kata, April 16, 2003, transcript, 13, box 1, SWE Pioneers.

159. Pickup to SWE Members at Large, [1960], folder: 3.30.5 Career Guidance; Professional Guidance and Education, 1956–59, Series 8: Committees (Career Guidance), SWE Records (unprocessed).

160. Margaret A. Kearney to Beatrice A. Hicks, December 10, 1952, folder: Board of Directors, Misc., 1953/54, Series 8: Committees (Newsletters, Sections, Students, Misc), SWE Records (unprocessed).

161. "Beatrice Hicks, Society's First President, Dies," 5.

162. "Special Report of Our Status on Subversive Activities" in Agenda for Meeting of Board of Directors of the SWE, January 13, 1951, folder 8, box 1, SWE Records (unprocessed); Kay Elsas Broughton, Report of the Incorporation Committee for the Board of Directors, Society of Women Engineers, March 10, 1951, folder 3, box 1, and Society of Women Engineers Minutes of Meeting, Board of Directors, January 14, 1951, folder 8, box 1, both in SWE Records (processed).

163. Beatrice Hicks to Margaret [?], May 1, 1952, folder: SWE Correspondence 1951–52, Series 8: Committees (Newsletter, Sections, Students, Misc), SWE Records (unprocessed).

164. Ibid.

165. Olive Mayer to Mickey Gerla, March 15, 1957, folder 30, box 1, SWE Records (unprocessed).

166. Ibid.

167. Olive Mayer, letter to the editor, *SWE Newsletter* 3, no. 7 (March 1957): 3.

168. Ibid.; Kata, "The Boundaries of Women's Rights," 40.

169. Kata, "The Boundaries of Women's Rights," 40; Margaret Kipilo quoted in ibid.

170. Margaret Kipilo quoted in Kata, "The Boundaries of Women's Rights," 40.

171. Catherine W. Eiden to Executive Committee, February 15, 1960, no folder, Series 3: SWE Officer Files—Unsorted, SWE Records (unprocessed); Society of Women Engineers, Amendment to Certificate of Incorporation, June 9, 1960, folder 4, box 1, SWE Records (processed); Kata, "The Boundaries of Women's Rights," 40–41.

172. Pat Brown, "IRS Ruling Prohibits Political Activity by SWE," *SWE Newsletter* 7, no. 7 (March 1961): 1–2; Kata, "The Boundaries of Women's Rights," 40–41.

173. Kindya, *Four Decades*, 28–29; Yvonne Clark and Irene Sharpe, interview by Lauren Kata, June 29, 2003, transcript, 1–4, 32, box 1, SWE Pioneers; Aileen Cavanagh to Arminta Harness, February 3, 1977, no folder, Series 12: Statistics and Surveys, SWE Records (unprocessed); Betty Jane Yost, Minutes of the Board of Directors Meeting, August 9–10, 12, folder 31, box 1, SWE Records (unprocessed). Although the society, like the engineering profession, was predominantly white, several African American women did belong to it at this time, but because SWE did not keep statistics on race, their precise numbers are not known.

174. "Eastern Regional Conference," October 27–28, 1956, folder 5.65.2 Eastern Seaboard Conference, 1955–57, Series 7: Conferences, SWE Records (unprocessed).

Chapter Three

1. Lloyd Shearer, "Meet Phyllis Weber—Housewife and Satellite Engineer," *Parade*, January 12, 1958, 6–7, clipping, folder EC83, carton 12, CEW Records.

2. Alice K. Leopold, "Wanted: More Phyllis Webers," *Parade*, January 12, 1958, 9, clipping, folder EC83, carton 12, CEW Records.

3. Clowse, *Brainpower for the Cold War*, 5–16.

4. Kevles, "Principles and Politics in Federal R&D Policy, 1945–90, xviii; Sherry, *In the Shadow of War*, 219–20, 226–28.

5. Dwight D. Eisenhower quoted in Sherry, *In the Shadow of War*, 226.

6. Public Law 85-864, 85th Cong., 2nd sess., September 2, 1958, http://www.gpo.gov/fdsys/pkg/STATUTE-72/pdf/STATUTE-72-Pg1580.pdf. For a fuller treatment of the National Defense Education Act, see Clowse, *Brainpower for the Cold War*, and Urban, *More than Science and Sputnik*.

7. Clowse, *Brainpower for the Cold War*, 162–67; Sherry, *In the Shadow of War*, 227–28; Kevles, "Principles and Politics in Federal R&D Policy, 1945–1990," xix.

8. National Manpower Council, *Womanpower*, 262.

9. Konstantin T. Galkin quoted in "Red Engineer Schools Loaded with Women," *Washington Post*, February 28, 1958, L5.

10. National Manpower Council, *Womanpower*, 262.

11. "Soviets Are Ahead with Womanpower," *Star*, February 9, 1958, no page, clipping in folder EC83, carton 12, CEW Records; "Women Add Much in Soviet Science," *New York Times*, February 16, 1958, no page, clipping, folder: SWE Newspaper Clippings, 1950s, Series 12: Clippings, SWE Records (unprocessed); "Red Engineering Schools Loaded with Women," *Washington Post*, February 28, 1958, L5.

12. Edward Gamarekian, "Talents of U.S. Women Being Wasted, 3 Soviet Scientists Say," *Washington Post*, January 25, 1959, B6.

13. Ethaline Cortelyou, "Utilizing Chemical Womanpower to Combat the Alleged Shortage of Chemists," *Chemical Bulletin* (June 1958): 18–19, clipping in folder EC83, carton 12, CEW Records.

14. Gamarekian, "Talents of U.S. Women Being Wasted," B6; see also "Top Soviet Woman" *New York Times*, February 28, 1956, 8, for a discussion of Ekaterina A. Furtseva, who is described as "Slavic-looking," tough, and renowned for her "Communist zeal." The main caption under her photo simply says "outranks her husband."

15. Fannie M. Pious, letter to the editor, *New York Times Magazine*, November 16, 1958, 17; Gertrude Samuels, "Why Russian Women Work like Men," *New York Times Magazine*, November 2, 1958, 22.

16. May, *Homeward Bound*, 16–20 (Richard Nixon quoted on 18).

17. Wahlin, *87-Year History of SDE-GWIS*, 13–15; Rossiter, *Women Scientists in America*, 1:300–301.

18. Wahlin, *87-Year History of SDE-GWIS*, 45, 50; Rossiter, *Women Scientists in America*, 1:300–301; Rossiter, *Women Scientists in America*, 2:346–47.

19. Wahlin, *87-Year History of SDE-GWIS*, 32; "The Sigma Delta Epsilon National Research Fellowship in Science," *Sigma Delta Epsilon News* 5, no. 2 (December 1939): 2; Margaret W. Sloss, "Greeting from the National President," *Sigma Delta Epsilon News* 9, no. 2 (January 1944): 1; Rossiter, *Women Scientists in America*, 2:347.

20. Program for Conference on the Participation of Women in Science, December 29, 1958, and notes from Conference on the Participation of Women in Science, December 29, 1958, both in folder 20, box 1, SDE Records; Rossiter, *Women Scientists in America*, 2:98–99, 101–3, 107–9, 347.

21. Program for Conference on the Participation of Women in Science, December 29, 1958, and notes from Conference on the Participation of Women in Science, December 29, 1958 (Elizabeth Wood quotation), both in folder 20, box 1, SDE Records; Elizabeth Ford, "Engineers Must Ditch Double Standard," *Washington Post*, December 30, 1958, C13; Rossiter, *Women Scientists in America*, 2:347–48.

22. Program for Conference on the Participation of Women in Science, December 29, 1958, folder 20, box 1, SDE Records; Bess Furman, "Flemming Backs Women in Science," *New York Times*, December 30, 1958, 18 (Anne Steinmann quotation).

23. Program for Conference on the Participation of Women in Science, December 29, 1958, folder 20, box 1, SDE Records; Ford, "Engineers Must Ditch Double Standard."

24. Arthur S. Flemming address at the Conference on Participation of Women in Science, December 29, 1958, folder H-8, box 4, SDE Records; Ford, "Engineers Must Ditch Double Standard"; Furman, "Flemming Backs Women in Science."

25. Betty Lou Raskin, "American Women: Unclaimed Treasures of Science" (paper presented at the American Association for the Advancement of Science Annual Meeting, Washington, D.C., December 1958), reprinted in *Goucher College Bulletin* 25, no. 4 (January 1959): no page numbers given, folder EC83, carton 12, CEW Records; "U.S. Wasting Female Brains, Scientist Says," *Los Angeles Times*, December 30, 1958, 3; Ford, "Engineers Must Ditch Double Standard." Raskin also gave the same speech in Chicago several months earlier. See Nicholas Shuman, "Girls Are Urged to Enter Science," *Chicago Daily News*, September 10, 1958, 45, clipping, folder: SWE Newspaper Clippings, 1950s, Series 12, SWE Records (unprocessed).

26. Raskin, "American Women."

27. Ibid.

28. Ibid.

29. Howes and Herzenberg, *Their Day in the Sun*, 76–77.

30. Although it was less feminized than other "hybrid" fields such as chemical librarianship, technical editing still claimed a high share of women, who made up 32.14 percent of the field in 1941 and 38.85 in 1955. Rossiter, *Women Scientists in America*, 2:263–64; Ethaline Cortelyou, "Counseling the Woman Chemistry Major," *Journal of Chemical Education* 32 (April 1955): 196, folder EC83, carton 12, CEW Records.

31. Cortelyou, "Utilizing Chemical Womanpower to Combat the Alleged Shortage of Chemists," 18–19.

32. Ibid.

33. "Brains Have No Sex," *Sigma Delta Epsilon News* 22, no. 2 (November 1958): 1; Virginia Kachan, "Distaff Brains Are Equal," *Washington Post*, May 26, 1958, B3.

34. Cortelyou, "The Status of the American Woman Scientists," 2.

35. Ibid., 3–4.

36. Ibid., 7.

37. Mary Louise Robbins, "Conference: December 29, 1958," *Sigma Delta Epsilon News* 23, no. 1 (May 1959): 1, 3; Mary Louise Robbins, "National Council: March 21, 1959," *Sigma Delta Epsilon News* 23, no. 1 (May 1959): 1, 12; Betty Lankford McLaughlin, "American Council on Women in Science," November 9, 1959, folder 2-3, box 2, SWE Records (unprocessed).

38. Robbins, "Conference: December 29, 1958," 1, 3; Robbins, "National Council: March 21, 1959," 1, 12; McLaughlin, "American Council on Women in Science," November 9, 1959, folder 2-3, box 2, SWE Records (unprocessed).

39. Robbins, "National Council: March 21, 1959," 12.

40. Rossiter, *Women Scientists in America*, 2:348.

41. Ibid., 348–49.

42. Betty Lou Raskin, "Woman's Place Is in the Lab, Too," *New York Times Magazine*, April 19, 1959, 17, 19–20; Ph.D. Research Chemist (Male) of Wilmington, Delaware, letter to the editor, *New York Times Magazine,* May 3, 1959, 6; Arthur H. Kahn, letter to the editor, *New York Times Magazine*, May 3, 1959, 6.

43. McLaughlin, "American Council on Women in Science," November 9, 1959, folder 2-3, box 2, SWE Records (unprocessed).

44. Alan T. Waterman quoted in Ethaline Cortelyou, "Encouraging Women to Select and to Advance in Scientific Careers (X2)," *Science* 131 (1960): 548; "The Conferences on Encouraging Women to Enter Science," box 5, SDE Records; McLaughlin, "American Council on Women in Science," November 9, 1959, folder 2-3, box 2, SWE Records (unprocessed); Robbins, *A History of Sigma Delta Epsilon*, 18; Cortelyou to Waterman, October 5, 1959, folder 19, box 1, SDE Records; Rossiter, *Women Scientists in America*, 2:349–51. Waterman's address was subsequently reprinted in Alan T. Waterman, "Scientific Womanpower—A Neglected Resource," *Science Education* 44, issue 3 (1960): 207–13.

45. Alan T. Waterman quoted in Ernestine B. Thurman, "Women in Science" (paper presented at the National League for Nursing Convention, Cleveland, Ohio, April 14, 1961), box 1, SDE Records.

46. See, for example, Cortelyou, "Encouraging Women to Select and to Advance in Scientific Careers (X2)"; Ernestine B. Thurman, "Women in Science" (paper presented at the National League for Nursing Convention, Cleveland, Ohio, April 14, 1961), box 1, SDE Records; Ernestine B. Thurman, "Needed: More Women in Science," *Nursing Outlook* 9 (October 1961), clipping in folder 6, box 7, Harding Papers.

47. "The Conferences on Encouraging Women to Enter Science," box 5, SDE Records; Robbins, *A History of Sigma Delta Epsilon*, 18; Raymond L. Taylor, "A Report of the Eighth New York Meeting," *Science* 133, no. 3451 (February 17, 1961): 476; "Programs Planned for the AAAS New York Meeting," *Science* 132, no. 3439 (November 25, 1960): 1560, 1562; Rossiter, *Women Scientists in America*, 2:350–51. The last record of the council is a handwritten notation on McLaughlin, "American Council on Women in Science," listing the officers as of September 1962 (November 9, 1959, folder 2-3, box 2, SWE Records [unprocessed]).

48. McLaughlin, Minutes of the National Council Meeting, August 28–31, 1961, Purdue University, West Lafayette, Indiana, 2, folder H-8, box 4, SDE Records.

49. Rossiter, *Women Scientists in America*, 2:350–51.

50. Helen Borton Parker, "Minutes of the Grand Chapter Meeting," December 27, 1957, Indianapolis, Indiana, 3, folder 22, box 1, SDE Records. The committee's name also appears in some places as the "Committee on Encouraging Women in Science."

51. Mary Louise Robbins, "The President's Column," *Sigma Delta Epsilon News* 22, no. 2 (November 1958): 2.

52. Robbins, "The President's Column"; Meta Ellis, "SDE Committee," *Sigma Delta Epsilon News* 23, no. 1 (May 1959): 1, 2; "G.M. of the Rockets," *Time*, June 30, 1958, 80. Biographical materials on Ellis can be found in folder 26, box 76, SWE Historical Membership Files.

53. Ellis, "SDE Committee," 2.

54. Ibid.

55. Ibid.; Helen Borton Parker, "Minutes of the Grand Chapter Meeting," Cosmos Club, Washington, D.C., December 29, 1958, 1, folder 21, box 1, SDE Records;

Meta Ellis to All Chapters of Sigma Delta Epsilon, May 1959, folder 2, box 2, SDE–Alpha Records.

56. Ellis to All Chapters of Sigma Delta Epsilon, May 1959, folder 2, box 2, SDE–Alpha Records.

57. Barbara Benson, "Supplemental History Nu Chapter," June 10, 1967, folder NU, box 5, SDE Records.

58. Hazeltene S. Parmenter, "Short History of Gamma Chapter Sigma Delta Epsilon," July 1968, and Almut Detmers, "Sigma Delta Epsilon—Xi Chapter," December 1966, both in box 5, SDE Records.

59. Committee on Encouraging Women in Science, "Encouraging Women in Science," *Sigma Delta Epsilon News* 24, no. 2 (November 1960): 6.

60. Sigma Delta Epsilon, welcome letter to new members, [1960], folder 17, box 1,SDE Records.

61. Committee on Encouraging Women in Science, "Encouraging Women in Science"; Marilyn Koering, "Sigma Delta Epsilon Beta Chapter," n.d., ca. 1965, box 5, SDE Records; Dorothy I. Fennell, "President's Report Sigma Delta Epsilon—Beta Chapter 1964–1965," July 1965, folder 10, box 1, SDE Records.

62. Fennell, "President's Report Sigma Delta Epsilon—Beta Chapter 1964–1965," July 1965, folder 10, box 1, SDE Records; Marilyn Koering, "Sigma Delta Epsilon Beta Chapter," n.d., ca. 1965, box 5, SDE Records.

63. "SDE: One Look Backward and One to the Future," n.d., ca. 1966, box 5, SDE Records; Meta Ellis to all chapters, May 15, 1959, folder 3, box 2, SDE–Alpha Records.

64. William Irving quoted in minutes, Inter-Society Educational Council, Sacramento, California, September 30, 1960, 2, folder 3, box 2, SDE–Alpha Records; Meta Ellis and Eunice Bonow, annual report of the Committee on Encouraging Women in Science, December 1960, box 1, SDE Records; Meta Ellis, "Excerpts from Our Responsibilities as Working Women," *Sigma Delta Epsilon News* (December 1961): 9; Meta Ellis, Summary, Inter-Society Meeting, May 5, 1960, box 2, SDE–Alpha Records.

65. Sigma Delta Epsilon, welcome letter to new members, [1960], folder 17, box 1, SDE Records; Committee on Encouraging Women in Science, "Encouraging Women in Science," *Sigma Delta Epsilon News* 24, no. 2 (November 1960): 6.

66. Ellis and Bonow, annual report of the Committee on Encouraging Women in Science, December 1960, box 1, SDE Records.

67. Delaphine G. R. Wyckoff, "The President's Column," *Sigma Delta Epsilon News* 25, no. 2 (December 1961): 3.

68. Ibid.

69. Arthur Lack, "Science Talent Hunt Faces Stiff Obstacle: 'Feminine Fallout,'" *Wall Street Journal*, January 16, 1958, 1; Rossiter, *Women Scientists in America*, 2:61.

70. Lack, "Science Talent Hunt Faces Stiff Obstacle."

71. Ibid. See, in particular, National Manpower Council, *Womanpower*.

72. Lack, "Science Talent Hunt Faces Stiff Obstacle," 1; Rossiter, *Women Scientists in America*, 2:61.

73. Susan Spaulding, letter to the editor, *Wall Street Journal*, January 29, 1958, 8; Rossiter, *Women Scientists in America*, 2:62.

74. Spaulding, letter to the editor, 8; Rossiter, *Women Scientists in America*, 2:62.

75. Spaulding, letter to the editor, 8; Rossiter, *Women Scientists in America*, 2:62. For more on Kathleen Morawetz, the faculty member to whom Spaulding referred, see Murray, *Women Becoming Mathematicians*.

76. For more on challenges faced by part-time female students, see Eisenmann, *Higher Education for Women in Postwar America*, 212–13.

77. Ruth V. Dippell, "Annual Report of the Fellowship Awards Board," December 1960, folder 18, box 1, SDE Records.

78. Ibid.

79. Patricia Grinager to Ruth V. Dippell, August 24, 1961, folder 17, box 1, SDE Records. Grinager would later write a biography of Margaret Mead, who was one of her mentors. See Grinager, *Uncommon Lives*.

80. Sigma Delta Epsilon Fellowship Board, Annual Report, November 27, 1964, and JoAnne Mueller, info sheet, n.d., ca. 1964, both in folder 11, box 1, SDE Records.

81. Natalie Miller, unknown article title, June 18, 1971, *Ithaca Journal,* clipping in box 4, SDE–Alpha Records; Acting Officers and Members of the Reactivation Committee to Member, n.d., ca. 1964, Reactivation Correspondence folder, box 5, SDE–Alpha Records; Rossiter, *Women Scientists in America*, 2:351.

82. Acting Officers and Members of the Reactivation Committee to Member, n.d., ca. 1964, Reactivation Correspondence folder, box 5, SDE–Alpha Records.

83. "Report of Interim Meeting," Sigma Delta Epsilon National Council and Board of Directors, Fort Washington, Pennsylvania, July 29, 1967, folder 6a, box 1, SDE Records; Rossiter, *Women Scientists in America*, 2:351.

84. Margaret Stone to Hazeltene S. Parmenter, October 1, 1964, box 5, SDE–Alpha Records.

85. Ibid.

86. "Biographical Brief: Mary I. Bunting, President of Radcliffe College," folder 11, box 1, Bunting Records; "Henry Ingraham, Lawyer, Is Dead," *New York Times*, September 20, 1962, 34; "University Planner, Mary Shotwell Ingraham," *New York Times*, December 14, 1960, 49; Peter Kihss, "Mary S. Ingraham Is Dead at 94," *New York Times*, April 20, 1981, D10; Yaffe, *Mary Ingraham Bunting*, 8–12; Lynn, *Progressive Women in Conservative Times*, 48–49, 55; Mary Ingraham Bunting, "Oral Memoir," interview by Jeannette Bailey Cheek, September–October 1978, transcript, 3–5, Schlesinger Library, Radcliffe Institute for Advanced Study, Harvard University, Cambridge, Massachusetts. Polly Bunting later remarked that while her mother "talk[ed] all the time about the importance of integration . . . it was all at arm's length." "I was not comfortable with the fact that Mother could work so hard for the cause of integration and never invite any blacks into the house." See Yaffe, *Mary Ingraham Bunting*, 12.

87. Bunting, "Oral Memoir," 17–20; Yaffe, *Mary Ingraham Bunting*, 14–21, 30–33.

88. Karen W. Arenson, "Mary Bunting-Smith, Ex-President of Radcliffe, Dies at 87," *New York Times*, January 23, 1998, D20; Bunting, "Oral Memoir," 31–34; Eisenmann, *Higher Education for Women in Postwar America*, 179–80; Yaffe, *Mary Ingraham Bunting*, 64.

89. Arenson, "Mary Bunting-Smith," D20; Bunting, "Oral Memoir," 35, 40, 50; Yaffe, *Mary Ingraham Bunting*, 101–7.

90. Mary Ingraham Bunting quoted in Yaffe, *Mary Ingraham Bunting*, 106; Bunting, "Oral Memoir," 49–50.

91. Yaffe, *Mary Ingraham Bunting*, 106–11.

92. *Newark Sunday News, Newark Evening News*, and Lewis Webster Jones quoted in Wheaton, "Challenging the 'Climate of Unexpectation,'" 22.

93. Yaffe, *Mary Ingraham Bunting*, 115, 118, 120–21, 137; photo number 15; Class of 1959 inscription quoted in Yaffe, *Mary Ingraham Bunting*, 137.

94. Rutgers historian Richard McCormick referred to Bunting as "a neophyte at the deaning business." Quoted in Yaffe, *Mary Ingraham Bunting*, 122.

95. Mary Ingraham Bunting quoted in Wheaton, "Challenging the 'Climate of Unexpectation,'" 23.

96. "New Dean for Douglass," *Douglass Alumnae Bulletin* (Fall 1955): 16–17; Yaffe, *Mary Ingraham Bunting*, 113.

97. Yaffe, *Mary Ingraham Bunting*, 122–23; Wheaton, "Challenging the 'Climate of Unexpectation,'" 23–24 (Mary Ingraham Bunting quoted on 23).

98. Mary Ingraham Bunting quoted in Wheaton, "Challenging the 'Climate of Unexpectation,'" 18.

99. Bunting, "Oral Memoir," 64.

100. Wheaton, "Challenging the 'Climate of Unexpectation,'" 76.

101. Ibid., 76–80; Eisenmann, *Higher Education for Women in Postwar America*, 102.

102. Wheaton, "Challenging the 'Climate of Unexpectation,'" 78–80.

103. Arthur S. Adams, Address on the Occasion of the Inauguration of Mary I. Bunting, Radcliffe College, May 19, 1960, folder 11, box 1, Bunting Records; Wheaton, "Challenging the 'Climate of Unexpectation,'" 80–81.

104. Hottel, *How Fare American Women?*, 1–2. For a fuller treatment of the Commission on the Education of Women, see Eisenmann, *Higher Education for Women in Postwar America*, chapter 3.

105. Hottel, *How Fare American Women?*, 14–15.

106. Alan T. Waterman to Bunting, December 24, 1957, folder: NSF 1957–58, box 71, Douglass College Dean Records; Bunting, "Oral Memoir," 65; Yaffe, *Mary Ingraham Bunting*, 146–47; Wheaton, "Challenging the 'Climate of Unexpectation,'" 87–89.

107. Rossiter, *Women Scientists in America*, 2:60–61.

108. Bunting, "From Serratia to Women's Lib and a Bit Beyond," New Brunswick Lecture given at a meeting of the American Society for Microbiology, Minneapolis, Minnesota, May 5, 1971, 4, folder 735, box 46, Bunting Records; Bunting, "Oral Memoir," 67–68.

109. Bunting, "Oral Memoir," 68–69.

110. Ibid., 69; Bunting, "Commencement Address," delivered at Woman's Medical College, Philadelphia, Pennsylvania, June 7, 1966, 2, folder 504, box 32, Bunting Records.

111. Helen M. Marston, "Report to the Ford Foundation of the Mathematics Study Project at Douglass: A Survey of the Potential Professional Utilization of Mathematically Trained College Women," n.d., and Carl W. Borgmann to Bunting, March 5, 1959, 1, both in folder: Mathematics Study Program, 1959–62, box 67, Douglass College Dean Records. Additional correspondence is located in Grant File #60–452, Ford Foundation Records.

112. Helen M. Marston, "Report to the Ford Foundation of the Mathematics Study Project at Douglass: A Survey of the Potential Professional Utilization of Mathematically Trained College Women," n.d., 2, folder: Mathematics Study Program, 1959–62, box 67, Douglass College Dean Records; Bunting, "Oral Memoir," 73–74.

113. Rutgers News Service, news release, October 2, 1959, 2, folder: Mathematics Study Program, 1959–62, box 67, Douglass College Dean Records.

114. "The Radcliffe Institute for Independent Study," November 1960, 1–5, folder 120, box 7, Bunting Records.

115. Ibid., 2.

116. Bunting to Robert A. Maes, Executive Secretary of the Donner Foundation, December 7, 1960, folder 121, box 7, Bunting Records.

117. Fred M. Hechinger, "Radcliffe Pioneers in Plan for Gifted Women's Study," *New York Times*, November 20, 1960, 1, 60.

118. "Radcliffe's Fine Plan," *Newsday*, November 21, 1960, 49.

119. "Advance in Woman's Education," *Harvard Crimson*, November 21, 1960, folder 120, box 7, Bunting Records.

120. Jackson Martindell to Mary Ingraham Bunting, May 11, 1961, folder 161, box 10, Bunting Records; cover and "One Woman, Two Lives," *Time,* November 3, 1961, 68–73.

121. Laughlin, *Women's Work and Public Policy*, 79–80; Kennedy, "Executive Order 10980 Establishing the President's Commission on the Status of Women," 207.

122. Harrison, *On Account of Sex*, 85–87, 110–11; Eisenmann, *Higher Education for Women in Postwar America*, 144.

123. Harrison, *On Account of Sex*, 74–76; Emma Guffey Miller and Doris Fleeson quoted in ibid., 76.

124. Harrison, *On Account of Sex*, 39, 110–11; Laughlin, *Women's Work and Public Policy*, 79–80; Eisenmann, *Higher Education for Women in Postwar America*, 144–45; Esther Peterson quoted in Harrison, *On Account of Sex*, 116.

125. Kennedy, "Executive Order 10980 Establishing the President's Commission on the Status of Women," 207.

126. Laughlin, *Women's Work and Public Policy*, 69–74. Some professional women's groups, however, actively opposed Peterson's appointment because of her ties to organized labor. These included the National Federation of Business and Professional Women's Clubs and the National Woman's Party.

127. Esther Peterson, speech to be given before the National Federation of Business and Professional Women," July 7, 1961, folder 2365, box 118, Peterson Papers.

128. U.S. Department of Labor, "Womanpower—A Great Resource for Progress," March 17, 1962, folder 2385, box 118, Peterson Papers. See also Sarah Evans, "U.S. Aide Lauds Gals' Space Role," *Detroit News*, February 28, 1962, 2E, and Pauline Sterling, "Mrs. Peterson Asserts: Space Program Opens New Doors to Women," *Detroit Free Press*, February 24, 1962, clipping, both in folder 8-2, box 8, SWE-Detroit.

129. Announcement of President's Commission on the Status of Women quoted in Dorothy Quiggle, "The President's Column," *Sigma Delta Epsilon News* (May 1962): 2.

130. Harrison, *On Account of Sex*, 112–14; Mead and Kaplan, *American Women*, 264–65.

131. Harrison, *On Account of Sex*, 114–15; Mead and Kaplan, *American Women*, 255–58.

132. Ernestine B. Thurman to John F. Kennedy, January 3, 1962, Katherine P. Ellickson to Dorothy Quiggle, February 15, 1962, and Dorothy Quiggle to Katherine P. Ellickson, March 2, 1962, all in folder: Grand Chapter Meeting, 1962, box 4, SDE Records.

133. Meta Ellis to Dorothy Quiggle, June 4, 1962, folder 15, box 1, SDE Records, and Meta Ellis to Patricia Brown, June 4, 1962, folder 26, box 76, SWE Historical Membership Files.

134. Dorothy Quiggle, "Notes on National Council Meeting Held in Washington, D.C., June 9 and 10, 1962," folder: Grand Chapter Meeting, 1962, box 4, and Hazeltene S. Parmenter, Sigma Delta Epsilon Minutes of the National Council and Board of Directors Meeting, December 26–30, 1963, folder 30, box 1, SDE Records.

135. Meta Ellis (Heller), Society of Women Engineers membership application, March 10, 1962, folder 26, box 76, SWE Historical Membership Files. Ellis's membership application lists her professional name of "Miss Meta Ellis" but includes her married name, Heller.

136. Ann Lawrence, Minutes of Board of Directors Meeting, Chicago, January 25 and 26, 1958, folder 29, box 1; Aileen Cavanagh to Lamona F. Cherry, "Memorandum to the Board of Directors—Society of Women Engineers," October 22, 1958, and Mary Ellen Russell, "1961-SWE Convention: PG&E Report, 1960–61, Pacific Northwest Section, SWE," both in folder: 3.99 Misc; Professional Guidance and Education Reports, 1954–61, Series 8: Committees (Newsletter, Sections, Students, Misc); and Mary V. Munger to Patricia L. Brown, January 23, 1962, folder 2-8, box 2, all in SWE Records (unprocessed).

137. "SWE Action Asked for by President's Committee on Scientists and Engineers," *SWE Newsletter* 6, no. 7 (March 1960): 1, 4; Beatrice A. Hicks to Catherine Eiden, December 5, 1960, folder: Arkansas Conference on Utilization of Engineers and Scientists, Series 12: Women in Engineering, SWE Records (unprocessed). Torpey was also the former "manpower" consultant to the President's Committee

on Scientists and Engineers. For information on Torpey, see American Political Science Association, "Other Activities," 1225.

138. Isabelle F. French, "Minutes of Executive Committee," June 21–22, 1961, folder 6, box 2, SWE Records (unprocessed); Donald Feight quoted in *Women in Professional Engineering,* 78–79.

139. "Bell Labs & GE, First Corporate Members," *SWE Newsletter* 7, no. 8 (April 1961): 1.

140. Isabelle F. French, "Minutes of Executive Committee," February 10–11, 1962, folder 8, box 2, SWE Records (unprocessed); "Women's Space Symposium Held," *SWE Newsletter* 8, no. 9 (May 1962): 1, 4.

141. See, for example, miscellaneous SWE recruitment materials [1963], no folder, Series 8: Committees (Newsletters, Sections, Students, Misc), SWE Records (unprocessed).

142. Meta Ellis to Patricia Brown, June 4, 1962, folder 26, box 76, SWE Historical Membership Files; Aileen Cavanagh to Patricia Brown, June 14, 1962, folder 1, box 181, National Records, SWE Records (processed).

143. Patricia Brown on Meta Ellis proposal, [June 1962], folder 1, box 181, National Records, SWE Records (processed).

144. Isabelle F. French, Minutes of Executive Committee, June 21, 1962, folder 9, box 2, SWE Records (unprocessed); Patricia L. Brown to Meta Ellis Heller, October 17, 1962, folder 26, box 76, SWE Historical Membership Files. SWE did report, however, on the PCSW from time to time. See, for example, "Committee Named to Study Working Women," *SWE Newsletter* 8, no. 9 (May 1962): 1, 4.

145. The most comprehensive account of the education committee's work can be found in Eisenmann, *Higher Education for Women in Postwar America,* 154–71.

146. Ibid., 155; Mead and Kaplan, *American Women,* 256; Esther Raushenbush, "Time Is a Vessel," Keynote Address at Job Forum, YWCA, Stamford, November 9, 1962, folder 12, carton 1, Raushenbush Papers.

147. "Summary of the First Meeting of the Education Committee," May 2, 1962, folder 42, and transcript of proceedings, President's Commission on the Status of Women Education Committee, May 2, 1962, 5–6, folder 43, both in box 7, PCSW Records.

148. "Summary of the First Meeting of the Education Committee," May 2, 1962, folder 42, box 7, PCSW Records; Eisenmann, *Higher Education for Women in Postwar America,* 158.

149. Transcript of proceedings, President's Commission on the Status of Women Education Committee, May 2, 1962, 9, folder 43, box 7, PCSW Records.

150. "Summary of the First Meeting of the Education Committee," May 2, 1962, folder 42, and transcript of proceedings, President's Commission on the Status of Women Education Committee, May 2, 1962, 75, 95–96, 110–14, folder 43, both in box 7, PCSW Records.

151. Eisenmann, *Higher Education for Women in Postwar America,* 165–68.

152. Mead and Kaplan, *American Women,* 29.

153. Committee on Education, "Summary of Report on Education," March 27, 1963, folder 41, box 6, PCSW Records.

154. Mead and Kaplan, *American Women*, 5, 9–12, 36–42, 48–53, 57, 118–27.

155. The President's Commission on the Status of Women quoted in Harrison, *On Account of Sex*, 133–34.

156. Harrison, *On Account of Sex*, 126–34; Linden-Ward and Green, *American Women in the 1960s*, 7.

157. Harrison, *On Account of Sex*, 155, 158.

158. Mead and Kaplan, *American Women*, 35–36.

Chapter Four

1. Stratton, "Welcoming Remarks," xi.

2. Van Aken, Foreword to *Women and the Scientific Professions*, v–vi.

3. Ibid., vi.

4. Mina Rees quoted in Bunting, "The Commitment Required of a Woman Entering a Scientific Profession," 34–36; Judy Green, Jeanne LaDuke, Saunders MacLane, and Uta C. Merzbach, "Mina Spiegel Rees (1902–1997)," *Notices of the American Mathematical Society* 45, no. 7 (August 1998): 866–73; Williams, *Improbable Warriors*, 169–99.

5. Chien-Shiung Wu quoted in Bunting, "The Commitment Required of a Woman Entering a Scientific Profession," 44–48; Rosenberg, *Changing the Subject*, 185–86; William Dicke, "Chien-Shiung Wu, 84, Dies; Top Experimental Physicist," *New York Times*, February 18, 1997, B7.

6. Rossiter, *Women Scientists in America*, 2:365; Rossi, "Equality between the Sexes"; Rossi, "The Biosocial Side of Parenthood."

7. Rossi, "Barriers to the Career Choice of Engineering, Medicine, or Science among American Women," 53.

8. Ibid., 52–53.

9. Harrison, *On Account of Sex*, 160–61.

10. Friedan, *The Feminine Mystique*, 13; Rosen, *The World Split Open*, 6–7. For a more nuanced account of Friedan's work, see Meyerowitz, "Beyond the Feminine Mystique," 229–62. For the impact of the book, see Coontz, *A Strange Stirring*.

11. Rosen, *The World Split Open*, xxiv, 68; Harrison, *On Account of Sex*, 89–105. Other treatments of working-class women's activism can be found in Cobble, "Recapturing Working-Class Feminism," and Gabin, *Feminism in the Labor Movement*.

12. Wandersee, *On the Move*, 104; Rosen, *The World Split Open*, 70–74; Harrison, *On Account of Sex*, 187–91.

13. Rosen, *The World Split Open*, 74–81; Harrison, *On Account of Sex*, 192–209; Lisa Hammel, "They Meet in Victorian Parlor to Demand 'True Equality'—NOW," *New York Times*, November 22, 1966, 44. See also Friedan, *It Changed My Life*. Although most accounts say that fifteen women attended the June meeting, recent research by Sonia Pressman Fuentes puts that number at twenty-eight. See "Honoring NOW's Founders and Pioneers," www.now.org/history/founders.html.

14. Rosen, *The World Split Open*, 78; National Organization for Women, "Statement of Purpose."

15. MacLean, *The American Women's Movement, 1945–2000*, 16.

16. Rosen, *The World Split Open*, 82–83.

17. Ibid., 81–83; Wandersee, *On the Move*, 19–20.

18. MacLean, *The American Women's Movement, 1945–2000*, 18; Harrison, *On Account of Sex*, 208. See also Evans, *Personal Politics*, and Echols, *Daring to Be Bad*.

19. MacLean, *The American Women's Movement, 1945–2000*, 19–20; Rosen, *The World Split Open*, 92–93.

20. Isserman and Kazin, *America Divided*, 228.

21. Ibid., 167–68; Pursell, *The Military-Industrial Complex*, 339. See also Rorabaugh, *Berkeley at War*.

22. Isserman and Kazin, *America Divided*, 228–29.

23. Farber, *The Age of Great Dreams*, 117, 136–37; Isserman and Kazin, *America Divided*, 187–92. See also Kaiser, *American Tragedy*.

24. Farber, *The Age of Great Dreams*, 138–39, 156–59. For one of the most comprehensive treatments of the antiwar movement to date, see Wells, *The War Within*.

25. Farber, *The Age of Great Dreams*, 156–57.

26. Clowse, *Brainpower for the Cold War*, 155. See also Urban, *More than Science and Sputnik*.

27. Eisenhower, "Farewell Address," 206; Roland, *The Military-Industrial Complex*, 6. According to the *Oxford English Dictionary*, the phrase "military-industrial complex" was first used in a 1931 *International Affairs* article. See "military, adj. and n." in *OED Online*, September 2013, Oxford University Press, http://www.oed.com.

28. Fulbright, "The War and Its Effects."

29. Leslie, *The Cold War and American Science*, 233–34.

30. Kevles, "Principles and Politics in Federal R&D Policy, 1945–1990," xxii.

31. Zelizer, *Arsenal of Democracy*, 218, 222, 234; Sherry, *In the Shadow of War*, 310–11.

32. Sherry, *In the Shadow of War*, 311.

33. Zelizer, *Arsenal of Democracy*, 238.

34. Freeman, Oldham, Cooper, Sinclair, and Achilladelis, "The Goals of R&D in the 1970s," 366.

35. Smith, *American Science Policy since World War II*, 81; Kevles, "Principles and Politics in Federal R&D Policy, 1945–1990," xviii.

36. Rossiter, *Women Scientists in America*, 2:373.

37. Sandra Blakeslee, "Young Physicists Find Fewer Jobs," *New York Times*, April 26, 1970, 50; Fred M. Hechinger, "Ph. D.s: The Degree That Has Become a 'Glut on the Market,'" *New York Times*, January 3, 1971, E7; Rossiter, *Women Scientists in America*, 2:373.

38. Rosen, *The World Split Open*, 304.

39. Wandersee, *On the Move*, 118–20; Rosen, *The World Split Open*, 89.

40. Margaret H. Stone, "Book Review Corner: Women and the Scientific Professions," *SDE News* 34, no. 1 (Spring 1970): 7.

41. Mrs. Victor [Jacquelyn] Mattfeld to L. Howard Bennett, October 26, 1964, folder: Affirmative Action: Negro Women in Science and Engineering, box 1,

Kistiakowsky Papers; Mabel Bell Crooks to Mrs. Victor H. [Jacquelyn] Mattfeld, October 17, 1964, folder: Women in Science and Engineering Symposium, Correspondence, 1964–65, box 9, MIT Associate Dean for Student Affairs Records.

42. "Tenn. State's Lady Engineer," *Ebony* 19, no. 9 (July 1964): 75.

43. Ibid., 75–82.

44. "The Ms. Factor in ASME," *Mechanical Engineering* (July 1973): 13, reprinted by the Society of Women Engineers, folder: 1973, carton 1, SWE-Boston. Additional biographical information about Clark can be found in Warren, *Black Women Scientists in the United States*, 37–39.

45. "The Ms. Factor in ASME," 14.

46. Eileen Duignan, Society of Women Engineers membership applications, March 13, 1958, and August 30, 1969, folder 60, box 187, National Records, SWE Records (processed); "The Ms. Factor in ASME," 15.

47. "The Ms. Factor in ASME," 15.

48. Jeanne Brodie to Winnie Gifford, May 7, 1966, folder: 3.30.17. Committees: Statistics, 1961–66, Series 8: Committees (Sections, Statistics, Student Activities), SWE Records (unprocessed).

49. Eileen Duignan-Woods to Priscilla J. Collins, December 4, 1972, folder: 1972, carton 1, SWE-Boston.

50. Naomi McAfee quoted in Kata, "The Boundaries of Women's Rights," 43.

51. Arminta J. Harness, "President's Letter," *SWE Newsletter* (December 1977): cover page.

52. Ibid.; Judy Klemesrud, "At Houston Meeting, 'A Kaleidoscope of American Womanhood,'" special to *New York Times*, November 19, 1977, 1; Rosen, *The World Split Open*, 291–94.

53. Arminta Harness, "The Significance of the National Women's Conference," *SWE Newsletter* (December 1977): 1.

54. Kindya, *Four Decades*, 28; Kata, "The Boundaries of Women's Rights," 44.

55. Aileen Cavanagh to Arminta Harness, February 3, 1977, no folder, Series 12: Statistics and Surveys, SWE Records (unprocessed).

56. Kindya, *Four Decades*, 28; "Convention Speaker Urges: Work for Equality," *SWE Newsletter* (September 1978): 8.

57. "Convention Speaker Urges: Work for Equality," *SWE Newsletter* (September 1978): 8.

58. Naomi McAfee, interview by Lauren Kata, May 30, 2003, transcript, 53–54, box 2, SWE Pioneers.

59. Kata, "The Boundaries of Women's Rights," 44.

60. Hayes, *Five Decades of the Society of Women Engineers*, unpaginated.

61. Bix, "Supporting Females in a Male Field," 337. The statistics regarding women's engineering degrees come from Rossiter, *Women Scientists in America*, 3:41–47.

62. Kindya, *Four Decades*, 27.

63. "SWE Conventioneers to 'Reach for the Skies,' Literally and Figuratively," *SWE Newsletter* (Spring 1976): 8–9, and Region IV advertisement for student conference, *SWE Newsletter* (Spring 1976): 10.

64. Peden, "Ceiling Unlimited," 85.

65. Ibid., 85.

66. McAfee, "The Society of Women Engineers—Past and Present," 6–7.

67. Ibid., 1–7; Bix, "Supporting Females in a Male Field," 340–41.

68. Aileen Cavanagh to Kathy Fowler, May 2, 1977, folder: 1977, carton 1, SWE-Boston.

69. Arminta J. Harness, "President's Letter," *SWE Newsletter* (December 1977): cover page; "SWE Membership Profile" in Hayes, *Five Decades of the Society of Women Engineers*, unpaginated.

70. Janet Christensen, "12 Intruders Protest Women's 'Inferior Role,'" clipping, folder E-3, box 3, SDE Records.

71. "Equality for Women in Science," folder E-3, box 3, SDE Records.

72. Ibid.

73. Sigma Delta Epsilon, Interim Board Meeting, minutes, December 28 and 19, 1969, folder E-4, box 3, SDE Records; Margaret Stone, "The National Organization of Graduate Women in Science," n.d., ca. 1971, folder: 50th anniversary meeting, box 5, SDE–Alpha Records.

74. Margaret Stone, "The National Organization of Graduate Women in Science," n.d., ca. 1971, folder: 50th anniversary meeting, box 5, SDE–Alpha Records.

75. Wahlin, *87-Year History of SDE-GWIS*, 17; Grace E. Jacobs to Presidents and Liaison Officers, April 23, 1970, folder: Grand Chapter Meeting, June 19–21, 1970, box 9, SDE Records.

76. Marie H. Berg, "President's Resume, 1969–1970," June 20, 1970, folder: Grand Chapter Meeting, June 19–20, 1970, box 9, SDE Records.

77. Bernice J. Austrheim, "Chi Chapter Annual Report, 1971–1972," n.d., folder: Grand Chapter Meeting, June 16–17, 1972, box 9, SDE Records.

78. Margaret Stone, "The National Organization of Graduate Women in Science," n.d., ca. 1971, folder: 50th anniversary meeting, box 5, SDE–Alpha Records; Wahlin, *87-Year History of SDE-GWIS*, 17.

79. May Wright, "Xi (Minnesota) Chapter Report, 1969–1970," n.d., folder: Grand Chapter Meeting, June 19–21, 1970, and Ruth Dickie, Beta Chapter President's Report, June 10, 1976, folder: Grand Chapter Meeting, June 10–12, 1976, both in box 9, SDE Records.

80. "Activities of Pi Chapter—1970–1971," n.d., and Zoe E. Anderson, "President's Report of Activities for 1970–1971," June 10, 1971, unmarked folder, both in box 8, SDE Records.

81. Jean E. Simmons, "Report of the President," [1971], folder: Grand Chapter Meetings, June 18–20, 1971; Eva Lurie Weinreb to Elizabeth O'Hern, "Interim Report for 1975–76," folder: Interim Meetings Feb. 18–24, 1976; B. A. Lewis, "Report of the President—1971–1972—Alpha Chapter," folder: Grand Chapter Meeting, June 16–17, 1972; "Minutes of the Grand Chapter Meeting and National Council, June 18 thru 20, 1971," folder: National Council and Grand Chapter Meetings; and Naomi M. Hawkins, "Omicron President's Report for 1977–78," May 1978, folder: Grand Chapter Meeting, June 8–11, 1978, all in box 9, SDE Records; "News from the Chapters," *Sigma Delta Epsilon News* 27, no. 2 (November 1963): 6.

82. Alice S. Rossi, "Women Scientists: Problems and Prospects," *Sigma Delta Epsilon News* (May 1967): 2–7.

83. Simmons, "Report of the President," [1971], folder: Grand Chapter Meetings, June 18–20, 1971; Ruth S. Dickie, "Report of the President," June 8, 1979, folder: Grand Chapter Meeting, June 7–10, 1979; Sigma Delta Epsilon–Graduate Women in Science, Program for Interim Meetings, February 25–28, 1974, folder: Interim Meetings Feb. 26 and 27, 1974, all in box 9, SDE Records.

84. Jean Simmons, preliminary program, folder E-4, box 3, SDE Records; Rossiter, *Women Scientists in America*, 2:98, 100, 111.

85. Jean Simmons, preliminary program, folder E-4, box 3, SDE Records.

86. Wahlin, *87-Year History of SDE-GWIS*, 48; Jean E. Simmons, "Women in Science," *Science* (October 9, 1970): 201; Sigma Delta Epsilon, "Symposium on Women in Science," program, and "Minutes of the Interim Meeting of the National Council," December 28, 1970, both in folder: Interim Meeting December 1970, box 3, SDE Records. For Weisstein, see Rossiter, *Women Scientists in America*, 2:370–71, and Weisstein, "Adventures of a Woman in Science."

87. Sheffield, *Women and Science*, 165; Hubbard, *The Politics of Women's Biology*, 1. For more on Wald, see Dowling, "George Wald, 1906–1997."

88. Handwritten notes, Women in Science Symposium, December 27, 1970, folder: Interim Meeting December 1970, box 3, SDE Records.

89. Sigma Delta Epsilon, "Symposium on Women in Science," program and handwritten notes, Women in Science Symposium, December 27, 1970, folder: Interim Meeting December 1970, box 3, SDE Records.

90. Ibid.

91. Arthur J. Snider, "Women in Science: Why There Aren't More of Them," *Chicago Daily News*, December 28, 1970, clipping, folder: Interim Meeting December 1970, box 3, SDE Records.

92. Beatrice A. Smith, "Annual Report of the President—Xi Chapter," [1972], folder: Grand Chapter Meeting, June 16–17, 1972, and Bette Barnes, "Annual Report 1974–1975" (Beta Chapter), folder: Grand Chapter Meeting, June 13–14, 1975, box 9, SDE Records.

93. "Roster Progress March 1967–February 1968," folder: Professional Skills Roster, box 5, SDE–Alpha Records; "Professional Opportunities for Women in Science (POWS)," *Sigma Delta Epsilon News* (Spring 1969): clipping, in box 3, Farley Papers.

94. Briscoe, "Phenomenon of the Seventies."

95. Ibid., 154; Pat Dalton, "Hope Seen for Women Scientists," *Tuscaloosa News*, October 29, 1975, 5; Oldman, "Women in the Professional Caucuses."

96. Warren, *Black Women Scientists in the United States*, 237–43.

97. Eva Ruth Kashket, Mary Louise Robbins, Loretta Leive, and Alice S. Huang, "Status of Women Microbiologists: A Study of Microbiologists Based on Objective and Subjective Criteria Is Presented," *Science* 183, no. 4124 (February 8, 1974): 488–94; see also Splaver, *Nontraditional Careers for Women*.

98. Rita Guttman, curriculum vitae, folder 1, and Rita Guttman, "A Lab of One's Own" ca. 1981, unpublished manuscript, 2, folder 2, Guttman Papers. Rita

Guttman to Vera Kistiakowsky, July 5, 1972, folder: AWIS, 1982, box 6, Kistiakowsky Papers.

99. Rita Guttman, "A Lab of One's Own," ca. 1981, unpublished manuscript, 65, folder 2, Guttman Papers.

100. Ibid., 65–66. The description of Apter comes from Rossiter, *Women Scientists in America*, 3:3.

101. Rita Guttman, "A Short History of the Caucus of Women Biophysicists," delivered to the Caucus of Women Biophysicists, February 16, 1982, folder 1, Guttman Papers.

102. "Meet a Member: Vera Kistiakowsky," *AWIS Newsletter* 4, no. 5 (September/October 1975): 9–11; Oakes, *Encyclopedia of World Scientists*, 403.

103. "Meet a Member: Vera Kistiakowsky," 10; Vera Kistiakowsky, interview by Shirlee Sherkow, April 27, 1976, transcript, 62–63, 73–75, 78, box 2, MIT Oral History.

104. Vera Kistiakowsky, interview by Shirlee Sherkow, April 27, 1976, transcript, 77, box 2, MIT Oral History; "Meet a Member: Vera Kistiakowsky," 10.

105. Transcription of Vera Kistiakowsky's remarks from "Escape from the Circle" conference, attached to November 29, 1972, letter from Irma L. Rabbino to Vera Kistiakowsky, folder: Mount Holyoke College, box 20, Kistiakowsky Papers.

106. Ibid.

107. Vera Kistiakowsky, interview by Shirlee Sherkow, April 27, 1976, transcript, 117–18, box 2, MIT Oral History; Vera Kistiakowsky to Robert Serber, April 14, 1971, box 3, "A.P.S. Committee on Women in Physics," [1971?], box 3, and Vera Kistiakowsky, "Women in Physics?," address delivered at West Chester State College, February 16, 1972, folder: Talk—Women in Physics, box 29, Kistiakowsky Papers. See also Gloria Lubkin, "Women in Physics," *Physics Today* 24, no. 4 (April 1971): 23–27.

108. Vera Kistiakowsky, interview by Shirlee Sherkow, April 27, 1976, transcript, 118, box 2, MIT Oral History.

109. Ibid., 118–19; "Report of the Committee on the Status of Women in Physics," January 1974, folder: APS-CWP, 1973–75, and Nancy M. O'Fallon and Caroline L. Herzenberg, "The American Physical Society Committee on the Status of Women in Physics: A Brief History," August 26, 1977, folder: APS Committee on the Status of Women in Physics: A Brief History, both in box 2, Kistiakowsky Papers.

110. Vera Kistiakowsky, interview by Shirlee Sherkow, April 27, 1976, transcript, 116, 221, box 2, MIT Oral History; Mackenzie Carpenter, "Pioneering Women Professor at Pitt Shuns Spotlight," *Pittsburgh Post-Gazette*, May 31, 2004, B-11 and B-12.

111. Carpenter, "Pioneering Women Professor at Pitt Shuns Spotlight," B-12; "Election Winners: Pake, Baranger, Vineyard, and Werthamer," *Physics Today* 28, no. 3 (March 1975): 67. Baranger returned to the University of Pittsburgh after her marriage broke up in the early 1970s, just four years after arriving at MIT.

112. Murray, *Women Becoming Mathematicians*, 191–92. Pless remained at MIT until 1975, when she accepted a tenured full professorship in mathematics and computer science at the University of Illinois at Chicago.

113. Vera Kistiakowsky, interview by Shirlee Sherkow, April 27, 1976, transcript, 116, box 2, MIT Oral History; "Women in Science and Engineering, Boston," [1971], box 29, Kistiakowsky Papers. See also M. E. Law, "Women in Science and Engineering, Boston," *AWIS Newsletter* 4, no. 5 (September/October 1975): 8.

114. Law, "Women in Science and Engineering, Boston," 8.

115. Ibid.; Law, *Goals for Women in Science*. Hornig is also mentioned in Williams, *Improbable Warriors*, 10.

116. Alice T. Schafer quoted in Murray, *Women Becoming Mathematicians*, 79; Anne Leggett, ed., "Alice Turner Schafer (1915–2009): Remembrances," *Notices of the American Mathematical Society* 57, no. 9 (October 2010): 1116–19.

117. Murray, *Women Becoming Mathematicians*, 44, 119–20, 217; Leggett, "Alice Turner Schafer (1915–2009)," 1116.

118. Fasanelli, "Mary Gray," 71–75.

119. Ibid., 72.

120. Ibid., 73.

121. Ibid.; Lenore Blum, "A Brief History of the Association for Women in Mathematics: The Presidents' Perspectives," *Notices of the American Mathematical Society* 38, no. 7 (September 1991): 738–74.

122. Fasanelli, "Mary Gray," 73; Murray, *Women Becoming Mathematicians*, 218; Blum, "A Brief History of the Association for Women in Mathematics," 738–74.

123. AWIS, press release, April 16, 1971, folder 7, box 6, Harding Papers.

124. "AWIS—Ten Years Later: G. Virginia Upton," *AWIS Newsletter* 5, no. 3 (May/June 1976): 8–9; Rossiter, *Women Scientists in America*, 3:1–2.

125. Briscoe, "Scientific Sexism: The World of Chemistry," 154–58; Anne Fleckenstein, "35 Years of AWIS," *AWIS Magazine* (Summer 2006): 25–26.

126. "Association of Women in Science," list of charter members and press release, April 16, 1971, folder 7, box 6, Harding Papers; Judith Pool obituary, reprinted in "President's Remarks," *AWIS Newsletter* 4, no. 4 (July/August 1975): 1; "Committee Chairmen," *AWIS Newsletter* 1, no. 1 (Summer 1971): 2; Neena B. Schwartz, *A Lab of My Own* (Amsterdam: Rodopi, 2010), 267–71; Briscoe, "Scientific Sexism: The World of Chemistry," 156; Rossiter, *Women Scientists in America*, 3:2–4.

127. Robert Q. Marston to Jan Keithly, July 19, 1971, folder 8, and Jules Asher, "HEW Bias Charged in Women's Suit," *Washington Post*, March 29, 1972, clipping, folder 9, both in box 6, Harding Papers; Julia Apter to AWIS members, May 14, 1973, folder 2, box 7, Harding Papers; "Adele Edison Reports: AWIS Explores Impact of Federal Guidelines at a HEW Forum," *AWIS Newsletter* 1, no. 1 (Summer 1971):1; "AWIS et al. vs. Richardson and Marston," *AWIS Newsletter* 1, nos. 3, 4 (Winter–Spring 1972): 1, 4; Rossiter, *Women Scientists in America*, 3:3, 289 (n. 6); Rossiter, *Women Scientists in America*, 2:380.

128. Neena Schwartz to Florence J. Hicks, August 28, 1972, folder 1, and Fann Harding, "Memorandum," September 26, 1973, folder 3, both in box 7, Harding Papers.

129. Rossiter, *Women Scientists in America*, 3:5, 290 (n. 10).

130. AWIS pamphlet, 1974–75, folder 5, box 10, and Helene N. Guttman to J. Weis, October 2, 1973, folder 8, box 6, both in Harding Papers.

131. "Report of the AWIS Affirmative Goals and Actions Committee," *AWIS Newsletter* 3, no. 1 (Autumn 1973): 5; "Outgoing President Reports on the State of AWIS," *AWIS Newsletter* 5, no. 2 (March/April 1976): 3.

132. "Local Chapters—What's New?," *AWIS Newsletter* 7, no. 3 (May/June 1978): 8–9; Fleckenstein, "35 Years of AWIS," 26.

133. Estelle Ramey, "AWIS President's Message," *AWIS Newsletter* 3, no. 2 (Winter 1974): 1; "AWIS Educational Foundation," *AWIS Newsletter* 4, no. 4 (July/August 1975): 9; Fleckenstein, "35 Years of AWIS," 26.

134. Estelle Ramey, curriculum vitae; Estelle Ramey, "Well, Fellows, What Did Happen at the Bay of Pigs? And Who Was in Control?" *McCalls*, January 1971, clipping; Nancy L. Ross, "Dr. Ramey: The Mort Sahl of Women's Lib," *Washington Post*, November 14, 1972, C2; and *People* clipping, January 19, 1976, all in folder 7, box 1, Harding Papers; Margalit Fox, "Estelle R. Ramey, 89, Who Used Medical Training to Rebut Sexism, Is Dead," *New York Times*, September 12, 2006, http://www.nytimes.com/2006/09/12/obituaries/12ramey.html#.

135. Estelle R. Ramey to Membership of AWIS, August 1, 1972, and Betty Beale, "Outraged Women and a Sexy Medical Tome," *Sunday Star and Daily News*, September 24, 1972, clipping, both in folder 7, box 1, Harding Papers; "Evolution of AWIS," *AWIS Newsletter* 2, no. 1 (Autumn 1972): 3–4.

136. Estelle R. Ramey to Membership of AWIS, August 1, 1972, folder 7, box 1, Harding Papers.

137. Ibid.

138. Estelle Ramey quoted in "There's Only One Way . . . Together," *Federation Newsletter* (Spring 1973): 3, limited distribution, folder 3, box 8; summary of minutes of AWIS steering committee, April 10–11, 1972, folder 9, box 6; Fann Harding to Members of Planning Committee, n.d., folder 7, box 7; "History," n.d., folder 2, box 8, all in Harding Papers.

139. Fann Harding, "Divide and Be Conquered—Unite and Proceed," address at American Association for the Advancement of Science meeting, December 27, 1972, folder 7, box 7; Fann Harding to attendees, November 22, 1972, folder 2, box 8; Fann Harding, list of receipts for Federation of Women's Professional Organizations Conference, November 17–18, 1972, folder 2, box 8, all in Harding Papers.

140. Anne Briscoe, "AWIS President's Greetings," *AWIS Newsletter* 3, no. 3 (May–June 1974): 1; "Federation Activities," *Federation Newsletter* (Spring 1973): 2, limited distribution, folder 3, box 8, Harding Papers.

141. Rossiter, *Women Scientists in America*, 3:12; "Federation ERA Task Force Organizes for 1979," clipping, folder 6, box 10, Harding Papers; Russo and Cassidy, "Women in Science and Technology."

142. Nancy Tooney, "Meet a Member," *AWIS Newsletter* 6, no. 5 (September/October 1977): 8–12; Anne Perusek, "In Memoriam: Lt. Col. Arminta J. Harness," *SWE Magazine* 56, no. 3 (Summer 2010): 125; "SWE's Corporate Sponsors: A Gauge of Growth," *SWE Newsletter* 22, nos. 1 and 2 (Winter 1975–76): 35; U.S. Atomic Energy Commission, advertisement, "We Want to Make Your Future Brighter," *SWE Newsletter* 21, no. 3 (January–March 1975): 5; U.S. Energy Research

and Development Administration, advertisement, "Brain Power. Our most important energy resource," *SWE Newsletter* 21, no. 4 (Spring Special 1975): 3.

143. Arminta J. Harness, "President's Letter," *SWE Newsletter* 24, no. 3 (February/March 1978): inside cover.

144. Judith Pool to McGeorge Bunting, December 15, 1971, folder 8, box 6, Harding Papers.

145. Ibid.

146. "Betty McGee Vetter," *Washington Post*, November 21, 1994, B3; "Scientific Manpower Commission," folder: Scientific Manpower Commission, box 37, Roscher Papers; "Bulletin Board," *AWIS Newsletter* 5, no. 5 (September/October 1976): 13; WISE announcement for December 4, 1975, event, featuring lecture by Betty Vetter titled "Supply and Demand: Labor Markets for Women Scientists and Engineers," folder: WISE meetings and speakers, box 29, Kistiakowsky Papers. See also box 7, Vetter Papers.

147. Jean E. Simmons, "Annual Report of the Finance and Fund Raising Committee, 1973–1974," folder 2, box 9, and Federation of Organizations for Professional Women, Participation of Women in the Sciences, National Science Foundation Proposal, [1974], folder 7, box 8, Harding Papers.

148. "Science Career Facilitation Project for Women at the University of Lowell," announcement, n.d., folder: WISE 1976, box 29, Kistiakowsky Papers.

149. Rutherford, "The Role of the National Science Foundation," 276–78; "WISE News" and "Science Career Facilitation Project for Women at the University of Lowell," announcements, n.d., folder: WISE 1976, box 29, Kistiakowsky Papers. Additional information regarding the Women in Science Program can be found in the Roscher Papers as well as in the NSF Records.

150. Rutherford, "The Role of the National Science Foundation," 278–79.

151. Hood College, Women in Science Careers Workshop agenda, March 10, 1978, folder 1a, box 1, Harding Papers; "Women in Science: Re-Entry," *AWIS Newsletter* 7, no. 6 (November–December 1978): 8.

152. Estelle Ramey to Mrs. Tobin Armstrong, July 20, 1973, folder 3, box 7, Harding Papers; "Anne Armstrong, 1927–2008; Longtime GOP Stalwart, Former Ambassador to Britain," *Los Angeles Times*, July 31, 2008, B7.

153. Estelle Ramey to Warren Magnuson, July 27, 1973, folder 3, box 7, Harding Papers.

154. "Anne Armstrong"; Pam Jacklin to AWIS Steering Committee, August 24, 1973, folder 3, box 7, Harding Papers.

155. Elizabeth Urey Baranger, "Admission and Attrition of Women in Graduate School" (paper presented at American Association for the Advancement of Science session, "Bicentennial Retrospectives and Prospectives: Science Education for Women," February 23, 1976), folder: Elizabeth Baranger, 1976, box 8, Kistiakowsky Papers.

156. Edward M. Kennedy to H. Guyford Stever, June 10, 1975, folder: Kennedy, Edward M., 1980, box 12, Kistiakowsky Papers.

157. Ibid.

158. Rossiter, *Women Scientists in America*, 3:8–11.

159. National Science Foundation, *Increasing the Participation of Women in Scientific Research*; Rossiter, *Women Scientists in America*, 3:9–11. See also Ambrose, Dunkle, Lazarus, Nair, and Harkus, *Journeys of Women in Science and Engineering*, 68–71.

160. National Science Foundation, *Increasing the Participation of Women in Scientific Research*, 4, 16–17; "AAAS Conference Looks at Women in Science," *Chemical and Engineering News* 55 (October 24, 1977): 5–6.

161. "AAAS Conference Looks at Women in Science," 5–6; S. 2550, 95th Cong., 2nd sess., copy in folder: Grand Chapter Meeting, June 8–11, 1978, box 9, SDE Records; Rossiter, *Women Scientists in America*, 3:16.

162. Rossiter, *Women Scientists in America*, 3:16–17.

163. Pfafflin, "Equal Opportunity for Women in Science," 341; Briscoe, "Introduction"; Anne M. Briscoe, "The Kennedy Bill: A Pipe Dream?" *AWIS Newsletter* 8, no. 3 (May/June 1979): 7–8.

164. Barasko, *Governing NOW*, 70–71.

165. Kevles, "Principles and Politics in Federal R&D Policy, 1945–1990," xxiv.

166. *Women in Science and Technology Equal Opportunity Act, 1979*; *Women in Science and Technology Equal Opportunity Act, 1980*.

167. Anne M. Briscoe, testimony, in *Women in Science and Technology Equal Opportunity Act, 1979*.

168. Margaret C. Dunkle, testimony, in *Women in Science and Technology Equal Opportunity Act, 1980*.

169. *Women in Science and Technology Equal Opportunity Act, 1980*; Rossiter, *Women Scientists in America*, 3:18–19.

170. Sheila Pfafflin, "President's Remarks," *AWIS Newsletter* 9, no. 2 (March/April 1980): 3; Sheila M. Pfafflin to voting members of the AWIS Executive Board, March 7, 1980, folder: 1980 AWIS, box 6, Kistiakowsky Papers.

171. Anne M. Briscoe, testimony, in *Women in Science and Technology Equal Opportunity Act, 1979*; Russo and Cassidy, "Women in Science and Technology," 259. The name of the act underwent several revisions and was finally enacted as the National Science Foundation Authorization and Science and Technology Equal Opportunities Act. See Library of Congress, Bill Summary and Status, 96th Cong. (1979–80), S. 568. http://thomas.loc.gov/cgi-bin/bdquery/z?d096:SN00568:@@@T.

172. Sheila M. Pfafflin, "The Women in Science Bill," *AWIS Newsletter* 9, no. 5 (September/October 1980): 3; Russo and Cassidy, "Women in Science and Technology," 258–59.

Epilogue

1. Geri Denterlein, "Reception Honors Senator Kennedy," *AWIS Newsletter* 11, no. 2 (April/May 1982): 10; Deboran S. Kals, "Kennedy Attacks Budget Cuts in Women's Science Programs," *Harvard Crimson*, February 13, 1982, http://www.thecrimson.com/article/1982/2/13/kennedy-attacks-budget-cuts-in-womens. The New England chapter of AWIS had recently absorbed WISE.

2. Edward Kennedy quoted in Kals, "Kennedy Attacks Budget Cuts in Women's Science Programs."

3. Stephanie Bird quoted in Denterlein, "Reception Honors Senator Kennedy," 10.

4. Kevles, "Principles and Politics in Federal R&D Policy, 1945–1990," xxiv–xxv.

5. Freeman, "Labor Market Imbalances," 171. Freeman explains that the shortage announced by the National Science Foundation in the early 1980s was based on erroneous use of data and elicited a number of counterclaims.

6. David Wessel and Ronald Rosenberg, "Engineer Shortage Has Employers Beating the Drums," *Boston Globe*, January 3, 1982, 1.

7. Ibid.

8. Blanche M. Ralston quoted in verbatim transcript, meeting of the Women's Advisory Committee of the War Manpower Commission, May 13, 1943, Washington, D.C., Records of the Women's Advisory Committee, minutes (verbatim), January 13, 1943–March 21, 1945, box 2, entry 21, WMC Records.

9. Vetter, "Changing Patterns of Recruitment and Employment," 60–61.

10. Rossiter, *Women Scientists in America*, 3:45–46.

11. Peggy Schmidt, "For the Women, Still a Long Way to Go," *New York Times*, March 24, 1985, HT14.

12. Vetter, "Changing Patterns of Recruitment and Employment," 62–63.

13. Some major works include Bleier, *Science and Gender*; Harding, *The Science Question in Feminism*; and Keller, *Reflections on Science and Gender*.

14. Carol C. Halpern, "I Dream of a Feminist Science," *AWIS Newsletter* 11, no. 1 (February/March 1982): 10–12; Nancy M. Tooney, "Editor's Note," *AWIS Newsletter* 11, no. 1 (February/March 1982): 10.

15. Halpern, "I Dream of a Feminist Science," 10–12.

16. Ibid., 12.

17. Nancy M. Tooney, "Letters," *AWIS Newsletter* 11, no. 3 (June/July 1982): 6; Ruth Berman, letter to the editor, *AWIS Newsletter* 11, no. 3 (June/July 1982): 7.

18. Berman, letter to the editor, 7.

19. Alpha Chapter program announcement, March 13, 1987, folder 1-33, box 5, SDE–Alpha Records.

20. See, for example, Goodman, *Gender and Science*.

21. Rosser, *Female-Friendly Science*. See also Halpern and Samuelson, "Our Progress and Struggles as Feminists Teaching Biology."

22. "Become a Big Sister in Science," *Sigma Delta Epsilon Graduate Women in Science Bulletin* 49, no. 2 (Summer 1985): 6, 13.

23. Hayes, *Five Decades of the Society of Women Engineers*, unpaginated.

24. Rossiter, *Women Scientists in America*, 3:108–9; Fort, *A Hand Up*.

25. Rosser and Lane, "A History of Funding for Women's Programs at the National Science Foundation," 328–29; Rossiter, *Women Scientists in America*, 3:215.

26. Rossiter, *Women Scientists in America*, 3:74; John Travis, "Making Room for Women in the Culture of Science," *Science* 260 (April 16, 1993): 412–15.

27. Kathleen Teltsch, "Rutgers Reserves a Dorm for Women in Science: Schools Nationwide Lack Female Scientists," *New York Times*, October 11, 1989, B6; Travis, "Making Room for Women in the Culture of Science," 415.

28. Fort, *A Hand Up*, x; Robert D. McFadden, "Bernadine P. Healy, a Pioneer at National Institutes of Health, Dies at 67," *New York Times*, August 8, 2011, http://www.nytimes.com/2011/08/09/us/09healy.html.

29. Teltsch, "Rutgers Reserves a Dorm for Women in Science," B6.

30. Betty M. Vetter, "Forget Affirmative Action. Think National Survival," *The Scientist* (October 19, 1987): 11, clipping, folder 4, box 7, Vetter Papers.

31. Congressional Budget Office, *Federal Support for Research and Development*, xviii.

32. Freeman, "Labor Market Imbalances," 171–73. See also Richard C. Atkinson, "Supply and Demand for Scientists and Engineers: A National Crisis in the Making," *Science* 248, no. 4954 (April 27, 1990): 425.

33. National Research Council, *Science and Security in a Post 9/11 World*, 52.

34. Congressional Budget Office, *Federal Support for Research and Development*, ix.

35. Neil Swidey, "The Provocateur; Two Words—'Intrinsic Aptitude'—Sparked a National Debate about Women and Science and Nearly Toppled the Presidency of Larry Summers," *Boston Globe*, December 18, 2005, BGM27; Rosser, *Breaking into the Lab*, 1; Lawrence H. Summers, "Remarks at NBER Conference on Diversifying the Science and Engineering Workforce," Cambridge, Massachusetts, January 14, 2005, http://www.president.harvard.edu/speeches/summers_2005/nber.php.

36. Summers, "Remarks at NBER Conference," http://www.president.harvard.edu/speeches/summers_2005/nber.php.

37. Marcella Bombardieri, "Summers' Remarks on Women Draw Fire," *Boston Globe*, January 17, 2005, A1; Daniel J. Hemel, "Summers' Comments on Women and Science Draw Ire," *Harvard Crimson*, January 14, 2005, http://www.thecrimson.com/article/2005/1/14/summers-comments-on-women-and-science; Rosser, *Breaking into the Lab*, 2; Rossiter, *Women Scientists in America*, 3:282.

38. Denice D. Denton et al. to Senators Ron Wyden and George Allen, May 11, 2005, http://www.mentornet.net/wyden-allen.

39. Ibid.

40. Jo Handelsman, Nancy Cantor, Molly Carnes, Denice Denton, Eve Fine, Barbara Grosz, Virginia Hinshaw, Cora Marrett, Sue Rosser, Donna Shalala, and Jennifer Sheridan, "More Women in Science," *Science* 309, no. 5738 (August 19, 2005): 1190.

41. Barack Obama quoted in White House Office of the Press Secretary, "Remarks by the President on Securing Our Nation's Cyber Infrastructure," May 29, 2009, http://www.whitehouse.gov/the_press_office/Remarks-by-the-President-on-Securing-Our-Nations-Cyber-Infrastructure.

42. Leon E. Panetta quoted in Elisabeth Bumiller and Thom Shanker, "Panetta Warns of Dire Threat of Cyberattack on U.S.," *New York Times*, October 11, 2012, http://www.nytimes.com/2012/10/12/world/panetta-warns-of-dire-threat-of-cyberattack.html.

43. See, for example, David E. Sanger, "In Cyberspace, New Cold War," *New York Times*, February 24, 2013, http://www.nytimes.com/2013/02/25/world/asia/us-confronts-cyber-cold-war-with-china.html.

44. Mohana Ravindranath, "Obama's Budget Proposal Would Increase Spending on Cybersecurity," *Washington Post*, April 14, 2013, http://articles.washingtonpost.com/2013-04-14/business/38537681_1_budget-proposal-cyber-federal-agencies; CyberWatch K-12, "Annual Cool Careers in CyberSecurity," http://www.edtechpolicy.org/cyberk12/c3workforcecareers.html; Society of Women Engineers, "SWE Scholarships," http://societyofwomenengineers.swe.org/index.php/scholarships#activePanels_3,4.

45. Tara Maller, "Half the Homeland: Mobilizing Women for National Security," *Huffington Post*, December 21, 2012, http://www.huffingtonpost.com/tara-maller/women-national-security_b_2325563.html.

46. Steve Wang, response to Kingsley Brown, "Putting Women in Combat Is a Disastrous Decision," *U.S. News and World Report*, January 25, 2013, http://www.usnews.com/debate-club/should-women-be-allowed-to-fight-in-combat/putting-women-in-combat-is-a-disastrous-decision.

47. See, for example, Stephen M. Walt, "Why Gay Marriage Is Good for U.S. Foreign Policy," *Foreign Policy*, March 29, 2013, http://walt.foreignpolicy.com/posts/2013/03/29/why_gay_marriage_is_good_for_us_foreign_policy.

48. International Trade Center, "The Global Platform for Action on Sourcing from Women Vendors," http://www.intracen.org/projects/women-and-trade/.

Bibliography

Archival Sources

Ames, Iowa
  Special Collections Department, Iowa State University Library
    Fann Harding Papers, MS 320
    Records of Iota Sigma Pi, MS 321
    Jean Nickerson Patterson, Curtiss-Wright Engineering Cadettes Records, RS 21/7/148
    Nina Matheny Roscher Papers, MS 578
    Betty M. Vetter Papers, MS 582
    Women in Chemistry Oral History Project, MS 650
Cambridge, Massachusetts
  Institute Archives and Special Collections, Massachusetts Institute of Technology
    Vera Kistiakowsky Papers, MC 485
    Massachusetts Institute of Technology, Oral History Program, oral history interviews on women in science and engineering, MC86
    Records of the Office of the Associate Dean for Student Affairs, AC 22
  Schlesinger Library, Radcliffe Institute for Advanced Study, Harvard University
    American Council on Education, Commission on the Education of Women Records, 1953–61, B-22
    Mary Ingraham Bunting, "Oral Memoir," interview by Jeannette Bailey Cheek, September–October 1978, transcript
    Mary Ingraham Bunting Records of the President of Radcliffe College, 1960–72, RG II, Series 4, Radcliffe College Archives
    Rita Guttman Papers, A/G985
    Institute of Women's Professional Relations Papers, 1928–41, B-5
    Alice Koller Leopold Papers, 1953–56, A-30
    Esther Peterson Papers, 1884–1998, MC 450
    Esther Raushenbush Papers, 1945–79, 80-M243
    Elizabeth Reynard Papers, 1934–62, A-128
    Catherine Filene Shouse Papers, 1878–1998, MC448
    Records of the Society of Women Engineers—Boston Section, 2001-M17 and 2001-M58
    United States, President's Commission on the Status of Women Records, 1961–63, B-26
College Park, Maryland
  National Archives and Records Administration, Archives II

Record Group 12: Records of the Office of Education
Record Group 86: Records of the Women's Bureau
Record Group 211: Records of the War Manpower Commission
Record Group 307: Records of the National Science Foundation

Detroit, Michigan
Walter P. Reuther Library, Wayne State University
Profiles of SWE Pioneers
Society of Women Engineers—Detroit Section
Society of Women Engineers National Records
Society of Women Engineers National Records: Historical Membership Files

Ithaca, New York
Division of Rare and Manuscript Collections, Cornell University Library
Jennie Farley Papers, #25-3-2710
Sigma Delta Epsilon, Alpha Chapter Records, #37-4-835
Sigma Delta Epsilon Records, #3605

New Brunswick, New Jersey
Special Collections and University Archives, Rutgers University
Records of the Dean of Douglass College (Group I), 1887–1973 (RG 19/A0/01)

New York, New York
Barnard College Archives, Barnard Library, Barnard College
Dean's Office and Departmental Correspondence, 1904–60
Personal Papers of Virginia Crocheron Gildersleeve, ca. 1910–63
Rare Book and Manuscript Library, Columbia University
Columbia University in World War II Collection, University Archives
Virginia Crocheron Gildersleeve Papers, 1898–1962

Sleepy Hollow, New York
Rockefeller Archive Center
Ford Foundation Archive

Washington, D.C.
American Association of University Women Archives
American Association of University Women Archives, 1881–1976, microfilm edition
National Federation of Business and Professional Women's Clubs Archives
Records of the National Federation of Business and Professional Women's Clubs

West Lafayette, Indiana
Karnes Archives and Special Collections, Purdue University Libraries
Frank and Lillian Gilbreth Papers

Newspapers, Serials, Periodicals, and Reference Works

AWIS Magazine
AWIS Newsletter
Barnard Bulletin
Boston Globe
Bulletin of Atomic Scientists
Chemical and Engineering News
Christian Science Monitor
Current Biography Yearbook
Douglass Alumnae Bulletin
Ebony
Educational Record
Foreign Policy
Harvard Crimson
Higher Education and National
  Defense
Huffington Post
Independent Woman
The Iotan
Journal of Applied Physics
Journal of Higher Education
Journal of the American Association
  of University Women
Journal of the Society of Women
  Engineers
Los Angeles Times
Mechanical Engineering
Memorial Tributes

National Cyclopaedia of American
  Biography
Newsday
New York Times
New York Times Magazine
Notices of the American Mathematical
  Society
OED Online
Physics Today
Pittsburgh Post-Gazette
Science
Science Education
Sigma Delta Epsilon Graduate Women in
  Science Bulletin
Sigma Delta Epsilon News
Smith College Associated News
Sunday Denver Post
Sun Sentinel
SWE Newsletter
Time
Tuscaloosa News
U.S. News and World Report
U.S. Woman Engineer
Wall Street Journal
Washington Post
Woman Engineer
Woman's Journal
Women's Work and Education

Other Published Primary Sources

American Council on Education, ed. *Higher Education and the War: The Report of a National Conference of College and University Presidents, Held in Baltimore, Md., January 3–4, 1942*. Washington, D.C.: American Council on Education, 1942.

American Political Science Association. "Other Activities." *American Political Science Review* 53, no. 4 (December 1959): 1221–25.

Armsby, Henry H. *Engineering, Science, and Management War Training Final Report*. Prepared for the Federal Security Agency, Bulletin 1946, no. 9. Washington, D.C.: Government Printing Office, 1946.

Baumgartner, Evelyn, and Nancy Petersen, eds. *Quair*. New Brunswick, NJ: Rutgers University, 1944.

Baxter, James Phinney, III. *Scientists against Time*. Boston: Little, Brown, 1946.

Blaeuer, Maybelle. "The History of the National Roster of Scientific and Specialized Personnel." Revised draft. July 9, 1951 (limited circulation). National Science Foundation Library, Arlington, Virginia.

Bleier, Ruth. *Science and Gender: A Critique of Biology and Its Theories on Women.* Elmsford, NY: Pergamon, 1984.

Briscoe, Anne M., and Sheila M. Pfafflin. "Introduction." In *Expanding the Role of Women in the Sciences*, edited by Anne M. Briscoe and Sheila M. Pfafflin, 1–5. New York: New York Academy of Sciences, 1979.

———. "Scientific Sexism: The World of Chemistry." In *Women in Scientific and Engineering Professions*, edited by Violet B. Haas and Carolyn C. Perrucci, 147–59. Ann Arbor: University of Michigan, 1984.

Briscoe, Anne M., and Sheila M. Pfafflin, eds. *Expanding the Role of Women in the Sciences.* New York: New York Academy of Sciences, 1979.

Brown, Francis J., ed. *Organizing Higher Education for National Defense.* Washington, D.C.: American Council on Education, 1941.

Brown, Patricia L., ed. *Women in Engineering.* New York: Society of Women Engineers, 1955.

Bunting, Mary I. "The Commitment Required of a Woman Entering a Scientific Profession." In *Women and the Scientific Professions: The MIT Symposium on American Women in Science and Engineering*, edited by Jacquelyn A. Mattfeld and Carol G. Van Aken, 20–48. Cambridge, MA: MIT Press, 1965.

Bush, Vannevar. *Endless Horizons.* Washington, D.C.: Public Affairs Press, 1946.

———. *Pieces of the Action.* New York: William Morrow, 1970.

———. "Science and National Defense." *Journal of Applied Physics* 12, no. 12 (December 1941): 823–26.

———. *Science, the Endless Frontier: A Report to the President on a Program for Postwar Scientific Research.* Washington, D.C.: Government Printing Office, 1945.

Cole, Charles C., Jr. *Encouraging Scientific Talent: A Study of America's Able Students Who Are Lost to College and of Ways of Attracting Them to College and Science Careers.* New York: College Entrance Examination Board, 1956.

Conant, James B. *My Several Lives: Memoirs of a Social Inventor.* New York: Harper and Row, 1970.

Congressional Budget Office. *Federal Support for Research and Development.* Washington, D.C.: Congress of the United States, June 2007.

Cortelyou, Ethaline. "The Status of the American Woman Scientists." Address, Luncheon for All Women in Science, sponsored by Sigma Delta Epsilon at the American Association for the Advancement of Science meeting, Washington, D.C., December 30, 1958 (limited circulation). Schlesinger Library, Radcliffe Institute for Advanced Study, Harvard University.

CyberWatch K-12. "Annual Cool Careers in CyberSecurity." http://www.edtechpolicy.org/cyberk12/c3workforcecareers.html (accessed May 14, 2013).

Denton, Denice D., et al. to Senators Ron Wyden and George Allen, May 11, 2005. http://www.mentornet.net/wyden-allen (accessed September 15, 2010).

Eisenhower, Dwight D. "Farewell Address." In *The Military-Industrial Complex*, edited by Carroll W. Pursell Jr., 4–208. New York: Harper and Row, 1972.

Engineers' Council for Professional Development. *Engineering: A Creative Profession*. New York: Engineers' Council for Professional Development, 1953.

———. *Engineering as a Career: A Message to Young Men, Teachers, and Parents*. New York: Engineers' Council for Professional Development, 1942.

Filene, Catherine. *Careers for Women*. Boston: Houghton Mifflin, 1920.

Fitzroy, Nancy D., and Sandford S. Cole, eds. *Career Guidance for Women Entering Engineering*. Proceedings of an Engineering Foundation Conference. Henniker, NH, New England College, August 19–24, 1973.

Flemming, Arthur S. "Some Personnel Needs of the Government War Agencies." In *Higher Education and the War: The Report of a National Conference of College and University Presidents, Held in Baltimore, Md., January 3–4, 1942*, edited by the American Council on Education, 96–107. Washington, D.C.: American Council on Education, 1942.

Fort, Deborah C., ed. *A Hand Up: Women Mentoring Women in Science*. Washington, D.C.: AWIS, 1993.

Freeman, C., C. H. G. Oldham, C. M. Cooper, T. C. Sinclair, and B. G. Achilladelis. "The Goals of R&D in the 1970s." *Science Studies* 1, no. 3/4 (October 1971): 357–406.

Friedan, Betty. *The Feminine Mystique*. New York: W. W. Norton, 1963; reprint, with new preface and introduction, New York: Laurel, 1983.

———. *It Changed My Life: Writings on the Women's Movement*. New York: Random House, 1976.

Fulbright, William J. "The War and Its Effects: The Military-Industrial-Academic Complex." In *Super-State: Readings in the Military-Industrial Complex*, edited by Herbert I. Schiller and Joseph D. Phillips, 173–78. Urbana: University of Illinois Press, 1970.

Gilbreth, Frank Bunker, Jr., and Ernestine Gilbreth Carey. *Cheaper by the Dozen*. New York: Thomas Crowell, 1948.

Gildersleeve, Virginia Crocheron. *Many a Good Crusade*. New York: Macmillan, 1954.

Goodman, Julie, ed. *Gender and Science: A Panel Discussion Sponsored by the New England Chapter of the Association for Women in Science, February 19, 1987*. Washington, D.C.: Association for Women in Science, 1987.

Groves, Leslie R. *Now It Can Be Told: The Story of the Manhattan Project*. New York: Harper, 1962.

Haas, Violet B., and Carolyn C. Perrucci, ed. *Women in Scientific and Engineering Professions*. Ann Arbor: University of Michigan, 1984.

Halpern, Carol C., and Marlene Samuelson. "Our Progress and Struggles as Feminists Teaching Biology." *Feminist Teacher* 1, no. 4 (Summer 1985): 10–14, 34.

Harding, Sandra. *The Science Question in Feminism*. Ithaca, NY: Cornell University Press, 1986.

Harper, Ida Husted, ed. *History of Woman Suffrage*, vol. 5, *1900–1920*. [Washington, D.C.?]: National American Woman Suffrage Association, 1922.

Hicks, Beatrice. "Our Untapped Source of Engineering Talent." In *Women in Engineering*, edited by Patricia L. Brown, 2–6. New York: Society of Women Engineers, 1955.

Hottel, Althea. *How Fare American Women?* Washington, D.C.: American Council on Education, 1955.

Hubbard, Ruth. *The Politics of Women's Biology*. New Brunswick, NJ: Rutgers University Press, 1990.

Institute of Women's Professional Relations, ed. *War and Post-War Demands for Trained Personnel: Proceedings of the Conference Held at the Mayflower Hotel, Washington, D.C., April 9 and 10, 1943*. New London: Institute of Women's Professional Relations, 1943.

———. *War and Post-War Employment and Its Demands for Educational Adjustments: Proceedings of the Conference Held at the Mayflower Hotel, Washington, D.C., May 4 and 5, 1944*. New London: Institute of Women's Professional Relations, 1945.

———. *War Demands for Trained Personnel: Proceedings of the Conference Held at the Mayflower Hotel, Washington, D.C., March 20 and 21, 1942*. New London: Institute of Women's Professional Relations, 1942.

International Trade Center. "The Global Platform for Action on Sourcing from Women Vendors." http://www.intracen.org/projects/women-and-trade/ (accessed May 14, 2013).

Karzon, Allaire U. "Appendix A: A Tax Revision Proposal to Encourage Women into Careers." In *Encouraging Scientific Talent: A Study of America's Able Students Who Are Lost to College and of Ways of Attracting Them to College and Science Careers*, edited by Charles C. Cole Jr., 198–208. New York: College Entrance Exam Board, 1956.

Keller, Evelyn Fox. *Reflections on Science and Gender*. New Haven: Yale University Press, 1985.

Kennedy, John F. "Executive Order 10980 Establishing the President's Commission on the Status of Women," December 14, 1961. In *American Women: The Report of the President's Commission on the Status of Women and Other Publications of the Commission*, edited by Margaret Mead and Frances Kaplan, 207–9. New York: Charles Scribner's Sons, 1965.

Law, Margaret E., ed. *Goals for Women in Science*. Boston: Women in Science and Engineering, 1972 (limited circulation). Schlesinger Library, Radcliffe Institute for Advanced Study, Harvard University.

Library of Congress. Bill Summary and Status, 96th Cong. (1979–80), S. 568. http://thomas.loc.gov/cgi-bin/bdquery/z?d096:SN00568:@@@T (accessed October 15, 2013).

Mattfeld, Jacquelyn A., and Carol G. Van Aken. *Women and the Scientific Professions: The MIT Symposium on American Women in Science and Engineering*. Cambridge, MA: MIT Press, 1965.

McAfee, Naomi J. "The Society of Women Engineers—Past and Present." In *Career Guidance for Women Entering Engineering*, edited by Nancy D. Fitzroy and Sanford S. Cole, 1–7. Proceedings of an Engineering Foundation Conference,

Henniker, New Hampshire, New England College, August 19–24, 1973 (limited circulation). Schlesinger Library, Radcliffe Institute for Advanced Study, Harvard University.

McDowell, Lois. "Educating Women for Engineering." In *Women in Engineering*, edited by Patricia L. Brown, 7–10. New York: Society of Women Engineers, 1955.

Mead, Margaret, and Frances Kaplan, ed. *American Women: The Report of the President's Commission on the Status of Women and Other Publications of the Commission*. New York: Charles Scribner's Sons, 1965.

Moxon, Rosamond Sawyer, and Mabel Clark Peabody. *Twenty-Five Years: Two Anniversary Sketches of New Jersey College for Women*. New Brunswick, NJ: Rutgers University Press, 1943.

National Committee on Education and Defense and United States Office of Education. *Higher Education and the War: The Report of a National Conference of College and University Presidents, Held in Baltimore, Md., January 3–4, 1942*. Washington, D.C.: American Council on Education, 1942.

National Manpower Council. *A Report on the National Manpower Council*. New York: Columbia University Graduate School of Business, 1954.

———. *Womanpower*. New York: Columbia University Press, 1957.

National Organization for Women. "Statement of Purpose, October 29, 1966." In *Feminism in Our Time: The Essential Writings, World War II to the Present*, edited by Miriam Schneir, 95–102. New York: Vintage Books, 1994.

National Research Council. *Science and Security in a Post 9/11 World: A Report Based on Regional Discussions Between the Science and Security Communities*. Committee on a New Government-University Partnership for Science and Security. Committee on Science, Technology, and Law. Washington, D.C.: National Academies Press, 2007.

National Science Foundation. *Increasing the Participation of Women in Scientific Research. Summary of a Conference Proceedings, October 1977, and Research Study Project Report, March 1978*. Washington, D.C.: National Science Foundation, 1978.

Office of the Federal Register. *The United States Government Manual 2011*. Washington, D.C.: Government Printing Office, 2011.

Oldman, Ruth. "Women in the Professional Caucuses." *American Behavioral Scientist* 15 (November 1971): 281–302.

Peden, Irene Carswell. "Ceiling Unlimited." In *Career Guidance for Women Entering Engineering*, edited by Nancy D. Fitzroy and Sanford S. Cole, 79–86. Proceedings of an Engineering Foundation Conference, Henniker, New Hampshire, New England College, August 19–24, 1973 (limited circulation). Schlesinger Library, Radcliffe Institute for Advanced Study, Harvard University.

Pfafflin, Sheila M. "Equal Opportunity for Women in Science." In *Expanding the Role of Women in the Sciences*, edited by Anne M. Briscoe and Sheila M. Pfafflin, 341–44. New York: New York Academy of Sciences, 1979.

Public Law 507, 81st Cong., May 10, 1950. http://www.nsf.gov/about/history/legislation.pdf (accessed January 16, 2012).

Public Law 85-864, 85th Cong., 2nd sess., September 2, 1958. http://www.gpo.
gov/fdsys/pkg/STATUTE-72/pdf/STATUTE-72-Pg1580.pdf (accessed October
15, 2013).

Rosser, Sue V. *Breaking into the Lab: Engineering Progress for Women in Science.*
New York: New York University Press, 2012.

———. *Female-Friendly Science: Applying Women's Studies Methods and Theories to
Attract Students.* New York: Pergamon Press, 1990.

Rossi, Alice S. "Barriers to the Career Choice of Engineering, Medicine, or Science
among American Women." In *Women and the Scientific Professions: The MIT
Symposium on American Women in Science and Engineering,* edited by Jacquelyn
A. Mattfeld and Carol G. Van Aken, 51–127. Cambridge, MA: MIT Press, 1965.

———. "The Biosocial Side of Parenthood." *Human Nature* 1 (June 1978): 72–79.

———. "Equality between the Sexes: An Immodest Proposal." *Daedalus* 83 (1964):
607–52.

Russo, Nancy Felipe, and Marie M. Cassidy. "Women in Science and Technology."
In *Women in Washington: Advocates for Public Policy,* edited by Irene Tinker,
250–62. Beverly Hills: Sage Publications, 1983.

Rutherford, James F. "The Role of the National Science Foundation." In *Expanding
the Role of Women in the Sciences,* edited by Anne M. Briscoe and Sheila M.
Pfafflin, 276–82. New York: New York Academy of Sciences, 1979.

Science Service. *Youth Looks at Science and War.* Washington, D.C.: Science
Service; New York: Penguin Books, 1942.

Society of Women Engineers. "SWE Scholarships." http://
societyofwomenengineers.swe.org/index.php/scholarships#activePanels_3,4
(accessed May 14, 2013).

Splaver, Sarah. *Nontraditional Careers for Women.* New York: Julian Messner, 1973.

Steele, Evelyn. *Careers for Girls in Science and Engineering.* New York: E. P. Dutton,
1944.

Steelman, John R. *Science and Public Policy,* vol. 1, *A Program for the Nation.*
Washington, D.C.: Government Research Office, 1947.

———. *Science and Public Policy,* vol. 2, *The Federal Research Program.*
Washington, D.C.: Government Research Office, 1947.

———. *Science and Public Policy,* vol. 5, *The Nation's Medical Research.*
Washington, D.C.: Government Research Office, 1947.

Stewart, Irvin. *Organizing Scientific Research for War: The Administrative History of
the Office of Scientific Research and Development.* Boston: Little, Brown, 1948.

Stinson, Katharine. "Some Facts about Engineering as a Career for Women." In
Women in Engineering, edited by Patricia L. Brown, 21–23. New York: Society of
Women Engineers, 1955.

Stratton, Julius. "Welcoming Remarks." In *Women and the Scientific Professions:
The MIT Symposium on American Women in Science and Engineering,* edited by
Jacquelyn A. Mattfeld and Carol G. Van Aken, xi–xiii. Cambridge, MA: MIT
Press, 1965.

Summers, Lawrence H. "Remarks at NBER Conference on Diversifying the Science
and Engineering Workforce," Cambridge, MA, January 14, 2005. http://

www.president.harvard.edu/speeches/summers_2005/nber.php (accessed
September 15, 2010).

United States Census, 1950. http://www.census.gov/prod/www/abs/
decennial/1950.html (accessed March 31, 2012).

Van Aken, Carol G. Foreword to *Women and the Scientific Professions: The MIT
Symposium on American Women in Science and Engineering*, edited by Jacquelyn
A. Mattfeld and Carol G. Van Aken, v–viii. Cambridge, MA: MIT Press, 1965.

Vetter, Betty M. "Changing Patterns of Recruitment and Employment." In *Women
in Scientific and Engineering Professions*, edited by Violet B. Haas and Carolyn C.
Perrucci, 59–74. Ann Arbor: University of Michigan Press, 1984.

Weisstein, Naomi. "Adventures of a Woman in Science." *Federation Proceedings* 35,
no. 11 (September 1976): 2226–31.

White House Office of the Press Secretary. "Remarks by the President on Securing
Our Nation's Cyber Infrastructure," May 29, 2009. http://www.whitehouse.
gov/the_press_office/Remarks-by-the-President-on-Securing-Our-Nations-
Cyber-Infrastructure (accessed December 16, 2012).

Wolfle, Dael. *America's Resources of Specialized Talent: A Current Appraisal and a
Look Ahead*. New York: Harper and Brothers, 1954.

*Women in Professional Engineering: A Conference Held under the Auspices of the
Executive Office of the President of the United States and Sponsored by the
University of Pittsburgh and the Society of Women Engineers, April 23 and 24,
1962, at the University of Pittsburgh*. [New York]: SWE, 1962.

*Women in Science and Technology Equal Opportunity Act, 1979: Hearing before the
Subcommittee on Health and Scientific Research of the Committee on Labor and
Human Resources, United States Senate, 96th Congress, First Session on S. 568 . . .
August 1, 1979*. Washington, D.C.: Government Printing Office, 1979.

*Women in Science and Technology Equal Opportunity Act, 1980: Hearing before the
Subcommittee on Health and Scientific Research of the Committee on Labor and
Human Resources, United States Senate, 96th Congress, Second Session on S. 568 . . .
March 3, 1980*. Washington, D.C.: Government Printing Office, 1980.

Women's Bureau of the United States Department of Labor. *Employment
Opportunities for Women in Professional Engineering*, Bulletin 254. Washington,
D.C.: Government Printing Office, 1954.

———. *The Outlook for Women in Science*, Bulletin 223. Washington, D.C.:
Government Printing Office, 1948–49.

Zook, George, F. Foreword to *Organizing Higher Education for National Defense*,
edited by Francis J. Brown, iii–v. Washington, D.C.: American Council on
Education, 1941.

Secondary Sources

Akers, Regina T. "Horton, Mildred McAfee." In *Notable American Women: A
Biographical Dictionary Completing the Twentieth Century*, edited by Susan
Ware and Stacy Braukman, 311–13. Cambridge, MA: Belknap Press of Harvard
University Press, 2004.

Allison, David K. "U.S. Navy Research and Development since World War II."
In *Military Enterprise and Technological Change: Perspectives on the American Experience*, edited by Merritt Roe Smith, 289–328. Cambridge, MA: MIT Press, 1985.

Alonso, Harriet Hyman. "Mayhem and Moderation: Women Peace Activists during the McCarthy Era." In *Not June Cleaver: Women and Gender in Postwar America, 1945–1960*, edited by Joanne Meyerowitz, 128–50. Philadelphia: Temple University Press, 1994.

Ambrose, Susan A., Kristin L. Dunkle, Barbara B. Lazarus, Indira Nair, and Deborah A. Harkus. *Journeys of Women in Science and Engineering: No Universal Constraints*. Philadelphia: Temple University Press, 1997.

Anderson, Karen. *Wartime Women: Sex Roles, Family Relations, and the Status of Women during World War II*. Westport, CT: Greenwood, 1981.

Barasko, Maryann. *Governing NOW: Grassroots Activism in the National Organization for Women*. Ithaca, NY: Cornell University Press, 2004.

Bergen, Summer Chick. "Women in Engineering, 1940–1970: Struggle against the Gender System." Master's thesis, University of Houston-Clear Lake, 1998.

Bérubé, Allan. *Coming Out Under Fire: The History of Gay Men and Women in World War II*. New York: Free Press, 1990.

Bix, Amy Sue. "Feminism Where Men Predominate: The History of Women's Science and Engineering Education at MIT." *Women's Studies Quarterly* 28 (2000): 24–45.

———. "From 'Engineeresses' to 'Girl Engineers' to 'Good Engineers': A History of Women's U.S. Engineering Education." *NWSA Journal* 16, no. 1 (Spring 2004): 27–49.

———. "Hicks, Beatrice Alice." In *Notable American Women: A Biographical Dictionary Completing the Twentieth Century*, edited by Susan Ware and Stacy Braukman, 295–97. Cambridge, MA: Belknap Press of Harvard University Press, 2004.

———. "Supporting Females in a Male Field: Philanthropy for Women's Engineering Education." In *Women and Philanthropy in Education*, edited by Andrea Walton, 320–45. Bloomington: Indiana University Press, 2005.

Blanpied, William A. *Science and Public Policy: The Steelman Report and the Politics of Post-World War II Science Policy*. http://www.aaas.org/spp/yearbook/chap29.htm (accessed January 16, 2012).

Borstelmann, Thomas. *The Cold War and the Color Line: American Race Relations in the Global Arena*. Cambridge, MA: Harvard University Press, 2001.

Briscoe, Anne M. "Phenomenon of the Seventies: The Women's Caucuses." *Signs* 4, no. 1 (Autumn 1978): 152–58.

Campbell, D'Ann. *Women at War with America: Private Lives in a Patriotic Era*. Cambridge, MA: Harvard University Press, 1984.

Cardozier, V. R. *Colleges and Universities in World War II*. Westport, CT: Praeger, 1993.

Clowse, Barbara Barksdale. *Brainpower for the Cold War*. Westport, CT: Greenwood, 1981.

Cobble, Dorothy Sue. *The Other Women's Movement: Workplace Justice and Social Rights in Modern America*. Princeton: Princeton University Press, 2004.

———. "Recapturing Working-Class Feminism: Union Women in the Postwar Era." In *Not June Cleaver: Women and Gender in Postwar America, 1945–1960*, edited by Joanne Meyerowitz, 57–83. Philadelphia: Temple University Press, 1994.

Cochrane, Rexmond C. *The National Academy of Sciences: The First Hundred Years, 1863–1963*. Washington, D.C.: National Academy of Sciences, 1978.

Coontz, Stephanie. *A Strange Stirring:* The Feminine Mystique *and American Women at the Dawn of the 1960s*. New York: Basic Books, 2011.

Cowan, Ruth Schwartz. "Lillian Moller Gilbreth." In *Notable American Women: The Modern Period*, edited by Barbara Sicherman and Carol Hurd Green, 271–73. Cambridge, MA: Belknap Press of Harvard University Press, 1980.

Craven, Wesley Frank, and James Lea Cate. *The Army Air Forces in World War II*, vol. 6, *Men and Planes*. Chicago: University of Chicago Press, 1955; reprint, with new foreword, Washington, D.C.: Office of Air Force History, 1984.

D'Emilio, John. *Sexual Politics, Sexual Communities: The Making of a Homosexual Minority in the United States, 1940–1970*. Chicago: University of Chicago Press, 1983.

Des Jardins, Julie. *Lillian Gilbreth: Redefining Domesticity*. Boulder, CO: Westview, 2013.

Deslippe, Dennis A. *"Rights Not Roses": Unions and the Rise of Working-Class Feminism, 1945–1980*. Urbana: University of Illinois Press, 2000.

Dowling, John E. "George Wald, 1906–1997." In National Academy of Sciences, *Biographical Memoirs*, 78:299–317. Washington, D.C.: National Academy Press, 2000.

Dudziak, Mary L. *Cold War Civil Rights: Race and the Image of American Democracy*. Princeton: Princeton University Press, 2000.

Dupree, A. Hunter. "The Great Instauration of 1940: The Organization of Scientific Research for War." In *The Twentieth-Century Sciences: Studies in the Biography of Ideas*, edited by Gerald Holton, 443–67. New York: W. W. Norton, 1972.

———. *Science in the Federal Government: A History of Policies and Activities to 1940*. Cambridge, MA: Belknap Press of Harvard University Press, 1957.

Echols, Alice. *Daring to Be Bad: Radical Feminism in America, 1967–1975*. Minneapolis: University of Minnesota Press, 1989.

Edwards, Glynn. "Shouse, Catherine Filene." In *Notable American Women: A Biographical Dictionary Completing the Twentieth Century*, edited by Susan Ware and Stacy Braukman, 590–91. Cambridge, MA: Belknap Press of Harvard University Press, 2004.

Eisenmann, Linda. *Higher Education for Women in Postwar America, 1945–1965*. Baltimore: Johns Hopkins University Press, 2006.

England, J. Merton. *A Patron for Pure Science: The National Science Foundation's Formative Years, 1945–57*. Washington, D.C.: National Science Foundation, 1982.

Estrepa, Andrea. "Taking the White Gloves Off: Women Strike for Peace and 'the Movement,' 1967–74." In *Feminist Coalitions: Historical Perspectives on Second-Wave Feminism in the United States*, edited by Stephanie Gilmore, 84–112. Urbana: University of Illinois Press, 2008.

Evans, Sara. *Personal Politics: The Roots of Women's Liberation in the Civil Rights Movement and the New Left*. New York: Vintage Books, 1979.

Farber, David. *The Age of Great Dreams: America in the 1960s*. New York: Hill and Wang, 1994.

Fasanelli, Florence. "Mary Gray." In *Notable Women in Mathematics: A Biographical Dictionary*, edited by Charlene Morrow and Teri Perl, 71–76. Westport, CT: Greenwood, 1998.

Flemming, Bernice. *Arthur Flemming: Crusader at Large*. Washington, D.C.: Caring Publishing, 1991.

Foerstel, Karen. *Biographical Dictionary of Congressional Women*. Westport, CT: Greenwood, 1999.

Fox, Daniel M. "The Politics of the NIH Extramural Program, 1937–1950." *Journal of the History of Medicine and Allied Sciences* 42 (1987): 447–66.

Freeman, Richard B. "Labor Market Imbalances: Shortages, Surpluses, or What?" In *Global Imbalances and the Evolving World Economy*, edited by Jane Sneddon Little, 159–82. Boston: Federal Reserve Bank of Boston, 2008.

Gabin, Nancy. *Feminism in the Labor Movement: Women and the United Auto Workers, 1935–1975*. Ithaca, NY: Cornell University Press, 1990.

Galison, Peter. "Physics between War and Peace." In *Science, Technology, and the Military*, edited by Everett Mendelsohn, Merritt Roe Smith, and Peter Weingart, 51–65. Dordrecht: Kluwer Academic Publishers, 1988.

Gallo, Marcia M. *Different Daughters: A History of the Daughters of Bilitis and the Rise of the Lesbian Rights Movement*. Emeryville, CA: Seal Press, 2007.

Geiger, Roger L. *Research and Relevant Knowledge: American Research Universities since World War II*. New York: Oxford University Press, 1993.

Green, Rosalie E. "A Historical Study of Arthur S. Flemming: His Impact on Federal Education and Training Programs Relating to Aging during the Period 1958–1978." Ed.D. diss., Virginia Polytechnic Institute and State University, 1985.

Grinager, Patricia. *Uncommon Lives: My Lifelong Friendship with Margaret Mead*. Lanham, MD: Rowman and Littlefield, 1999.

Hall, Jacquelyn Dowd. "The Long Civil Rights Movement and Political Uses of the Past." *Journal of American History* 91, no. 4 (March 2005): 1233–63.

Harrison, Cynthia. *On Account of Sex: The Politics of Women's Issues, 1945–1968*. Berkeley: University of California Press, 1988.

Hart, David M. *Forged Consensus: Science, Technology, and Economic Policy in the United States, 1921–1953*. Princeton: Princeton University Press, 1998.

Hartmann, Susan M. *The Home Front and Beyond*. Boston: Twayne, 1982.

———. *The Other Feminists: Activists in the Liberal Establishment*. New Haven: Yale University Press, 1998.

———. "Women's Employment and the Domestic Ideal in the Early Cold War Years." In *Not June Cleaver: Women and Gender in Postwar America, 1945–1960*, edited by Joanne Meyerowitz, 84–100. Philadelphia: Temple University Press, 1994.

Hayes, Dianne Williams, ed. *Five Decades of the Society of Women Engineers*. N.p., n.d., ca. 2005.

Hewitt, Nancy A., ed. *No Permanent Waves: Recasting Histories of U.S. Feminism.* New Brunswick, NJ: Rutgers University Press, 2010.

Hewlett, Richard G., and Oscar E. Anderson Jr. *A History of the United States Atomic Energy Commission*, vol. 1, *The New World, 1939–1946*. University Park: Pennsylvania State University Press, 1962.

Hewlett, Richard G., and Francis Duncan. *A History of the United States Atomic Energy Commission*, vol. 2, *Atomic Shield, 1947–1952*. University Park: Pennsylvania State University Press, 1969.

Hogan, Michael J. *A Cross of Iron: Harry S. Truman and the Origins of the National Security State, 1945–1954*. Cambridge: Cambridge University Press, 1998.

Honey, Maureen. *Creating Rosie the Riveter: Class, Gender, and Propaganda during World War II*. Amherst: University of Massachusetts Press, 1984.

Horowitz, Daniel. *Betty Friedan and the Making of* The Feminine Mystique: *The American Left, the Cold War, and Modern Feminism*. Amherst: University of Massachusetts Press, 1988.

Howes, Ruth H., and Caroline L. Herzenberg. *Their Day in the Sun*. Philadelphia: Temple University Press, 1999.

Isserman, Maurice, and Michael Kazin. *America Divided: The Civil War of the 1960s*. New York: Oxford University Press, 2000.

Kaiser, David. *American Tragedy: Kennedy, Johnson, and the Origins of the Vietnam War*. Cambridge, MA: Harvard University Press, 2000.

Kata, Lauren. "The Boundaries of Women's Rights: Activism and Aspirations in the Society of Women Engineers, 1946–1980." *Journal of the Society of Women Engineers* 5 (2011): 36–49.

Kessler-Harris, Alice. *Out to Work: A History of Wage-Earning Women in the United States*. New York: Oxford University Press, 1982.

Kevles, Daniel J. "K_1S_2: Korea, Science, and the State." In *Big Science: The Growth of Large-Scale Research*, edited by Peter Galison and Bruce Hevly, 312–33. Stanford: Stanford University Press, 1992.

———. "The National Science Foundation and the Debate over Postwar Research Policy, 1942–1945: A Political Interpretation of *Science—The Endless Frontier*." *Isis* 68, no. 1 (March 1977): 4–26.

———. *The Physicists: The History of a Scientific Community in Modern America*. New York: Knopf, 1977; reprint, with new preface, Cambridge, MA: Harvard University Press, 1995.

———. "Principles and Politics in Federal R&D Policy, 1945–1990: An Appreciation of the Bush Report." Preface to the 40th Anniversary Edition of *Science: The Endless Frontier*, by Vannevar Bush, ix–xxv. Washington, D.C.: National Science Foundation, 1990.

Kindya, Marta Navia. *Four Decades of the Society of Women Engineers*. New York: Society of Women Engineers, 1990.

Kleinman, Daniel Lee. *Politics on the Endless Frontier: Postwar Research Policy in the United States*. Durham: Duke University Press, 1995.

Kohlstedt, Sally Gregory. "Sustaining Gains: Reflections on Women in Science and Technology in 20th-Century United States." *Feminist Formations* 16, no. 1 (Spring 2004): 1–26.

Lancaster, Jane. *Making Time: Lillian Moller Gilbreth—A Life Beyond "Cheaper by the Dozen."* Boston: Northeastern University Press, 2004.

Laughlin, Kathleen A. *Women's Work and Public Policy: A History of the Women's Bureau, U.S. Department of Labor, 1945–1970*. Boston: Northeastern University Press, 2000.

Laughlin, Kathleen A., and Jacqueline L. Castledine, eds. *Breaking the Wave: Women, Their Organizations, and Feminism, 1945–1985*. New York: Routledge, 2011.

Laughlin, Kathleen A., Julie Gallagher, Dorothy Sue Cobble, Eileen Boris, Premilla Nadasen, Stephanie Gilmore, and Leandra Zarnow. "Is It Time to Jump Ship? Historians Rethink the Waves Metaphor." *Feminist Formations* 22, no. 1 (Spring 2010): 76–135.

Leffler, Melvyn P. *A Preponderance of Power: National Security, the Truman Administration, and the Cold War*. Stanford: Stanford University Press, 1992.

Leslie, Stuart W. *The Cold War and American Science: The Military-Industrial-Academic Complex at MIT and Stanford*. New York: Columbia University Press, 1993.

Levine, Susan. *Degrees of Equality: The American Association of University Women and the Challenge of Twentieth-Century Feminism*. Philadelphia: Temple University Press, 1995.

Linden-Ward, Blanche, and Carol Hurd Green. *American Women in the 1960s: Changing the Future*. New York: Twayne, 1993.

Lynn, Susan. *Progressive Women in Conservative Times: Racial Justice, Peace, and Feminism, 1945 to the 1960s*. New Brunswick, NJ: Rutgers University Press, 1992.

Mack, Pamela E. "What Difference Has Feminism Made to Engineering in the Twentieth Century?" In *Feminism in Twentieth-Century Science, Technology, and Medicine*, edited by Angela N. H. Creager, Elizabeth Lunbeck, and Londa Schiebinger, 149–68. Chicago: University of Chicago Press, 2001.

MacLean, Nancy. *The American Women's Movement, 1945–2000: A Brief History with Documents*. Boston: Bedford/St. Martin's, 2009.

May, Elaine Tyler. *Homeward Bound*. New York: Basic Books, 1988.

McEnaney, Laura. *Civil Defense Begins at Home: Militarization Meets Everyday Life in the Fifties*. Princeton: Princeton University Press, 2000.

McIntire, Natalie Marie. "Curtiss-Wright Cadettes: A Case Study of the Effect of the World War II Labor Shortage on Women in Engineering." Master's thesis, University of Minnesota, 1993.

Meyerowitz, Joanne. "Beyond the Feminine Mystique: A Reassessment of Postwar Mass Culture, 1946–1958." In *Not June Cleaver: Women and Gender in Postwar America, 1945–1960*, edited by Joanne Meyerowitz, 229–62. Philadelphia: Temple University Press, 1994.

———. "Sex, Gender, and the Cold War Language of Reform." In *Rethinking Cold War Culture*, edited by Peter J. Kuznick and James Gilbert, 106–23. Washington, D.C.: Smithsonian Institution Press, 2001.

———, ed. *Not June Cleaver: Women and Gender in Postwar America, 1945–1960*. Philadelphia: Temple University Press, 1994.

Milkman, Ruth. *Gender at Work*. Urbana: University of Illinois Press, 1987.

Morgan, Agnes Fay, ed. *A History of Iota Sigma Pi*. Berkeley: Iota Sigma Pi, 1953; reprint, 1963.

Morrow, Charlene, and Teri Perl, eds. *Notable Women in Mathematics: A Biographical Dictionary*. Westport, CT: Greenwood, 1998.

Mosch, Theodore R. *The GI Bill: A Breakthrough in Educational and Social Policy in the United States*. Hicksville, NY: Exposition Press, 1975.

Mullins, James P. *The Defense Matrix: National Preparedness and the Military-Industrial Complex*. San Diego: Avant Books, 1986.

Murray, Margaret A. M. *Women Becoming Mathematicians: Creating a Professional Identity in Post–World War II America*. Cambridge, MA: MIT Press, 2000.

Oakes, Elizabeth H., ed. *Encyclopedia of World Scientists*. New York: Facts on File, 2007.

Oldenziel, Ruth. "Multiple-Entry Visas: Gender and Engineering in the U.S., 1870–1945." In *Crossing Boundaries, Building Bridges: Comparing the History of Women Engineers, 1870s-1990s*, edited by Annie Canel, Ruth Oldenziel, and Karin Zachmann, 11–49. Australia: Harwood Academic Publishers, 2000.

Olson, Keith W. *The GI Bill, the Veterans, and the Colleges*. Lexington: University Press of Kentucky, 1974.

Phares, Tom K. *Seeking—and Finding—Science Talent: A 50-Year History of the Westinghouse Science Talent Search*. Pittsburgh: Westinghouse Electric, 1990.

Pickren, W. E., and W. J. McKeachie. "Dael Wolfle (1906–2002)." *American Psychologist* 58, no. 9 (2003): 758–59.

Puaca, Laura Micheletti. "Cold War Women: Professional Guidance, National Defense, and the Society of Women Engineers, 1950–1960." In *The Educational Work of Women's Organizations*, edited by Anne Meis Knupfer and Christine Woyshner, 57–77. New York: Palgrave Macmillan, 2008.

Pursell, Carroll, ed. *The Military-Industrial Complex*. New York: Harper and Row, 1972.

———. "Science Agencies in World War II: The OSRD and Its Challengers." In *The Sciences in the American Context: New Perspectives*, edited by Nathan Reingold, 359–78. Washington, D.C.: Smithsonian Institution Press, 1979.

Reingold, Nathan. "Vannevar Bush's New Deal for Research: Or the Triumph of the Old Order." *Historical Studies in the Physical and Biological Sciences* 17, no. 2 (1987): 299–344.

Rife, Patricia. *Lise Meitner and the Dawn of the Nuclear Age*. Boston: Birkhauser, 1999.

Robbins, Mary Louise, ed. *A History of Sigma Delta Epsilon, 1921–1971*. N.p.: Graduate Women in Science, 1971.

Roland, Alex. *The Military-Industrial Complex*. Washington, D.C.: American Historical Association, 2001.

———. "Science and War." *Osiris*, 2nd ser., 1 (1985): 247–72.

Rorabaugh, W. J. *Berkeley at War: The 1960s*. New York: Oxford University Press, 1989.

Rosen, Ruth. *The World Split Open: How the Modern Women's Movement Changed America*. New York: Viking Penguin, 2000; reprint, New York: Penguin Books, 2006.

Rosenberg, David Alan. "American Atomic Strategy and the Hydrogen Bomb Decision." *Journal of American History* 66, no. 1 (June 1979): 62–87.

Rosenberg, Rosalind. *Changing the Subject: How the Women of Columbia Shaped the Way We Think about Sex and Politics*. New York: Columbia University Press, 2004.

———. "Virginia Gildersleeve: Opening the Gates." *Barnard Alumnae Magazine* (Summer 2001). http://www.columbia.edu/cu/alumni/Magazine/Summer2001/Gildersleeve.html (accessed February 1, 2004).

Ross, David R. B. *Preparing for Ulysses: Politics and Veterans during World War II*. New York: Columbia University Press, 1969.

Rosser, Sue V., and Eliesh O'Neil Lane. "A History of Funding for Women's Programs at the National Science Foundation: From Individual Power Approaches to the Advance of Institutional Approaches." *Journal of Women and Minorities in Science and Engineering* 8 (2002): 327–46.

Rossiter, Margaret W. "Science and Public Policy since World War II." In *Historical Writing on American Science*, edited by Sally Gregory Kohlstedt and Margaret W. Rossiter, 273–94. Baltimore: Johns Hopkins University Press, 1985.

———. *Women Scientists in America*, vol. 1, *Struggles and Strategies to 1940*. Baltimore: Johns Hopkins University Press, 1982.

———. *Women Scientists in America*, vol. 2, *Before Affirmative Action, 1940–1972*. Baltimore: Johns Hopkins University Press, 1995.

———. *Women Scientists in America*, vol. 3, *Forging a New World Since 1972*. Baltimore: Johns Hopkins University Press, 2012.

Rudolph, John L. *Scientists in the Classroom: The Cold War Reconstruction of American Science Education*. New York: Palgrave, 2002.

Rung, Margaret C. *Servants of the State: Managing Diversity and Democracy in the Federal Workforce, 1933–1953*. Athens: University of Georgia Press, 2002.

Rupp, Leila J. *Mobilizing Women for War: German and American Propaganda, 1939–1945*. Princeton: Princeton University Press, 1978.

Rupp, Leila J., and Verta Taylor. *Survival in the Doldrums: The American Women's Rights Movement, 1945 to the 1960s*. New York: Oxford University Press, 1987.

Sapolsky, Harvey. *Science and the Navy: The History of the Office of Naval Research*. Princeton: Princeton University Press, 1990.

Schiebinger, Londa. *Has Feminism Changed Science?* Cambridge, MA: Harvard University Press, 1999.

———. *The Mind Has No Sex? Women and the Origins of Modern Science*. Cambridge, MA: Harvard University Press, 1989.

Schiller, Herbert I., and Joseph D. Phillips, eds. *Super-State: Readings in the Military-Industrial Complex*. Urbana: University of Illinois Press, 1970.

Schrecker, Ellen. *Many Are the Crimes: McCarthyism in America*. Boston: Little, Brown, 1998.

Schweber, S. S. "The Mutual Embrace of Science and the Military: ONR and the Growth of Physics in the United States after World War II." In *Science, Technology, and the Military*, edited by Everett Mendelsohn, Merritt Roe Smith, and Peter Weingart, 3–45. Dordrecht: Kluwer Academic Publishers, 1988.

Sheffield, Suzanne Le-May. *Women and Science: Social Impact and Interaction*. Santa Barbara, CA: ABC-CLIO, 2004.

Sherry, Michael S. *In the Shadow of War: The United States since the 1930s*. New Haven: Yale University Press, 1995.

Smith, Bruce L. R. *American Science Policy since World War II*. Washington, D.C.: Brookings Institution, 1990.

Solinger, Rickie. "Extreme Danger: Women Abortionists and Their Clients before *Roe v. Wade*." In *Not June Cleaver: Women and Gender in Postwar America, 1945–1960*, edited by Joanne Meyerowitz, 335–57. Philadelphia: Temple University Press, 1994.

Solomon, Barbara Miller. *In the Company of Educated Women: A History of Higher Education in America*. New Haven: Yale University Press, 1985.

Storrs, Landon R. Y. "Attacking the Washington 'Femmocracy': Antifeminism in the Cold War Campaign against 'Communists in Government.'" *Feminist Studies* 33, no. 1 (Spring 2007): 118–52.

———. "Red Scare Politics and the Suppression of Popular Front Feminism: The Loyalty Investigation of Mary Dublin Keyserling." *Journal of American History* 90, no. 2 (September 2003): 491–524.

Strickland, Stephen P. *Politics, Science and Dread Disease: A Short History of United States Medical Research Policy*. Cambridge, MA: Harvard University Press, 1972.

Stuart, Douglas T. *Creating the National Security State: A History of the Law that Transformed America*. Princeton: Princeton University Press, 2008.

Swain, Donald. "The Rise of a Research Empire: NIH, 1930–1950." *Science* 138 (1962): 1233–37.

Swerdlow, Amy. *Women Strike for Peace: Traditional Motherhood and Radical Politics in the 1960s*. Chicago: University of Chicago Press, 1993.

Task Force on Science Policy, Committee on Science and Technology, House of Representatives, 99th Cong., 2nd sess. "A History of Science Policy in the United States, 1940–1985," Science Policy Study Background Report, No. 1. Washington, D.C.: Government Printing Office, 1986.

Terzian, Sevan G. "'Adventures in Science': Casting Scientifically Talented Youth as National Resources on American Radio, 1942–1958." *Paedagogica Historica* 44, no. 3 (June 2008): 309–25.

Tinker, Irene, ed. *Women in Washington: Advocates for Public Policy*. Beverly Hills: Sage Publications, 1983.

Trescott, Martha Moore. "Women in the Intellectual Development of Engineering: A Study in Persistence and Systems Thought." In *Women of Science: Righting the Record*, edited by G. Kass-Simon and Patricia Farnes, 147–87. Bloomington: Indiana University Press, 1990.

Tryon, Ruth Wilson. *Investment in Creative Scholarship: A History of the Fellowship Program of the American Association of University Women, 1890–1956.* Washington, D.C.: American Association of University Women, 1957.

Turner, Edna May. "Education of Women for Engineering in the United States, 1885–1952." Ph.D. diss., New York University, 1954.

Urban, Wayne J. *More than Science and Sputnik: The National Defense Education Act of 1958.* Tuscaloosa: University of Alabama Press, 2010.

Von Eschen, Penny M. *Race against Empire: Black Americans and Anticolonialism, 1937–1957.* Ithaca, NY: Cornell University Press, 1997.

Wahlin, Michelle D. *87-Year History of SDE-GWIS*. N.p.: Bordeaux Printers, 2009.

Walls, Patricia C. "Defending Their Liberties: Women's Organizations during the McCarthy Era." Ph.D. diss., University of Maryland, 1994.

Wandersee, Winifred D. *On the Move: American Women in the 1970s*. Boston: Twayne Publishers, 1988.

Wang, Jessica. *American Scientists in an Age of Anxiety: Scientists, Anticommunism, and the Cold War*. Chapel Hill: University of North Carolina Press, 1999.

Warren, Wini. *Black Women Scientists in the United States*. Bloomington: Indiana University Press, 1999.

Wasniewski, Matthew Andrew, ed. *Women in Congress, 1917–2006*. Washington, D.C.: Government Printing Office, 2006.

Weigand, Kate. *Red Feminism: American Communism and the Making of Women's Liberation*. Baltimore: Johns Hopkins University Press, 2001.

Wells, Tom. *The War Within: America's Battle over Vietnam*. Berkeley: University of California Press, 1994.

Wheaton, Kimberly Dolphin. "Challenging the 'Climate of Unexpectation': Mary Ingraham Bunting and American Women's Higher Education in the 1950s and 1960s." Ph.D. diss., Harvard University, 2001.

Williams, Kathleen Broome. *Improbable Warriors: Women Scientists and the U.S. Navy in World War II*. Annapolis, MD: Naval Institute Press, 2001.

Witzel, Morgen, ed. *The Encyclopedia of the History of American Management*. Bristol, England: Thoemmes Continuum, 2005.

Woods, Jeff. *Black Struggle, Red Scare: Segregation and Anti-Communism in the South, 1948–1968*. Baton Rouge: Louisiana State University Press, 2004.

Yaffe, Elaine. *Mary Ingraham Bunting: Her Two Lives*. Savannah: Frederic C. Beil, 2005.

Yergin, Daniel. *Shattered Peace: The Origins of the Cold War and the National Security State*. Boston: Houghton Mifflin, 1977.

York, Herbert F., and G. Allen Greb. "Military Research and Development: A Postwar History." In *Science, Technology, and National Policy*, edited by Thomas J. Kuehn and Alan L. Porter, 190–215. Ithaca, NY: Cornell University Press, 1981.

Zachary, G. Pascal. *Endless Frontier: Vannevar Bush, Engineer of the American Century*. New York: Free Press, 1997.

Zapoleon, Marguerite W., and Lois Meek Stolz. "Helen Bradford Thompson Woolley." In *Notable American Women: The Modern Period*, edited by Barbara Sicherman and Carol Hurd Green, 657–60. Cambridge, MA: Belknap Press of Harvard University Press, 1980.

Zarnow, Leandra. "The Legal Origin of 'The Personal Is Political': Bella Abzug and Sexual Politics in Cold War America." In *Breaking the Wave: Women, Their Organizations, and Feminism, 1945–1985*, edited by Kathleen A. Laughlin and Jacqueline L. Castledine, 28–46. New York: Routledge, 2011.

Zelizer, Julian E. *Arsenal of Democracy: The Politics of National Security from World War II to the War on Terrorism*. New York: Basic Books, 2010.

Index

Abzug, Bella, 140
Adams, Arthur S., 111, 112
Addams, Jane, 20
Aerojet General Corporation, 99
Affirmative action, 136, 144, 146, 152, 155–56, 157–58, 163, 175
African Americans, 2, 30, 53, 83, 133, 138, 149, 155, 156, 160, 164–65, 192 (n. 84), 198 (n. 41), 206 (n. 173), 211 (n. 86)
Alfred College, 92
Alfred P. Sloan Foundation, 151–52, 174
Alonso, Harriet, 4
American Association for the Advancement of Science, 90–91, 95, 96, 137, 143, 149, 157, 162, 163, 164, 167, 175–76, 188 (n. 31); Girls and Science Program, 174–75; "Participation of Women in Scientific Research" conference, 164–65; post-Sputnik conferences on encouraging women in science, 91–95, 96–98; "Women in Science" symposium, 146–48
American Association of Scientific Workers, 90, 95
American Association of University Women (AAUW), 5, 10, 16, 17, 20, 22, 24–25, 26, 38, 43, 51, 95, 103, 104, 111, 117–18, 160, 188 (nn. 27, 32); "College Women and War Industry" conference, 35; Committee on International Relations, 16; fellowship program, 55–56, 150
American Council on Education, 10, 16, 17, 26, 111, 112, 188 (n. 31); Commission on the Education of Women, 5,

112–14; Office of Statistical Information and Research, 111; Rye Conference, 111–12
American Council on Women in Science, 96–99, 145, 209 (n. 47)
American Geological Institute, 149
American Institute of Chemical Engineers, 27
American Institute of Physics, 136
American Mathematical Society, 154, 155
American Medical Women's Association, 81, 187 (n. 24)
American Physical Society, 47, 151; Committee on the Status of Women in Physics, 150, 151–52, 160
American Psychological Association, 60
American Society for Microbiology, 149, 160; Committee on the Status of Women Microbiologists, 149, 160
American Society of Biological Chemists, 149
American Society of Mechanical Engineers, 79, 139
American University, 154, 155
America's Resources of Specialized Talent, 60–61
Anticommunism, 5, 50–51, 80–81, 133, 135, 198 (n. 29)
Antidiscrimination legislation, 1, 81–82, 125, 130–31, 136–37, 143, 144, 145, 146, 148, 152, 153, 155–56, 157–58, 161, 163, 167, 177. *See also* Equal Rights Amendment; Women in science legislation
Antifeminist backlash, 6, 166, 169, 171

Antiwar protests (Vietnam War), 130,
133–35, 147
Apter, Julia, 150
Arditti, Rita, 144
Armour Research Foundation, 88, 99
Armstrong, Anne, 163
Association for Women in Mathemat-
ics, 154–56, 157, 160
Association for Women in Science
(AWIS), 156–59, 162, 166, 167,
169, 173, 174, 175, 178; *AWIS et al.
v. Richardson*, 157; Educational
Foundation, 158, 166, 167; "Expand-
ing the Role of Women in the Sci-
ences" conference, 166; *A Hand Up*,
174, 175; New England chapter, 169,
225 (n. 1)
Atkinson, Richard C., 175–76
Atomic energy, 4–5, 7, 9, 10, 44, 45,
46, 47, 49, 50, 53, 54, 55, 58, 59, 86,
104–5, 142, 152, 161
Atomic Energy Act, 47
Atomic Energy Commission, 47, 49, 50,
54, 55, 58, 59, 134, 161
Austrheim, Bernice, 144–45

Bailey, Dorothy, 51
Bailey, George, 24
Balancing family and professional life,
3, 6, 7, 86, 89, 94, 96, 103, 105–7,
109–10, 114–16, 120–21, 123–26, 130,
137, 143, 148, 155, 158, 171
Baltimore Conference, 21–22, 24, 60
Baranger, Elizabeth Urey, 152, 153, 160,
163–64, 221 (n. 111)
Barnard College, 9, 14–15, 17, 26, 28,
29, 66
Belknap, Fredericka, 33
Bell Laboratories, 33–34, 67, 91, 122
Bennett College, 17
Bennington College, 108, 109
Berg, Marie, 101, 144
Berman, Edgar, 158–59
Berman, Ruth, 173
Bérubé, Allan, 4

Bethune, Mary McLeod, 20
Bien, Esther, 36
Biophysical Society, 149–50; Caucus of
Women Biophysicists, 149–50; Com-
mittee on Professional Opportunities
for Women, 149–50
Bird, Stephanie, 169, 171
Bix, Amy Sue, 6
Blake, Lillie Devereux, 15
Blizard, Jane, 61–62
Blumstein, Rita, 163
Boyd, Harriet, 95
Brandeis University, 150, 151
Bridgman, Donald, 113
Briscoe, Anne, 156, 167
Brodie, Jeanne, 139
Brown, Janet Welsh, 164–65, 166, 167
Brown, Lynne, 171
Brown, Patricia, 74, 79, 82, 123, 178
Brown University, 19; Higher Educa-
tion Resource Service, 153. *See also*
Pembroke College
Bryn Mawr College, 30, 111, 117
Bucknell University, 30
Bunting, Henry, 108
Bunting, Mary "Polly" Ingraham, 4, 7,
107–16, 119, 123–24, 127, 137–38, 147,
171, 175, 211 (n. 86), 212
(n. 94)
Bunting-Cobb Residence Hall, 175
Bush, Vannevar, 11, 13, 17, 43–44, 45–46,
48, 61, 163, 197 (n. 16)
Butler, Nicholas Murray, 14

California State University, Haywood,
155
Career days, 77, 80, 100, 101–2, 137, 143,
158
*Careers for Girls in Science and
Engineering*, 36
Careers for Women, 22
Carmichael, Leonard, 24–25, 40
Carter, Jimmy, 166, 167, 168
Carter, Rosalynn, 140
Cassidy, Marie, 160

Dunkle, Margaret, 167
DuPont, 34, 40, 75

Earhart, Amelia, 20
Eaves, Elsie, 33, 36, 65–66, 69
Edgecomb, Hilda Counts, 65
Education Amendments Act of 1972 (Title IX), 1, 136–37, 148
Eisenhower, Dwight, 50, 62, 63–64, 73, 74, 87, 134, 150
Eisenmann, Linda, 5, 184 (n. 5)
Ellickson, Katherine, 120
Ellis, Meta (Heller), 99–100, 101–2, 120, 122–23, 145, 214 (n. 135)
Embrey, Lee Anna, 97
Emergency Committee for Employment, 20
Encouraging Scientific Talent, 61–62
Endocrine Society, 149
Energy Research and Development Administration, 161
Engineering, Science, and Management War Training (ESMWT) program, 29–30, 31, 40, 41, 192 (n. 83)
Engineering Society of Detroit, 76, 77
Engineers' Council for Professional Development (ECPD), 71–73
Engineers Week, 77
Equal Employment Opportunity Commission (EEOC), 131
Equal pay, 43, 70, 81–82, 125, 130, 144, 145, 156
Equal Pay Act, 130
Equal Rights Amendment (ERA), 2, 81–82, 118, 125, 132, 137, 139–41, 155, 160–61, 166; defeat of, 169
Equal Suffrage League, 15
Executive Order 11375, 136

Farber, David, 134
Federal Bureau of Investigation, 50
Federation of American Societies for Experimental Biology, 156, 157
Federation of Organizations for Professional Women (FOPW), 159–61, 162,

164, 166, 167, 169, 178; *Washington Women*, 160
Feight, Donald, 122
Feminine fallout, 103–6, 171. *See also* Women's employment patterns: intermittency in
The Feminine Mystique, 3–4, 130, 137, 150–51
Feminism, 2–3, 4–6, 7–8, 10, 130–32, 143, 148, 150–51, 168, 178; explicit embrace of, 5, 129–30, 137, 139–40, 141, 145–46, 148–61 passim; reluctance to be identified with, 2–3, 10, 16, 20, 51, 81–82, 110–11, 112. *See also* Labor feminism; Technocratic feminism
Filene, Lincoln, 22
Financial aid and funding for women scientists, 1, 6, 38–39, 54–56, 69–70, 79, 90, 105–6, 128, 147–48, 154–55, 158, 162–63, 165, 167, 174, 177, 178–79, 180
Finch, James Kip, 27–28
Finch College, 38
First International Women's Space Symposium, 122
Fleeson, Doris, 117
Flemming, Arthur S., 21, 24, 59–60, 61, 62, 70, 74, 75, 91, 96, 97, 100
Ford, Betty, 140
Ford Foundation, 114
Fowler, Evelyn Vernick, 66
Franklin, Eleanor, 156
Free Speech Movement, 133
Friedan, Betty, 3–4, 130, 131, 137, 150–51, 185 (n. 6)
Fulbright, J. William, 134–35

Gabin, Nancy, 4
Gallo, Marcia, 4
Gay and lesbian liberation, 5, 140, 179
Geiger, Roger, 48
General Aniline & Film Corporation, 40
General Electric, 32, 59, 122
General Motors, 75, 99
Geneva School of International Studies, 52

Relations, 22–23, 36, 190 (nn. 48, 51); "War Demands for Trained Personnel" conference, 24–25

Instrument Society of America, 101–2

Internal Revenue Service (IRS), 62, 82, 140

International Union of Electrical, Radio, and Machine Workers, 119

Intersociety councils, 102

Iota Sigma Pi, 35–36, 56

Iowa State University, 31

Johns Hopkins University, 38, 91–92, 108

Johnson, Lady Bird, 140

Johnson, Lyndon, 133, 136, 153

Joint Research and Development Board, 48, 197 (n. 16)

Jones, Barbara, 109

Jones, Lewis Webster, 109

Justin, Margaret, 17

Kahn, Arthur, 96

Kansas State College, 17

Karzon, Allaire, 61–62

Kearney, Margaret, 80

Keller, Evelyn Fox, 173–74

Keller, Helen, 20

Kennedy, Edward, 164, 165–66, 167, 169, 170, 171

Kennedy, John F., 116–18, 119–20, 124, 159

Kenyon, Dorothy, 51

Kerr, Clark, 133

Kessler-Harris, Alice, 73–74

Kevles, Daniel, 58

Khrushchev, Nikita, 89

Kilgore, Harley, 48

King, Earl S., 170–71

King, Martin Luther, Jr., 133

Kipilo, Margaret, 82

Kistiakowsky, George, 150

Kistiakowsky, Vera, 150–52, 153, 165, 166, 169

Kohlstedt, Sally Gregory, 6

Korean War, 58–59, 61, 68–69, 118

Kostalos, Mary, 167

Krueger, Geraldine Lynch, 39

Labor feminism, 4, 50–51, 73, 116–19, 125, 130, 132, 213 (n. 126)

Lack, Arthur, 103–4

Laughlin, Kathleen, 6, 118

Lawsuits, 132, 153, 156, 157, 158, 166, 168, 172

League of Nations Association, 16

Lemisch, Jesse, 146

Leopold, Alice, 73–74, 85, 118

Lewin, Arie, 147

Lloyd, Alice C., 37–38

Lockheed Missiles and Space Company, 161

Longobardo, Anna Kazanjian, 66

Long women's movement, 6, 178, 179–80, 185 (n. 23)

Los Alamos, 34, 153

Lynn, Susan, 4, 185 (n. 7)

Mack, Pamela, 6

Maffett, Minnie, 35

Magat, Phyllis Pollock, 38

Magnuson, Warren, 48, 163

Malcom, Shirley, 167

Manhattan Project, 9, 47, 59, 93, 128, 150, 152, 186 (n. 2)

Manpower studies, 1, 12, 43–44, 59, 60–65, 68, 70–71, 83–84, 87–88, 94, 96, 97, 112, 113, 118, 136, 137, 162, 163, 170–71, 175–76

Mansfield, Mike, 135

Mansfield Amendment, 135, 152

Masevich, Alla, 88

Massachusetts Institute of Technology (MIT), 11, 28, 34, 38, 61, 108, 150–51, 152, 153, 177; Association of Women Students, 127; research strike, 135; Symposium on American Women in Science and Engineering, 127–30, 137–38

May, Elaine Tyler, 4

Mayer, Olive, 81–82

(NOW), 131–32, 136, 139, 143, 145, 151, 153, 157, 160, 166, 167, 216 (n. 13)

National Register of Scientific and Technical Personnel, 49, 162

National Research Council, 12, 24, 41, 54–55, 70

National Resources Planning Board, 186–87 (n. 16)

National Roster of Scientific and Specialized Personnel, 12, 20–21, 24–25, 26, 34–35, 40, 41, 49, 52, 162, 186–87 (n. 16), 187 (n. 17)

National Science Foundation, 48–49, 55, 61, 70, 97, 99, 105, 113–14, 136, 162, 163, 164–65, 167; Committee on Equal Opportunities in Science and Technology, 167; "Cool Careers in Cybersecurity for Girls" workshops, 179; Divisional Committee for Scientific Personnel and Education, 113; grants and fellowships, 49, 55, 79, 87, 95, 128, 134, 146, 147, 148, 154–55, 162–63; Women in Science Program, 162–63, 166, 174

National Science Teachers Association, 71

National Scientific Register, 49, 70. *See also* National Roster of Scientific and Specialized Personnel

National Security Act, 48

National security concerns, 1, 4–5, 6, 7, 8, 9–13, 40, 41, 43–52, 53, 58–59, 64, 68, 83–84, 86–89, 133–36, 166, 169–71, 175–76, 178–79

National Security Council, 58

National Society of Professional Engineers, 77, 82

National Woman's Party, 117, 160, 213 (n. 126)

National Women's Conference, 140

Newark College of Engineering, 67

Newark Controls Company, 67

New Jersey College for Women, 29, 33. *See also* Douglass College

New Jersey Institute of Technology, 67

New School for Social Research, 119

New York Academy of Sciences, 166; "Expanding the Role of Women in the Sciences" conference, 166

New York Business and Professional Women's Club, 118

New York School of Social Work, 52

New York University, 30, 40, 104, 106, 147, 192 (n. 86); Institute of Mathematical Science, 104–5

Nienburg, Bertha, 35

Nixon, Richard, 89, 117, 135–36, 163

North Carolina College for Women, 23

North Carolina State College, 30

Northwestern University, 152, 192 (n. 87)

NSC-68, 58

Obama, Barack, 178

O'Brien, Ruth, 23

Occupational segregation, 3, 23, 32–35, 40–41, 43, 63, 64, 79, 90–91, 92–93, 146, 156, 172–73, 208 (n. 30)

Office of Civil and Defense Mobilization, 121

Office of Defense Mobilization, 59, 60. *See also* Office of Civil and Defense Mobilization

Office of Scientific Personnel, 12, 24, 70, 187 (n. 17)

Office of Scientific Research and Development (OSRD), 11–12, 13, 17, 24, 34, 40, 43, 46, 48, 61, 127, 187 (n. 17), 188 (n. 30); Committee on Medical Research, 46; Committee on Scientific Personnel, 12

Office of War Mobilization and Reconversion, 48

Ohio State University, 28, 167

Ohio Wesleyan University, 60

Oldenziel, Ruth, 6

Oppenheimer, J. Robert, 50

Packer Collegiate Institute, 107

Panetta, Leon, 178

Parmenter, Hazeltene, 107

Science, mobilization of: during Cold War, 1, 45–50, 58–59, 68, 86–87, 113, 169–70; and cybersecurity, 178–79; postwar, 43–44, 45–50; during Second World War, 1, 7, 9–13, 23; and "war on terror," 176

Science and Public Policy (Steelman Report), 48–49, 53

Science as masculine, 2, 3, 172–74

Science fairs and competitions, 13, 54, 76, 78, 100–101, 102, 148

Science Service, 13

Science Talent Search (Westinghouse), 13, 54, 101, 187 (n. 20)

Science, the Endless Frontier, 43–44, 48, 53, 61, 163

Scientific Manpower Commission, 162, 163. *See also* Committee on Professionals in Science and Technology

Scully, Marie, 77

Second Red Scare, 50–51. *See also* McCarthyism

Second World War, 1, 3, 7, 9–13, 16, 17, 20–22, 23–37 passim, 40–41, 44, 45–46, 49, 50, 55, 60–61, 63, 64, 65–66, 67, 70, 79, 83, 90, 92, 93, 127, 150, 153, 162, 171. *See also* Science, mobilization of

Sells, Lucy, 165–66

Senders, Virginia, 123

Shell Oil, 161

Sherry, Michael, 135–36

Shouse, Catherine Filene Dodd, 22, 23–24, 190 (n. 53)

Sigma Delta Epsilon/Sigma Delta Epsilon–Graduate Women in Science (SDE-GWIS), 7, 55, 56, 89–107 passim, 119–20, 137, 143–48, 149, 159–60, 171, 173-174, 178; All Women in Science Luncheon, 90, 92, 93–94, 143–44; Big Sisters program, 174; Committee to Encourage Women to Enter Science, 99–103, 120, 149; fellowships and grants, 55, 105–6; founding of, 89–90; name change,

144–45; post-Sputnik conferences on encouraging women in science, 90–95, 96–98; "Women in Science" symposium, 146–48

Simmons, Jean, 148, 160

Simmons College, 30, 163

Smeal, Eleanor, 167

Smith College, 4, 23, 28, 29, 30, 59, 130

Society of Women Engineers (SWE), 7, 65–84, 85, 86, 88, 100, 120–23, 138, 139–43, 160, 161, 166, 169, 170, 171, 174, 177–78; Big Sister program, 174; corporate memberships, 122, 161; Equal Rights Amendment, 139–41; founding of, 65–67, 68, 78, 201 (n. 102); membership in, 78, 141–42, 206 (n. 173); precursors to, 56, 57–58; Professional Guidance and Education Committee activities, 75–78, 80, 100, 139; scholarships, 69–70, 179; *Women in Engineering*, 74–76, 178

Solinger, Rickie, 4

Solomon, Barbara Miller, 39

Space race, 86–88, 99, 122

Spaulding, Susan, 104–5

Sperry Rand Corporation, 75

Sputnik launchings, 7, 85, 86–89, 90, 93, 98, 99, 102, 113, 120, 125, 148, 165

Stanford University, 38, 106; Medical School, 156

Stansberry, James W., 170

State commissions on status of women, 130, 131, 139, 145

Steele, Evelyn, 36

Steelman, John R., 48–49

Steinmann, Anne, 91

Stevens Institute of Technology, 31, 66, 67

Stinson, Katharine, 75

Stone, Margaret, 106–7, 137, 144, 160

Storrs, Landon, 50, 198 (n. 29)

Stratton, Julius, 127

Students for a Democratic Society, 134

Summers, Lawrence, 1, 176–77

Syracuse University, 38

Tarbell, Ida, 20
Taylor, Verta, 51
Technocratic feminism, 2–3, 5–8, 10,
    13, 16–17, 26, 31, 44–45, 51–52, 58,
    65, 85–86, 88–89, 107, 125–26, 128,
    129–30, 137, 161–68, 169–70, 175, 176,
    178, 179–80; advantages of, 3, 10, 41,
    83–84, 90, 171, 180; limits of, 3, 10,
    34, 40–41, 80–81, 171–72, 180
Tennessee A&I State University, 138
Terrorism, 8, 176, 178–79
Texas Christian University, 106
Thomas Alva Edison Foundation, 70–71
Thorndike, Edward, 18
Thurman, Ernestine, 95, 97–98, 119–20
Time and motion studies, 19
Title IX. See Education Amendments
    Act of 1972
Torpey, William G., 121, 214–15 (n. 137)
Truman, Harry S., 43, 45, 48–49, 58,
    59, 118
Tryon, Ruth, 56
Trytten, M. H., 70, 71
Tufts University, 40
Turner, Elsie Lee, 18

United Auto Workers, 130
United Nations, 16
U.S. Air Force, 122, 152, 161, 170
U.S. Department of Agriculture, 23, 119
U.S. Department of Defense, 48, 59,
    104, 134, 135, 166
U.S. Department of Health, Education,
    and Welfare, 91, 119, 157
U.S. Department of Labor, 116, 119; Em-
    ployment Opportunities for Women in
    Professional Engineering, 73–74, 203
    (n. 129); The Outlook for Women in
    Science, 52–55, 198 (n. 41); Women's
    Bureau, 35, 52, 62, 73–74, 83, 85, 95,
    111, 116, 130; Women's Division of the
    U.S. Employment Service, 22
U.S. Navy, 11, 35, 46, 47, 48, 70, 85;
    Office of Naval Research, 47, 49, 127,
    197 (n. 15); training facilities, 28–29;

Women Accepted for Voluntary
    Emergency Service (WAVES), 12, 16,
    17, 20, 28–29, 186 (n. 13), 193–94
    (n. 104)
U.S. Office of Education, 12–13, 70, 71
U.S. Steel Corporation, 122
U.S. War Department, 46, 47–48. See
    also U.S. Department of Defense
University of Arkansas, 121
University of Berlin, 23
University of California: at Berkeley, 18,
    128, 133, 150, 155; at Los Angeles, 28;
    at Santa Cruz, 177
University of Chicago, 23, 28, 52, 93,
    128, 146, 152, 154, 156, 158
University of Cincinnati, 29, 52
University of Colorado, 39, 65, 142
University of Connecticut, 30
University of Detroit, 76
University of Illinois: at Chicago, 221
    (n. 112); College of Medicine, 156; at
    Urbana-Champaign, 59, 101
University of Kansas, 154, 155
University of Lowell, 163
University of Maryland, 91, 153, 155
University of Massachusetts at Lowell,
    163
University of Michigan, 30, 37, 38,
    133–34
University of Minnesota, 31, 59, 101,
    123, 145
University of Missouri, 102
University of New Hampshire, 30
University of Pennsylvania, 95
University of Pittsburgh, 77, 121–22, 152,
    221 (n. 111)
University of Richmond, 154
University of Texas, 31
University of Wisconsin, 14, 38, 89–90,
    101, 102, 108, 144, 145, 148
Urey, Harold, 152

Van Aken, Carol, 127
Vander Wende, Christina, 147
Vassar College, 15, 29, 30, 38, 107–8, 111

World War II. *See* Second World War
Wu, Chien-Shiung, 128, 138, 150
Wyckoff, Delaphine G. R., 98, 102–3

Yale University, 61, 108–9, 146, 156;
  Medical School, 108

Young Women's Christian Association
  (YWCA), 107

Zapoleon, Marguerite Wykoff, 52–55,
  62, 73, 83, 111, 198 (n. 41)
Zarnow, Leandra, 4